NO
GODS
NO
MASTERS

Book Two

NO GODS NO MASTERS

Book Two

edited by
Daniel Guerín

translated by
Paul Sharkey

© Copyright: 1998
© 1998 Translation: Paul Sharkey

No Gods, No Masters: Book Two

ISBN 1 873176 69 4

Library of Congress Cataloging-in-Publication Data
   A catalog record for this title is available from the Library of Congress.

British Library Cataloguing-in-Publication Data
   A catalogue record for this title is available from the British Library.

The two books of *No Gods, No Masters* consist of the first complete English translation of the four volume French edition (original French title, English translation: *Neither God Nor Master*) published in 1980 by Francois Maspero. Book One consists of Volumes One and Two of the Maspero edition, Book Two consists of Volumes Three and Four of the Maspero edition.

Published by:

AK Press	AK Press	Kate Sharpley Library
P.O. Box 12766	P.O. Box 40682	BM Hurricane
Edinburgh, Scotland	San Francisco, CA	London, England
EH8 9YE	94140-0682	WC1 3XX

Translated by Paul Sharkey
Cover by Clifford Harper
Design and layout work donated by Freddie Baer.

TABLE OF CONTENTS

VOLUME THREE OF NO GODS, NO MASTERS

ERRICO MALATESTA (1853–1932) _____ 1
  Revolution and Reaction _____ 4
  Anarchy *by Errico Malatesta* _____ 6
  Malatesta and the Anarchists
  at the London Congress (1896) _____ 14
  Malatesta and the International Anarchist Congress
  in Amsterdam (1907) _____ 22
  Malatesta, the Anarchist International and War _____ 34
  A Prophetic Letter to Luigi Fabbri _____ 38

EMILE HENRY (1872-1894) _____ 40
  Letter to the Governor of the Conciergerie Prison _____ 43

THE FRENCH ANARCHISTS IN THE TRADE UNIONS _____ 49
  Fernand Pelloutier (1867–1901) _____ 51
    Anarchism and the Workers' Union _____ 51
  Emile Pouget (1860–1931) _____ 58
    Emile Pouget's Life as an Activist *by Paul Delesalle* _____ 58
    What is the Trade Union? *by Emile Pouget* _____ 66

THE SPANISH COLLECTIVES _____ 74
  Collectivization in Spain *by Augustin Souchy* _____ 75
  The Program of the Aragonese Federation of Collectives _____ 82
  Some Local Examples of Collectivization _____ 84
  In the Province of Levante *by Gaston Leval* _____ 88
  The Decree on Collectivization of the Catalan Economy _____ 93
  The Writings of Diego Abad de Santillán _____ 100

VOLINE (1882–1945) _____ 104
  The Unknown Revolution _____ 107
  Proceedings of *Nabat* _____ 117
  Third Congress of the Anarchist Organizations of the
  Ukraine (Nabat) (September 3-8, 1920) _____ 119

Volume Four of No Gods, No Masters

Nestor Makhno (1889–1935) — 123
- Nestor Makhno, Anarchist Guerrilla — 123
- Makhno's Visit to the Kremlin — 125
- The Makhnovist Movement — 139
- Trotsky and the "Makhnovshchina" (1919) — 148
- Manifesto of the Insurgent Army of the Ukraine (1920) — 157
- Program/Manifesto of April 1920 — 159
- Anarchism and the "Makhnovshchina" — 161

Kronstadt (1921) — 163
- Memories of Kronstadt — 165
  by Emma Goldman
- Resolution Passed by the General Assembly of the 1st and 2nd Squadrons of the Baltic Fleet — 181
- The Official Journal of the Kronstadt Uprising (Extracts from the Kronstadt *Izvestia*) — 183
- Petritchenko's Testimony — 206

Anarchists Behind Bars (1921) — 209
by Gaston Leval

Anarchism in the Spanish Civil War — 219
- Anarchism in Spain from 1919 to 1936 — 220
- The Spanish Revolution (1936) In Response to Fascism: A General Strike! — 226

Durruti and Libertarian Warfare — 230
- Buenaventura Durruti — 230
- The Spirit of Durruti — 240
- Durruti Speaks — 248
- Militians, Yes! Soldiers, Never! — 250

Anarcho-syndicalism in Government — 259

NO GODS, NO MASTERS: VOLUME 3

ERRICO MALATESTA (1853–1932)

Errico Malatesta was born in Italy's Caserta province on December 14, 1853, into a family of modest rural landowners. At the early age of fourteen years, he sent an insolent threatening letter to King Victor Emmanuel II, as a result of which he was arrested. He received his education in Naples at the seminary of the Scalloped Friars, going on to read medicine at university. A one-time republican who later repudiated Mazzini's patronage, he joined the International in 1871, a few months before the Paris Commune, falling in with its Bakuninist wing. In October 1876, he played an active part in the Berne congress of the "anti-authoritarian" International, where, straying somewhat from Bakunin's ideological legacy, he repudiated "collectivism" to become an exponent of "libertarian communism" (See Volume II of this anthology) and also to broach the notion of "propaganda by deed." From then on, Malatesta, Carlo Cafiero and Kropotkin were inseparable.

In the province of Benevento in 1877, the first two named attempted to put their activism into effect, Blanquist-fashion. At the head of around thirty Internationalists, armed and following red flags, they seized the village of Lentino, issued arms to the population and put the public records to the torch. But the population remained passive onlookers and the army stepped in. Malatesta and Cafiero were arrested on the spot. Although they conceded that they had fired shots at the carabinieri, they were acquitted when brought to trial.

After lots of adventures in the Middle East, Malatesta left Marseilles for Geneva, where he joined Kropotkin in publishing the newspaper *Le Révolté*. Expelled from Switzerland and then from a number of other countries, he finally settled in London, where he turned his hand to a number of minor trades.

In 1881 the anarchists assembled in London for an international congress, and Malatesta suggested, to no avail, that an Anarchist International be formed (See below). Returning to Italy, he was able to resume his revolutionary activity and founded two newspapers there, *La Questione sociale* and *L'Anarchia*, which were anti-patriotic and anti-parliamentarist in tone. But soon, by 1884, he fell victim to repression once again. While a political trial was in progress, he managed to escape hidden in the crate of a sewing machine bound for South America. Meanwhile, he had published a "draft for reorganization of the International on exclusively anarchist foundations."

The year 1885 found him in Buenos Aires, where he launched another *Questione sociale* and became a trade union organizer. In 1889, after a lot of picaresque adventures, he turned his back on Latin America for France, then England, then Spain. This tireless little man was forever on the move. In London in 1896, (See below) Malatesta took part in the international socialist labor congress, attending as the delegate of the Spanish anarcho-syndicalists.

Returning illegally to Italy, he waged war there simultaneously against parliamentarism, individualism and marxism and parted company with Kropotkin, of whose "spontaneism" he was critical. He insisted upon the necessity of organizing anarchism as a party and became an advocate of trade union action as well as direct labor action.

But further adventures awaited him. Deported to the Italian islands, he escaped from there in 1889, making his way to England and thence to the United States and Cuba, returning to London in 1900, where he brought out a number of newspapers like *L'Internazionale* and *Lo Sciopero generale* (The General Strike).

In 1907 he was an active participant in the international anarchist congress in Amsterdam (See below). Not until 1913 did he quit England for Italy, where he met Mussolini, who was at that time a left-wing socialist and director of the newspaper *Avanti*. He had lengthy conversations with the future fascist "Duce," finding him rather a skeptic when it came to the prospect of social revolution: to his friend Luigi Fabbri he confided that this guy was revolutionary only on paper and there was nothing to be expected of him.

In Ancona Malatesta published the newspaper *Volontà*, which he had launched earlier in London and proved himself a tireless agitator. In June 1914, he lit the fuse of the "Red Week." Disturbances erupted after the forces of law and order massacred unarmed demonstrators. The people took over the city. The trade unions called a nationwide general strike. The army stepped in. Malatesta was forced to flee, returning to England.

The First World War found him faithful to working class internationalism and he indignantly upbraided Kropotkin for his support for the war (See below). By the end of 1919 he was able to leave London to return to Italy, where he was greeted by enthusiastic crowds. The *Corriere della Sera* of January 20, 1920 portrayed him as "one of the greatest figures in Italian life." His newspaper *Umanità Nova* had a print-run of 50,000 copies and he became a leading light of an anarcho-syndicalist labor organization, the Unione Sindacalista Italiana (USI).

The years 1919 to 1922 saw Malatesta at the height of his career as a revolutionary militant and agitator. He transferred his newspaper to Rome and attempted to conclude an antifascist "Labor Alliance" with the political parties and trade unions: in July 1922, the Alliance called a general strike, but the attempt was smashed by the rising power of the fascist blackshirts. *Umanità Nova* was banned shortly after the March on Rome and Malatesta's picture was burned in public. Even so, he managed to bring out a bimonthly review, *Pensiero e Volontà,* in 1924: though frequently censored, it survived into 1926. It carried articles of consummate maturity from him.

From the end of 1926 onwards, the aged Malatesta, whom fascist totalitarianism had reduced to silence (except for a few articles which he managed to smuggle out of the country), was living under house arrest, which is what stopped him from joining the republican revolution in Spain in 1931 as he would have wished. He died on July 22, 1932.

Revolution and Reaction

Revolution: is the creation of new, living institutions, new groupings and new social relations. It is also the destruction of privilege and monopoly, the spirit of a new justice and fraternity, of that liberty which should overhaul the whole life of society, the moral level and material circumstances of the masses, prompting them to look to their own future through intelligent direct action.

Revolution: is organization of all public services by those working in them, in their own interest as much as in the public's interest.

Revolution: is abolition of all constraint, autonomy for groups, communes and regions.

Revolution: is free federation conjured into existence by the yearning for human brotherhood, by individual and collective interests and by the demands of production and defense.

Revolution: is the constitution of countless free groupings rooted in such ideas, desires and tastes of all sorts as are to be found in men.

Revolution: is the formation and proliferation of thousands of communal, regional and national representative bodies which, while possessed of no legislative authority, are of service in articulating and coordinating people's wishes, over short distances and long, operating by means of reports, advice and example.

Revolution: is liberty tempered in the crucible of action: it survives as long as independence does, which is to say, until such time as others, seizing upon the weariness descending upon the masses, and the inevitable disappointment that comes in the wake of the unduly high hopes, probable errors and failings of men, manage to found a power which, sustained by an army of conscripts or mercenaries, lays down the law and halts the movement in its tracks, at which point the reaction begins.

Organization without Authority[1]

Believing, under the sway of received authoritarian education, that authority is the essence of social organization, they [certain anarchists] have, in order to combat the former, resisted and denied the latter (. . .) The fundamental error of those anarchists who are opposed to organization is believing that organization is not feasible without authority and, having once accepted that hypothesis, preferring to abjure all organization rather than countenance the slightest authority (. . .) If we held that organization could not exist without authority, we would be authoritarians, because we would still prefer the authority that hobbles life and makes it miserable over the dis-organization that renders it an impossibility.

On the Necessity of Organization[2]

Organization is only the practice of cooperation and solidarity, the natural and necessary condition of social life, an ineluctable fact forcing itself upon everyone, upon human society generally as well as upon any group of people with a common aim to strive for.

Man does not wish, nor has he the ability, to live in isolation. He cannot even become truly a man and meet his material and moral requirements other than in society and through cooperation with his fellows. So it is inevitable that all who do not organize themselves freely, either because they cannot, or because they are not alive to the urgent necessity of so doing, should have to endure the organization established by other individuals ordinarily constituted as a ruling class or group, for the purpose of exploiting other people's labor for their own benefit.

And the age-old oppression of the masses by a tiny number of privileged has always been the consequence of most individuals' inability to come to some accommodation, to organize alongside other workers on the basis of shared interests and persuasions, for the purposes of production and enjoyment and self-defense against the exploiters and oppressors. Anarchism offers a remedy for this state of affairs, with its underlying principle of free organization, generated and sustained by the free will of the associated with no authority of any sort, which is to say, without any individual's having the right to foist his wishes upon anyone else. So it is only natural that anarchists should seek to apply to their private lives and party life, this very same principle upon which, they hold, the whole of human society should be founded.

Certain controversies have created the impression that there are some anarchists inimical to all organization, but in fact the many, the all too many disputations we have had upon this matter, even when they have been obscured by semantics or poisoned by personality issues, essentially have had to do with the modality and not the principle of organization. Thus some comrades who are verbally loudest in their opposition to organization organize like everyone else and, often, better than the rest, whenever they are seriously intent upon achieving something.

Notes for Revolution and Reaction

1. *L'Agitazion*, Ancona Nos. 13 and 14 (June 4 and 11, 1897).
2. *Anarchiè et organisation* (1927) republished 1967.

Errico Malatesta — Anarchy I

The word Anarchy comes to us from the Greek and signifies without government, the condition of a people governing itself without benefit of constituted authority.

Before a whole category of thinkers ever deemed such organization possible and desirable, before it was ever adopted as a goal by a party which has since become one of the prime factors in modern social struggles, the word Anarchy was generally taken in the sense of disorder, confusion: to this very day it is taken by the ignorant masses and by adversaries concerned to hide the truth to mean just that.

As government was held to be necessary, in that it was accepted that without government there could be naught but disorder and confusion, it is only natural, and indeed logical, that the term Anarchy, signifying absence of government, should also signify absence of order.

The phenomenon is not without precedent in the history of words. In the days and in the countries where the people believed in the necessity of government by one person (monarchy), the term **republic,** signifying government by majority, was taken in the sense of disorder and confusion: the very same meaning still attaches to it in the popular parlance in virtually every country.

Do but change minds and persuade the public that not only is government not a necessity, but that it is extremely dangerous and harmful, and the word Anarchy, precisely because it signifies absence of government, would imply, as far as everyone is concerned: natural order, harmony of everyone's needs and interests, utter freedom in solidarity.

It is argued, incorrectly, that the anarchists made a poor choice of name, since that name is misconstrued by the masses and susceptible to misinterpretation. The error resides, not in the word, but in the thing: and the difficulty encountered by anarchists in their propaganda springs, not from the name they espouse, but from the fact that their outlook sits ill with all of the age-old prejudices which people cherish regarding the function of government or, to use the common parlance, regarding the State.

What is government?

The metaphysical tendency (which is an affliction of the mind whereby man, having, by means of logic, abstracted the qualities of an entity, succumbs to a sort of hallucination whereby he mistakes the abstraction for the reality), the metaphysical tendency, shall we say, which, for all of the buffeting of positive science, is still deeply rooted in the minds of most contemporaries, ensures that many think of government as a moral entity, endowed with certain attributes of reason, justice and equity quite separate from the personnel of the government.

For them, the government, or rather, the State, is the abstract power of society: it is the representative, albeit the abstract representative, of the general interest: it is the expression of the rights of all, construed as a limit upon the rights of each. This way of thinking about government is supported by interested parties preoccupied with salvaging the principle of authority and seeing it outlive the shortcomings and errors of those who succeed one another in the exercise of power.

We see government as the collectivity of those who govern: and governments, kings, presidents, ministers, deputies, etc., are those endowed with the faculty of making laws in order to regulate the relations between men and of having those laws carried out; of prescribing and levying taxes; of enforcing military service; of judging and punishing those who trespass against the laws, of supervising and sanctioning private contracts, of monopolizing certain areas of production and certain public services, or, should they so desire, the whole of production and every public service; of expediting or obstructing the exchange of products; of declaring war or concluding peace with governments from other countries; of granting or withholding franchises, etc. Governors, in short, are those who, to a greater or lesser extent, are empowered to make use of society's resources, or of everyone's physical, intellectual and economic wherewithal, in order to compel everyone to do their will. As we see it, this faculty constitutes the principle of government, the principle of authority.

But what is government's raison d'être?

Why abdicate our own freedom, our own initiative into the hands of a few individuals? Why empower them to arrogate the power of all to themselves, with or without the consent of the individual, and to do with it what they will? Are they so exceptionally gifted that they can, with some semblance of reason, supplant the masses and look to men's interests better than the people concerned could do? Are they so infallible and incorruptible that the fate of each and every one can prudently be entrusted to their kind hearts?

And even were there men of boundless kindness and learning in existence, and, to take a hypothesis which has never been proved in history and which, we believe, is not susceptible to verification, even if the power of government were to be bestowed upon the most competent and the best, the possession of power would add nothing to their power of beneficence, and would, rather, paralyze and destroy it on account of their finding themselves confronted with the necessity of concerning themselves with so many things beyond their understanding and above all of squandering the greater part of their energies upon keeping themselves in power, appeasing friends, quelling malcontents and thwarting rebels.

Moreover, be they good or bad, wise or ignorant, what are governments? Who appoints them to their elevated position? Do they prevail of themselves by right of war, conquest or revolution? In which case, what assurance does the people have that they are prompted by considerations of general usefulness? It is a straightforward matter of usurpation; and their subjects, should they be unhappy, have no recourse but force if they are to shrug off the yoke. Are they chosen by a class, by a party? In which case it is the interests and ideas of that class which will prevail, while others' wishes and interests will be sacrificed. Are they elected by universal suffrage? In which case the sole criterion is numbers, which is assuredly no proof either of equity, reason or competence. Those elected will be the ones best able to gull the masses, and the minority, which may well be a half minus one, will be sacrificed: and that is without taking into account the fact that experience teaches there is no way of devising an electoral machinery to ensure that those elected are at least truly representative of the majority.

Many and varied are the theories by means of which attempts have been made to explain away and justify the existence of government. All in all, they are all founded upon the presumption, confessed or not, that men have contrary interests and that it takes an outside force to compel some to respect the interests of the rest, by prescribing and imposing such a such a line of conduct which would, insofar as possible, reconcile the conflicting interests and afford each of them as much gratification as possible with the least possible sacrifice.

If, say authoritarianism's theoreticians, an individual's interests, inclinations and desires are at odds with those of another individual, or even of society as a whole, who is to be entitled and empowered to compel him to respect the interests of the others? Who is to prevent such a citizen from trespassing against the general will? The freedom of each, they contend, is bounded by the freedom of others, but who is to set such boundaries and enforce respect for them? The natural antagonisms of interests and enthusiasms create the need for government and justify authority's posing as moderator in the social strife, marking out the boundaries of everyone's rights and duties.

So runs the theory: but, if they are to be just, theories must be founded upon facts and have the capacity to explain them, and we know that in social economy, theories are all too often devised in justification of facts, which is to say, in defense of privilege and in order to have it blithely accepted by those who are its victims.

Let us examine the facts instead.

Throughout the whole course of history, as well as in our own day, government has been, either the brutal, violent, arbitrary rule of a few over the mass, or a tool designed to guarantee the rule and the privilege those who, on foot of force or guile or heredity, have laid claim to all of the wherewithal of existence, particularly the soil, and utilize it in order to keep the people in servitude and to have it work for them. Men are doubly oppressed: either directly, by brute force and physical violence; or indirectly, by being denied the means of subsistence, thereby reducing them to powerlessness. The former mode is the source of power, that is, political privilege; the second is the root of economic privilege.

Men can further be oppressed by working upon their intellect and their feelings, as represented by religious or "academic" power, but since the mind is merely a product of material forces, falsehood and the bodies set up in order to peddle it have no reason to exist except insofar as they are the product of economic and political privilege, a means of defending and consolidating the latter.

Today, government, made up of property-owners and of people in their service, is wholly at the disposal of the propertied: so much so that the wealthiest often even disdain to belong to it. Rothschild has no need to be either deputy or minister: it is enough that he has deputies and ministers to do his bidding.

In many countries, the proletariat nominally enjoys a greater or lesser part in the election of the government. This is a concession granted by the bourgeoisie, either in order to secure popular backing in its struggle against royal or aristocratic power, or in order to divert the people away from the notion of self-emancipation, by affording it a semblance of sovereignty. Whether or not the bourgeoisie anticipated this, from the moment it granted the people the right to vote, it is a certainty that that right turned out to be quite illusory, good only for consolidating the power of the bourgeoisie, by affording the most vigorous portion of the proletariat the illusory hope of achieving power.

Even with universal suffrage, we might indeed say particularly with universal suffrage, government has remained the bourgeoisie's serf and gendarme. Were it otherwise, were the government to threaten to turn hostile, if democracy could be anything other than a means of deceiving the people, the bourgeoisie, its interests in jeopardy, would make ready for revolt and would utilize all of the strength and influence afforded it by its possession of wealth in order to call the government to order as a mere gendarme doing its bidding.

At all times and everywhere, whatever the name by which government has been known, whatever its origins and its organization, its essential function has always been that of oppressing and exploiting the masses and defending the oppressors and usurpers: its chief organs and vital characteristics are the gendarme and tax-collector, the soldier and the jailer, unfailingly joined by the peddler of lies, priest or professor, paid and protected by the government to enslave minds and make them suffer the yoke without complaint.

A government cannot exist for long unless it conceals its nature behind some semblance of general serviceability: it cannot ensure respect for the life of the privileged without seeming to seek respect for everyone's life; it cannot secure acceptance for the privileges of some without going through the motions of safe-guarding everybody's rights. "The law," Kropotkin says, which is to say, those who make the law, meaning the government, "the law has played upon man's social sentiments in order to secure the passage, along with moral precepts readily acceptable to man, orders servicing the minority of despoilers against whom he would have revolted."

A government can scarcely want the break-up of society, because that would signify the disappearance of victims for it and the ruling class to exploit. It cannot allow society to regulate itself without official interference, because then the people would very quickly realize that government serves no purpose, other than to defend the property-owners who keep it hungry, and would make preparation for ridding itself of governments and property-owners.

Today, faced with the urgent and menacing demands of the proletariat, governments display a tendency to meddle in dealings between employers and workers. In so doing, they try to derail the workers' movement and, by dint of a few deceitful reforms, to prevent the poor for seizing for themselves all that they need, which is to say, as great a morsel of well-being as the others.

Furthermore, it has to be borne in mind that, on the one hand, the bourgeois, which is to say the property-owners, are themselves continually in the process of waging war on one another and gobbling one another up, and, on the other, that the government, although child, slave and protector of the bourgeoisie, tends, like any other serf, to seek its own emancipation, and, like any protector, to lord it over the protected. Hence, among the conservatives, this see-sawing, this tug of war, these concessions awarded and then withdrawn, this questing after allies against the people, this game which constitutes the science of those who govern and which deludes the ingenuous and the lazy into forever waiting for salvation from above.

The government, or, as it is called, the referee "State," arbitrating in social struggles, impartial administrator of public interests, is a lie, an illusion, a utopia never attained and never attainable.

If men's interests were necessarily in conflict one with another, if strife between men was a necessary law of human society, if the liberty of some set a boundary upon the liberty of others, then everyone would always want to see his interests succeed over those of others: everyone would seek to expand his freedom at the expense of his neighbor's. If there had to be government, not because it might be of greater or lesser use to every member of a society, but because the victors would like to assure themselves of the fruits of their victory, by firmly subjugating the vanquished, and spare themselves the burden of being forever on the defensive, by entrusting its defense to men specially trained for gendarme duties, then humanity would be doomed to perish or to remain forever torn between the tyranny of the victors and the rebellion of the vanquished.

(. . .) Today, the tremendous expansion which has taken place in production, the spread of these needs which can never be met except with the assistance of a huge number of men from every country, the communications media, the habit of travel, science, literature, trade, and indeed wars have knit and increasingly are knitting humanity into a single body, the mutually solidary parts of which look no further than the welfare of the other parts and of the whole for their own scope and freedom to develop.

Abolition of government does not and cannot signify destruction of the social bond. Quite the opposite: the cooperation which today is forced and which is today directly beneficial to a few, will be free, voluntary and direct, working to the advantage of all and will be all the more intense and effective for that.

The social instinct, the sentiment of solidarity, would flourish in the highest degree: every man will do all that he can for the good of other men, in order to satisfy his feelings of affection as well as out of a properly understood self-interest.

Out of the free collaboration of everyone, thanks to the spontaneous combination of men in accordance with their needs and sympathies, from the bottom up, from the simple to the complex, starting from the most immediate interests and working towards the most general, there will arise a social organization, the goal of which will be the greatest well-being and fullest freedom of all, and which will bind the whole of humanity into one fraternal community; which will amend and improve itself in accordance with the amendments, circumstances and lessons of experience.

Such a society of free men, such a society of friends, is Anarchy.

But suppose that government does not, of itself, constitute a privileged class and that it can live without creating about itself a new class of privileged, while remaining the representative, the slave if you will, of the whole of society. Of what further use would it be? In what and how would it add to the strength, intelligence, spirit of solidarity and concern for the welfare of all and of future humanity which would, by then, be present in the society?

Here again we have the old saw about the bound man who, having managed to survive despite his bonds, regards them as a necessary circumstance of his existence.

We have grown accustomed to living under a government that commandeers all of the strength, intelligence and resolution which it can bend to its purposes and hobbles, paralyses and does away with any that are not useful or hostile to it, and we imagine that everything done in society is the handiwork of government, and that, without government, society would be bereft of strength, intelligence and goodwill. Thus, the property-owner who has staked claim to the land has it worked to his private benefit, leaving the worker no more than is strictly needed so that he can willingly carry on working and the enslaved worker thinks that, but for the employer, he could not live, as if the latter had created the earth and the forces of nature.

(. . .) The existence of a government, even were it, to take our hypothesis, the ideal government of the authoritarian socialists, far from giving a boost to society's productive, organizational and protective forces, would stunt them beyond measure, by restricting initiative to a few and affording that few the right to do anything, without, of course, affording them the gift of omniscience.

Indeed, if you remove from legislation and from all of the works of government everything included therein to defend the privileged and which represents the wishes of the privileged themselves, what is there left, other than the results of everybody's activity?

Moreover, in order to understand how a society can live without government, one need only look into the depths of the present society, and one will see how in fact the greater part, the essential part of the life of society, carries on, even today, outside of government intervention, and how government intervenes only in order to exploit the masses, to defend the privileged and, finally, to sanction, quite pointlessly, everything that gets done without it and indeed despite and against it.

Men work, trade, study, travel and observe how they will the rules of morality and hygiene, capitalize upon the advances of science and art, and sustain an infinite range of dealings with one another, without being sensible of any need for someone to prescribe the manner in which these should be conducted. And it is precisely those affairs into which government has no input that go best, engender the least strife and conform to everybody's wishes, in such a way that everybody affords them their custom and consent.

(. . .) Government, let me say again, is the body of individuals who have received or have assumed the right and the wherewithal to make laws and to force people to obey; the administrator, the engineer, etc., are, by contrast, men who receive or who assume the task of performing some task and who do so. "Government" signifies delegation of power, which is to say the abdication of everyone's initiative and sovereignty into the hands of a few. "Administration" signifies delegation of work, which is to say, task assigned and task accepted, and free exchange of services on the basis of free contracts.

He who governs is a privileged person, since he has the right to command others and utilize others' strengths in order to bring about the triumph of his own ideas and wishes. The administrator, the technical director, etc., are workers like all the rest — provided, of course, that we are speaking of a society wherein everyone has equal access to growth, where everyone is, or can be simultaneously brainworkers and manual workers, wherein all tasks, all duties entail equal entitlement to enjoyment of social amenities. The function of government should not be confused with the function of administration, for they are different in essence, for, whereas today they may be mistaken one for the other, this can be attributed to economic and political privilege.

But let us move on speedily to the functions for which government is regarded — by all who are not anarchists — as truly indispensable: the defense of a society, within and without, which is to say, "war," "policing" and "justice."

Once governments have been done away with and society's wealth placed at the disposal of all, all of the antagonisms between different peoples will very quickly evaporate and there will be no more justification for war.

(...) Let us suppose, though, that the governments of countries as yet unemancipated should attempt to reduce a free people to servitude again. Will the latter require a government in order to defend itself? The waging of warfare requires men with the requisite geographical and technical expertise, and, above all, masses willing to fight. A government can add nothing to the competence of the one, nor to the resolution and courage of the other. Historical experience teaches us how a people truly desirous of defending its own country is invincible: in Italy, everybody knows how thrones collapsed and regular armies made up of conscripts or enlisted men melted away before the volunteer corps (an anarchistic formation).

And what of "policing"? What of "justice"? Many imagine that if there were no gendarmes, police and judges around, everyone would be at liberty to kill, rape and maim his neighbor: that the anarchists, in the name of their principles, would like to see respected this queer freedom that rapes and destroys the liberty and life of other folk. They are all but convinced that, once we have destroyed government and private property, we would blithely allow both to be re-established, out of regard for the "liberty" of those who might feel the need to be governors and proprietors. A truly queer construction to place upon our ideas! True, it is easier, with a shrug of the shoulders, to dispose of them that way rather than take the trouble to refute them.

The liberty we seek, for ourselves and for others, is not that absolute, abstract, metaphysical liberty which, in practice, inevitably translates into oppression of the weak, but rather, real liberty, the achievable liberty represented by conscious community of interests and willing solidarity. We proclaim the maxim: "Do what you will," and we condense our program, so to speak, into that, because, as will readily be understood, we are convinced that in a harmonious society, in a society without government and without property, "each will want what will be his duty."

(...) Were it not for the equivocation by means of which an attempt is made to head off the social revolution, we might assert that anarchy is a synonym for socialism.

Notes for Anarchy

1. Excerpts from *L'Anarchia* 1891.

Malatesta and the Anarchists at the London Congress (1896)

The "anti-authoritarian" International was defunct, on account of its lack of homogeneity, following the Verviers congress in 1877. In 1881 the anarchists had tried to meet for an international congress in London in order to launch a purely anarchist International there. But the proposal, emanating from Malatesta (see above) had come to nothing, primarily because of the French anarchists' display of repugnance as far as organization was concerned. Not that Malatesta was discouraged by this. In 1884, he returned to his suggestion that a new International be launched that would, according to him, have had to be at once "communist, anarchist, anti-religious, revolutionary and anti-parliamentary." But this plan was a slow burner and anarchists had become increasingly isolated from the laboring masses whom the reformists had had growing success in marshaling: in 1889, Social Democrats from several countries met in Paris to lay the groundwork for what was to become the Second International. A few anarchists who showed up at this gathering were made to feel unwelcome and there were violent incidents: the Social Democrats, by sheer force of numbers, silenced any contradictions from the libertarians.

There was a similar to-do at the international socialist congress in Brussels in 1891, with the anarchists being expelled to cat-calls. This time, though, a significant number of British, Dutch and Italian workers' delegates had pulled out of the congress by way of a protest.

At the next congress held in Zurich in 1893, the Social Democrats decided, by way of a precaution, that henceforth, in addition to trade union organizations, they would admit only socialist parties and groupings in agreement with the need for political activity, by which they meant taking power through the ballot-box.

When a new international socialist congress met in London in July 1896, a few French and Italian anarchists had seen fit to ensure that they were delegated to represent labor unions. But this way of circumventing the obstacle did nothing to defuse the reformists' venom, and the latter's behavior, as a pile of documents will reveal, was nothing short of despicable.

Thus, as the libertarian writer Victor Serge was to write "anarchism has been a profoundly healthy backlash against the corruption of late 19th century socialism."[1] Lenin's view was not far removed from that.[2]

---

*Most of the texts that follow are taken from Paul Delesalle's historical introduction to the minutes of the *Congrès anarchiste internationale de 1907* (Paris 1908) and from Augustin Hamon's book *Les Socialistes au Congrés de Londres* 1897.

Paul Delesalle[3]: In France the divorce between anarchists and social democrats dates from 1880. The previous year, at the Marseilles congress, all tendencies had rubbed shoulders: possibilists, collectivists and anarchists had lined up under the same banner.

Eugene Fourniere[4]: We were then separated from the anarchists by an extremely narrow, rather idealistic, or rather semantic margin (. . .) There were anarchists inside the *L'Egalité* group itself, right up until 1890. Not until the point where the young Parti ouvrier made up its mind to contest elections did they walk out on us, and it was at the Le Havre congress (November 1880) that the program drafted in London at the dictation of Karl Marx and offered to us for approval by [Benoit] Malon[5] and which set the seal upon the split between anarchists and [socialists] was adopted.

Paul Delesalle: The divorce was final and was quickly to extend to anarchists and social democrats in every country. However the anarchists, or, to be more precise, a number of them, never stopped, in spite of everything, thinking of themselves spiritually as members of the great family of worldwide socialism. So when, in Paris in 1889 and in Brussels in 1891, the social democrats attempted to revive the practice of international socialist congresses, some anarchists reckoned they could participate in this.

Their presence triggered the most acrimonious clashes. The social democrats, with the force of numbers behind them, stifled any contradiction from their adversaries who where expelled to the sound of catcalls. "It is true," wrote Bernard Lazare (*Echo de Paris* July 1896), "that a great number of the English, Dutch and Italian workers' delegates walked out in protest. However, as the victors did not yet feel sufficiently strong, they passed no resolution of significance and chose to side-step the issue of parliamentarism and that of alliance with governmental parties. Nevertheless, the attitude of the majority plainly signified: we are no longer going to concern ourselves with economic struggles but with political struggles, and we will replace revolutionary action with lawful, peaceful action."

At the following congress, which was held in Zurich in 1893, the social democrats finally succeeded (or so they believed, at any rate) in disposing of their adversaries.

Circular Passed at the Zurich Congress and Issued in 1895

All workers' trades councils will be admitted to congresses; so too will those socialist parties and organizations that acknowledge the necessity of organizing the workers and of political action. By political action is meant that, as far as possible, the workers' organizations seek to utilize or capture political rights and the machinery of law-making, in order to bring about the triumph of the proletariat's interests and the conquest of political power.

Gustave Rouanet[6]: "The anarchists' doctrines are the very antipodes of ours (. . .) Socialism and anarchy are mutually exclusive terms."

Article by Domela Nieuwenhuis[7]: Shame on those who will exclude, on those who will divide instead of uniting. The world is to witness a re-enactment of the contest between Marx and Bakunin in 1872. It will be a fresh contest between authority and liberty. Just imagine men like Kropotkin, Tcherkessoff, Cipriani[8] and lots of others barred from the congress and you have to concede that this is no longer going to be a socialist congress, but only a parliamentary congress, a reformist congress of social democrats, a congress of one sect. Make up your mind what you want to be: a serious congress of socialists discussing all of the issues of interest to socialists, or a congress of sectarians which has excluded as heretics many a man who has fought and suffered for the people's cause.

PAUL DELESALLE

At the following congress (London July 26 to August 1, 1896), numerous anarchists showed up, not, it is true, in their capacity as anarchists, but as trade union members, delegates from trades councils (Jean Grave, Errico Malatesta, Emile Pouget, Fernand Pelloutier, Tortelier, Paul Delesalle, etc.)[9] At which point the social democrats, following a three day battle in which they failed to gain the upper hand, issued these famous resolutions, barring from future congresses all groupings, even trades bodies, which might decline to acknowledge the "necessity" of parliamentarism.

At the opening of the proceedings of the London Congress, on July 27, 1896, Paul Delesalle took the rostrum and attempted to speak. The interpreter, a young French student, seized him in a bear-hug and flung him violently down the steps, in which action Delesalle suffered bruising.

Jean Jaures[10] — If the anarchists, who have evolved considerably, have entered the trade unions in order to turn them into revolutionary groups, let them say so (. . .) We will repudiate the organizations that have delegated them, for we cannot countenance anarchist theories.

Fernand Pelloutier — By selecting me as its delegate the Federation of Bourses du Travail meant to signify that the economic movement should take priority over electioneering. Mr. Jaures is well aware that the workers do not, at any price, want their money to be used for electoral activity.

Gustave Delory[11] — The anarchists are the adversaries of all organization, and we are here in order to get organized and come to agreement on concerted action. So there is no possibility of their being admitted.

Jules Guesde — Parliamentary action is the socialist principle par excellence. There is no place here for its enemies. We must first take government (...) Anything else is only mystification, and, what is more, treachery. Those who dream of different action have nothing for it but to hold another congress.

Jean Jaures — I ask you formally to endorse the crucial decision taken at the Zurich Congress, which is to say, the absolute necessity of political action.

H. M. Hyndman[12] — Anarchy is disorder: it has no place at this congress.

Domela Nieuwenhuis — It is true that this congress is not an anarchist congress, but it is also true that it is not a social democratic congress. Every socialist is entitled to attend.

Jean Jaures — We are elected socialists and we are more entitled to be at a congress than with a mandate from some insignificant trades unions with a membership of four or five people.

Alexandre Millerand[13] — We formally refuse to have any association with them [the anarchists] (...) Socialism can only come to pass if it remains true to itself and refrains from lining up alongside anarchy.

Domela Nieuwenhuis — We are withdrawing, having no desire to participate any longer in a sham mounted by the social democracy for the greater glory of a few ambitious individuals.

M. van Kol[14] — Bon voyage!

August Bebel[15] — Far from saying to the workers, as the anarchists do "Vote no more!" I will tell them, "Vote again and keep on voting!"

Wilhelm Liebknecht[16] — [For the next congress] I ask that anarchists be excluded, no matter the capacity in which they may show up.

Augustin Hamon's Comments

The speeches were abridged (...) while Mrs. Marx-Aveling [Karl Marx' daughter] was translating.

The English at all times voted in favor of exclusion, meaning to bar the individualist anarchists hostile to all organization of whatever sort. They reckoned that they were chasing away dynamiters and bandits.

This congress was characterized by a brazen authoritarianism (...) an extraordinary intolerance.

The Germans were the directors. Assisted by Mr. and Mrs. Aveling, they were the true masters of the congress. The bureau decided whatever (. . .) Liebknecht wanted it to.

The social democracy showed itself up for what it is: intolerant, narrow-minded, so authoritarian that Keir Hardie[17] described it as Bismarckian.

Little by little the socialists from beyond the Rhine have been seen to abandon socialism's principles. They are leaning towards radicalism.

They are automata.

Mrs. Marx-Aveling — All anarchists are madmen.

JEAN JAURES — (*PETIT REPUBLIQUE* JULY 31, 1896)

No collaboration is possible between socialists and the anarchists, who cannot even plead sincerity in their aberration, and who arrived in order to disorganize the congress just as they disorganize the unions, to the great advantage of the reaction.

Notes for Malatesta and the Anarchists at the London Congress

1. Victor Serge "La pensée anarchiste" in *Le Crapouillot* January 1938.
2. Lenin *The State and Revolution* 1917.
3. On Paul Delesalle, see below for French anarchists and syndicalism.
4. Eugène Fournière (1857–1914), one-time lapidary, founder along with Gustave Rouanet of the *Revue socialiste,* Paris municipal councilor and deputy, lecturer in labor history. This has been taken from his book *La Crise socialiste.*
5. Benoit Malon (1841–1893) French socialist and author of *Le Socialisme intégral.*
6. Gustave Rouanet (1855–1927) journalist and socialist deputy for the Seine from 1893 to 1914. Taken from *La Petite Republique* July 15, 1896.
7. Ferdinand Domela Nieuwenhuis (1846–1919), Dutch anarchist and former Lutheran pastor turned revolutionary socialist and libertarian, advocate of the general strike. Author of *Socialism in Danger* (1894) and *Libertarian Socialism and Authoritarian Socialism* (1895).
8. Vladimir Tcherkessoff (1854–1925), Russian anarchist born in Georgia: fled to London in 1891: friend to Kropotkin and Malatesta: anti-marxist and advocate of revolutionary syndicalism: author of *Teachings and Actions of the Social Democracy* (1896) and translator of Bakunin, Kropotkin, Malatesta, Reclus, etc.
Amilcare Cipriani (1844–1918), Italian libertarian revolutionary, former colleague of Garibaldi's on the Sicilian expedition, took part, in London, in the launch of the First International in 1864 and participated in the Paris Commune.
9. Jean Grave (1854–1939), French anarchist of working class extraction, published *Le Révolté* in Geneva, then *Les Temps nouveaux* in Paris: author, notably of *Society the*

Day after the Revolution (1882) and of *The Moribund Society and Anarchy* (1893), which book resulted in his being brought before the courts.

For Fernand Pelloutier and Emile Pouget, see below on French anarchists and syndicalism.

Joseph Tortelier (1854–1925), carpenter, took part in direct action against unemployment and property-owners along with Louise Michel and Emile Pouget: turned anarchist in 1884, advocated the general strike, abstention from elections, supply of bread, accommodation and clothing free of charge, by way of an overture to consumption based upon needs.

10. Jean Jaures (1859–1914), Republican and Social Democratic leader, journalist and historian, assassinated on the eve of the First World War.

11. Gustave Delory (1857–1925) of working class extraction, one of the first socialist activists in the North of France, arrested during the strike wave of May 1, 1890, elected mayor of Lille in 1896, councilor-general and deputy in 1902.

12. For Jules Guesde and H. M. Hyndman, see Malatesta's letter to Luigi Fabbri, below.

13. Alexandre Millerand (1859–1943) reformist socialist who became a minister in 1899 and president of the Republic from 1920 to 1924.

14. Henri van Kol (1852–1925) Dutch Social Democrat deputy, specializing in colonial matters, and author of a pamphlet *Anarchism* (1893) under the *nom de plume* of Rienzi.

15. August Bebel (1840–1913), one of the founding fathers of the German Social Democracy.

16. For Wilhem Liebknecht see volume I of this anthology.

17. Keir Hardie (1856–1915), Scottish ex-miner and left-wing Laborite, founder of the Independent Labor Party in 1893.

Manifesto by the Anarchists Present at the Congress

We think that it may be useful to offer a proper explanation of the anarchists' position *vis à vis* the workers' movement generally and this congress in particular.

With the object of making the workers look upon us with suspicion and in order to gain the upper hand over the movement, the social democrats allege that anarchists are not socialists.

Well now! if there are anarchists fond of calling themselves by that title and who are unwilling to be socialists, they certainly have no place in a socialist congress and they will be the first to want no truck with it.

But we communist or collectivist anarchists seek the complete abolition of classes and of all exploitation and domination of man by his fellow man.

We want the land and all instruments of production and exchange, as well as all the wealth amassed through the toil of past generations, to become, through expropriation of the present holders, the common property of all men, so that all, by working, may enjoy the products of labor amid full-fledged communism.

We want to replace competition and strife between men with fraternity and solidarity in labor for the sake of the happiness of all. And the anarchists have spread this ideal and fought and suffered for its realization, for many a long year, and in certain countries, like Italy and Spain, well before the inception of parliamentary socialism.

What well-informed man of good faith would dare argue that we are not socialists?

Might we not be socialists because we want the workers to gain their rights through their organized efforts? Or because we want them not to cling to the — as we see it, chimerical — hope of securing them through the concessions of some government? Because we hold that parliamentarism is not merely a weapon of no avail for proletarians but also, by virtue of its being incapable, by its very nature, even should the bourgeoisie not resist, of representing the interests and wishes of all, remaining at all times the instrument of ascendancy of a class or a party? Or because we believe that the new society should be organized with the direct participation of all concerned, from the periphery to the center, freely and spontaneously, at the prompting of the sentiment of solidarity and under pressure of the natural needs of society? Because we believe that if, instead, that reorganization was carried out by means of decrees from some central body, be it elected or self-imposed, it would start off as an artificial organization, doing violence to everyone and making them unhappy, and would culminate in the creation of a new class of professional politicians, which would claim all manner of privileges and monopolies for itself?

It could be argued with much more reason that we are the most logical and most complete of socialists, since we demand for every person not just his entire measure of the wealth of society but also his portion of social power, which is to say, the real ability to make his influence felt, along with that of everybody else, in the administration of public affairs.

So socialists we are. Plainly, it follows that a congress from which we might be excluded could not honestly describe itself as an international socialist congress of the workers. So it ought to assume the particular title of the party or parties which would be granted admission to it. Thus, none of us would have thought of having any truck with a congress that would have described itself as being a social democratic congress or a congress of parliamentary socialists.

It is in the interest of every enemy of capitalist society that the workers should be united and stand by one another in the fight against capitalism. That fight is necessarily economic in nature. Not that we fail to appreciate the importance of political issues. We believe not only that government, the State, is an evil in itself: but also we are convinced that it is capitalism's armed defender. We think that the people will not be able to lay hands upon property without trampling the gendarme's body underfoot, literally or figuratively, according to circumstances. So, of necessity, we should concern ourselves with the political struggle against governments.

But politics is of course a great source of division. Doubtless this is because of the different conditions and temperaments obtaining in various countries, the fact that relations between a country's political constitution and its people's circumstances are very complex, less assimilable and less likely to be handled in a manner universally applicable. In fact, the conscious workers of various countries, whom the economic struggle might easily marshal and harness together, are split into countless factions on account of politics.

As a result, an understanding between all workers fighting for their emancipation is feasible on the economic terrain only. Anyway, that is what counts the most, for the proletariat's political action, whether it be parliamentary or revolutionary, is equally unavailing as long as the proletariat does not constitute an organized, conscious economic power.

Any attempt to foist a single political view upon the workers' movement would lead to that movement's disintegration and would prevent advancement of economic organization.

Apparently, the social democrats intend to force their special program upon the workers. It is almost as if they wanted to forbid those who do not accept their party's decisions from fighting for human emancipation.

We do not ask — far from it — that the various parties and schools abjure their programs and their tactics. We stand by our ideas and we understand others standing by theirs.

All we ask is that the division is not carried over into a sphere where it has no reason to exist: we ask that every worker have the right to fight against the bourgeoisie, hand in hand with his brothers, without regard to political ideas. We ask that each person should fight howsoever he may see fit, in accordance with like-minded folk, but that they all stand by one another in the economic struggle.

Should the social democrats seek to persist in their efforts to regiment and thereby sow division among the workers, may the latter understand and ensure that victory goes to Marx's great dictum: Workers of the world, unite!

— E. Malatesta and A. Hamon.

Malatesta and the International Anarchist Congress in Amsterdam, August 24-31, 1907

Thereafter the anarchists, having had their fingers burned, abandoned any attempt to rub shoulders with social democrats at international congresses. They resolved to hold congresses of their own. As they did in Amsterdam in 1907. Below the reader will find lengthy extracts from the minutes of the proceedings, lifted from *La Publication sociale* Paris, 1908, published by Paul Delesalle. Other excerpts from the proceedings of this congress have been reprinted by Jean Maitron in *Ravachol et les Anarchistes* Collection Archives, 1964, pp. 141-158: they relate to the Monatte-Malatesta exchanges on the relationship between syndicalism and anarchism, which we do not deal with here, but which is dealt with later in this volume by Fernand Pelloutier.

Tuesday, August 27

Amedee Dunois — It is not so long ago that most anarchists were opposed to any notion of organization. Then, the scheme we have before us, would have drawn countless objections from them and its authors would have been suspected of backward-looking ulterior motives and authoritarian intent.

Those were the days when anarchists, isolated from one another, and even more isolated from the working class, seemed to have lost all social sensibility: when anarchism, with its endless appeals for reformation of the individual, appeared to many as the highest expression of the old bourgeois individualism.

Individual action, "individual initiative" was held to be all-sufficing. Generally speaking, no one gave a fig for study of economics, of the factors of production and exchange, and indeed, some of us, denying that the class struggle had any substance to it, refused to see in the existing society anything other than conflicts of opinion for which it was the precise task of "propaganda" to equip the individual.

As an abstract protest against the social democracy's opportunistic and authoritarian tendencies, anarchism has played a considerable role over the past twenty five years. So why, instead of sticking to that, has it attempted, in the face of parliamentary socialism, to build up an ideology of its very own? In its daring aerobatics, that ideology has all too often lost sight of the solid ground of reality and practical action, and, all too often also, it had ended up coming in to land, willy-nilly, upon the farther shores of individualism. This is why, among us, organization cannot be thought of any longer in anything other than terms which are inevitably oppressive of the "individual" and why we have come systematically to repudiate any collective endeavor. However, on this matter of organization, which is the one we have before us, a telling shift is taking place. Without the shadow of a doubt, this particular shift should be seen in the context of the overall evolution which anarchism has undergone in France over the past few years.

By taking a more active hand than hitherto in the workers' movement, we have bridged the gulf separating the pure idea, which so readily turns into inviolable dogma, from the living reality. Less and less have we any interest in our former abstractions and more and more in the practical movement, in action: trade unionism and anti-militarism have claimed first place in our considerations. Anarchism appears to us much less in the guise of a philosophical and moral doctrine than as a revolutionary theory, a concrete program for social transformation. It is enough that we should see in it the most comprehensive theoretical expression of the proletarian movement's tendencies.

Anarchist organization still provokes objections. But those objections differ greatly, depending upon whether they emanate from individualists or from syndicalists.

Against the former, we need only appeal to the history of anarchism. The latter evolved as an outgrowth from the "collectivism" of the International, which is to say, in the final analysis, from the workers' movement. So it is not a recent, not the most rounded form of individualism, but rather one of the modalities of revolutionary socialism. Thus, what it refutes is not organization: but, quite the contrary, government, with which, Proudhon tells us, organization is incompatible. Anarchism is not individualist: it is primarily federalist, "association-ist." It might be defined as: unalloyed federalism.

Moreover, we fail to see how an anarchist organization could harm the individual growth of its members. No one, in fact, would be compelled to join it, nor, having joined, prevented from quitting.

The objections raised from the individualist viewpoint against our schemes for anarchist organization do not stand up to scrutiny; they might as readily be voiced against any form of society. Those from the syndicalists have more substance. Let us dwell upon those for a moment.

The existence of a workers' movement of plainly revolutionary outlook is currently, in France, the great fact which any attempt at anarchist organization is likely to run into, if not founder upon, and this great historical phenomenon forces upon us certain precautions which, I imagine, our colleagues abroad need no longer bother with.

"The workers' movement" — they tell us — "offers you a pretty well unlimited theater of activity. Whereas your groups of believers, tiny little cliques visited by none but the faithful, cannot hope to expand their membership indefinitely, trade union organization does not lose hope of eventually enfolding the entire proletariat within its supple and elastic embrace."

"Now" — they continue — " your place as anarchists is in the labor union, there and nowhere else. The labor union is not simply a combat organization: it is the living germ of the future society, and the latter will be whatever we make of the trade union. The fault lies in keeping company with the initiated, forever re-hashing the same old doctrinal issues, endlessly spinning within the same thought radius. Under no circumstances must we be separated from the people, for, backward and slow-witted though the people may still be, it — and not the ideologue — is the essential locomotive in every revolution. Have you, then, just like the social democrats, interests different from those of the proletariat to pursue, party interests, sectarian, factional interests? Is it for the proletariat to come to you or for you to go out to it and share its life, earn its trust and incite it, by word and example, to resistance, revolt and revolution?"

I cannot see however that such objections apply to us. Organized or not, anarchists (by which I mean those of our persuasion who do not separate anarchism from the proletariat) do not pretend to the role of "supreme saviors." Long since persuaded that the workers' emancipation will be the doing of the workers themselves, or will not take place, we gladly afford the workers' movement pride of place in our battle order. Meaning that, as far as we are concerned, the trade union is not called upon to play a purely corporative, blandly professional role, as the Guesdists, and, along with them, certain anarchists who cling to obsolete formulas, contend. Corporatism has had its day: that fact may, to begin with, have upset older outlooks, but we, for our part, accept it with all of its consequences.

So our role, the role of us anarchists who regard ourselves as the most advanced, most daring and most liberated fraction of that proletariat, constantly marching at its side, is to fight the same battles, mingling with it. Far be it from us to subscribe to the inane notion that we should isolate ourselves in our study groups: organized or not, we will remain faithful to our mission as educators and agitators of the working class. And if we reckon today that we ought to combine with other comrades, it is, among other reasons, so that we can invest our trade union activity with maximum force and continuity. The stronger we will be, the stronger also will be the currents of ideas that we can direct through the workers' movement.

But should our anarchist groups confine themselves to completing militants' education, conserving their revolutionary vigor and allowing them to make one another's acquaintance and get together? Should they not be engaged in activity of their own? We think that they should.

The social revolution cannot be carried out except by the mass. But every revolution necessarily entails acts which, by virtue of their, so to speak, technical character, can only be carried out by a small number, by the boldest, most expert fraction of the seething proletariat. In every district, every city, every region, in times of revolution, our groups would represent so many little combat organizations, assigned to carry out special, delicate tasks, for which the broad masses are most often not equipped.

But the essential, ongoing object of a group would be, and at last I come to it, anarchist propaganda. Yes, we would all band together primarily in order to spread our theoretical outlook, our direct action methods and our federalism. Thus far, propaganda has been conducted on an individual basis. Individual propaganda has produced very considerable results in the past, but it has to be confessed that this is not the case today.

For several years now, anarchism has been stricken with a sort of crisis. The virtually complete absence of agreement and organization among us is a major factor in that crisis. In France, anarchists are very numerous. On theoretical matters, they are already greatly divided; in terms of practice, they are even more so. Everybody acts how and when he chooses. Considerable though they may be, individual efforts are diffuse and often turn out to be a complete waste. There are anarchists everywhere: what is missing is an anarchist movement to marshal all of the forces hitherto battling in isolation, on a common platform.

Just such an anarchist movement will grow out of our common action, our concerted, coordinated action. Needless to say, the anarchist organization would not seek to unify every element professing, sometimes very mistakenly, to subscribe to the anarchist idea. It would be enough if it would rally around a program of practical action all comrades subscribing to our principles and desirous of working alongside us.

The floor was given to comrade H. Croiset of Amsterdam, representing the individualist tendency at the congress.

H. Croiset — What matters above all else is that I offer a definition of anarchy which will serve as the basis for my reasoning. We are anarchists in this sense, that we seek to bring about a social condition in which the individual will find his complete liberty assured, in which everyone will be able to live his life to the full: to put that another way, in which the individual will be afforded the right to live without constraints of any sort, his whole life his own, and not, as it is today, the life others would have him lead. I mean to say the life that others force upon him.

My motto is: Me, me me . . . and then the rest!

Individuals ought to combine only when it has been shown that their individual efforts cannot enable them to accomplish their aim unaided. But combination, organization ought never, on any account, to become a constraint upon him who enters freely into it. The individual was not made for society: instead, it is society that was made for the individual.

Anarchy seeks to place every individual in a position where he can develop all his faculties freely. Now, the inevitable outcome of organization is that it always limits the freedom of the individual to a greater or a lesser extent. Anarchy thus opposes any system of standing organization. In their pointless ambition to become practical, anarchists have made their peace with organization. It is a slippery slope on to which they are stepping, there. Some day or another they will wind up making their peace with authority itself, just as the social democrats have done!

Anarchist ideas must retain their ancient purity, rather than incline to become more practical. So let us revert to the ancient purity of our ideas.

Siegfried Nacht — I will not follow Croiset on to the ground where he has taken his stand. It strikes me that what is in need of elucidation above all else is the relationship between anarchism, or, to be more precise, anarchist organizations, and the labor unions. It is in order to facilitate the work of the latter that we, as anarchists, ought to set up special groups to offer training and education for revolution.

The workers' movement has a mission of its own, arising out of the living conditions foisted upon the proletariat by the present society: that mission is the conquest of economic power, and collective appropriation of all of the wellsprings of production and life. That is what anarchism aspires to, but the latter could not attain it with its ideological propaganda groups alone. However fine it may be, theory makes no deep impression upon the people, and it is primarily through action that it is educated. Little by little, action will invest it with a revolutionary mentality.

The general strike and direct action ideas have a very seductive impact upon the consciousness of the laboring masses. In the revolution to come, those masses will, so to speak, make up the foot-soldiers of the revolutionary army. Our anarchist groups, specializing in technical matters, will, so to speak, represent its artillery, which, though less numerous, is no less vital than the infantry.

George Thonar — In the anarchist idea taken as a whole, communism and individualism are equal and inseparable. Organization, concerted action, is indispensable to the growth of anarchism and in no way contradicts our theoretical premises. Organization is a means and not a principle: but it goes without saying that if it is to be acceptable, it should be constituted in a libertarian way.

Organization may have been useless in the days when there was only a very small number of us anarchists, all familiar with one another and in frequent contact with one another. We have become legion, and we must take care lest our strength be squandered. So let us organize ourselves, not just for anarchist propaganda, but also and above all for direct action.

I am far from being hostile to trade unionism, especially when its inclinations are towards revolution. But after all the workers' organization is not anarchist, and as a result, inside it we will never be absolutely ourselves; our activity there can never be undilutedly anarchist. Hence the need for us to set up libertarian groupings and federations, founded upon respect for the liberty and initiative of each and every one.

K. Vohryzek — It is as an individualist that I wish to argue the case for organization. There is no way to pretend that anarchism, by virtue of its very principles, could not countenance organization. The self-proclaimed individualist makes no radical condemnation of association between individuals.

To say, as is sometimes done, either Stirner or Kropotkin, thereby pitting these two thinkers one against the other, is a mistake. Kropotkin and Stirner cannot be contrasted one with the other: they set out the same idea from differing points of view. That is all. And the proof that Max Stirner was not the dyed-in-the-wool individualist that has been claimed is that he spoke up in favor of "organization." He even devoted a whole chapter to the "Association of Egoists."

Our organization, having no executive power, will not be at odds with our principles. Inside the trade unions, we champion the workers' economic interests. But for everything else, we should combine separately, to create organizations with libertarian foundations.

Emma Goldman — I too am favorable, in principle, to organization. However, I fear that the latter may, some day or another, lapse into exclusivism.

Dunois spoke against the excesses of individualism. But such excesses have nothing to do with true individualism, any more than the excesses of communism have anything to do with real communism. I have set out my views in a report, the conclusion of which is that organization always tends, more or less, to erode the individual personality. That is a danger which we have to anticipate. So I will agree to anarchist organization on one condition only, that it be based upon absolute respect for all individual initiative and is able to hamper neither its operation nor its evolution.

The essential principle of anarchy is individual autonomy. The International will be anarchist only if it abides by that principle completely.

Pierre Ramus — I favor organization and every effort to be made among us in that direction. Yet it does not strike me that the arguments advanced in Dunois's submission are quite of the quality to be desired. We should strive to return to anarchist principles as formulated just now by Croiset, but at the same time we ought systematically to organize our movement. In other words, individual initiative should depend upon the strength of the collective and the collective should express itself through individual initiative.

But if this is to be achieved in practice, we must keep our basic principles intact and undiluted. What is more, we are far from devising anything new. In reality, we are the immediate successors of those who, in the old International WorkingMen's Association, stood with Bakunin against Marx. So we are not offering anything new, and the most that we can do is to inject fresh life into our old principles, by encouraging the trend towards organization everywhere.

As for the aim of the new International, that ought not to be to constitute an auxiliary to the force of revolutionary syndicalism, but rather to work on the dissemination of anarchism in its totality.

Errico Malatesta — I have listened attentively to everything that has been said in my presence regarding this business of organization, and my very clear impression is that what divides us is words which we interpret differently. We are quibbling over words. But with regard to the very crux of the issue, I am persuaded that everybody is in agreement.

All anarchists, whatever the tendency to which they belong, are, in some sense, individualists. But the reverse is far from being true: all individualists are not — if only they were! — anarchists. Individualists are thus divided into two quite distinct types: some demand, for every human individual, themselves and others alike, the right to full development — others have a care only for their own individuality and never hesitate to sacrifice others to it. The tsar of all the Russias belongs to these latter individualists. We belong among the former.

Ibsen's cry, that the most powerful man in the world is the one who is most alone, is taken up. What utter nonsense! Dr. Stockmann, in whose mouth Ibsen places that maxim was not a solitary in the full sense of the word: he lived in a constituted society and not on some desert island. The "solitary" man is disbarred from performing the tiniest useful and productive task: and if anybody needs a master to watch over him, it is the man who lives in isolation. What sets the individual free, what allows him to develop all his faculties, is not solitude but association.

In order to accomplish truly useful work cooperation is essential, today more than ever. Of course, the association must leave its component individuals complete autonomy, and the federation ought to respect that same autonomy in its groups: preserve us from the belief that lack of organization is a guarantee of liberty. All of the evidence indicates otherwise.

To take one example: there are French anarchist newspapers which close their columns to all whose ideas, style or simply personality has had the misfortune to incur the displeasure of their customary editors. The upshot is that those editors are invested with a personal power that sets limits upon the comrades' freedom of opinion and expression. Things would be different if those newspapers, instead of being the personal property of such and such an individual, belonged to groups: whereupon every opinion might contend freely with every other opinion.

There is much talk of authority and authoritarianism. But we have to be clear here. Against the authority embodied in the State and having no purpose other than to preserve economic slavery in society, we revolt with all of our might and will never cease revolting. But there is a purely moral authority which arises out of experience, intelligence or talent, and, anarchists though we may be, there is not one of us but respects that authority.

It is wrong to portray the "organizers," the federalists as authoritarians, and it is also a no less great error to represent the "anti-organizers," the individualists, as deliberately dooming themselves to isolation. In my view, let me repeat, the squabble between individualists and organizers is purely a semantic quibble that does not stand up to attentive scrutiny of the facts. In practical reality, what then do we see? That the "individualists" are sometimes better organized than the "organizers" for the reason that the latter all too often restrict themselves to preaching organization without practicing it. Then again, it happens that one finds a lot more actual authoritarianism in the groupings noisily invoking the "absolute freedom of the individual" than in the ones ordinarily regarded as authoritarian on the grounds that they have a bureau and make decisions.

To put this another way: organizers or anti-organizers, they are all organizing. Only those who do nothing or next to nothing can exist in isolation and be content with it. That is the truth: why not acknowledge it?

Evidence to back up my argument: in Italy all of the comrades currently in the struggle invoke my name, the "individualists" and the "organizers" alike, and I really think that they are all right, for, whatever their theoretical discrepancies, they all practice collective action equally.

Enough of the semantics! Let us stick to actions! Words divide and action unites. It is time that we all set to work together to exercise effective influence over social happenings. It pains me to think that in order to wrest one of our people from the clutches of the executioners, we were obliged to look to parties other than our own. And yet, Ferrer would not be indebted to the freemasons and bourgeois free-thinkers for his liberty, had the anarchists, banded together into a mighty and fearsome International been able themselves to take charge of the worldwide protests against the criminal infamy of the Spanish government.

So let us strive to ensure that the anarchist International becomes a reality at last. If we are to be in a position to make quick appeal to all our comrades, in order to struggle against the reaction, as well as display our revolutionary initiative, when the time comes, we have to have our International!

Max Baginsky — A serious mistake, all too often made, is the belief that individualism repudiates all organization. On the contrary, the two terms cannot be dissevered. Individualism signifies a very special effort in the direction of inner, moral liberation of the individual; organization signifies association between conscious individuals with an eye to some aim to be achieved or some economic need to be satisfied. However, it is important that it should never be forgotten that a revolutionary organization has need of especially energetic and conscious individuals.

Amedee Dunois — Let me place it on record that I was trying to bring the discussion down from the heaven of vague abstractions to the *terra firma* of concrete, precise, humbly relative ideas. Croiset on the other hand lifted it into the heavens again, to the metaphysical heights where I refuse to follow.

The resolution which I move be adopted by congress is not inspired by speculative ideas about the individual's entitlement to integral development. It starts from quite practical considerations of the need which exists for our propaganda and combat efforts to be organized and orchestrated.

Christian Cornelissen — There is nothing more relative than the notion of the individual. Individuality per se does not exist in reality, where we find it forever bounded by other individuals. The individualists are too apt to forget about these de facto limits, and the great boon of organization resides precisely in its making the individual conscious of such limits by accustoming him to reconciling his right to personal development with the entitlements of others.

G. Rinjnders — I too am not hostile to organization either. Moreover there is not one anarchist who is not, deep down, in favor of it. It all depends on the way in which organization is construed and established. What has to be avoided above all else is personalities. In Holland, for example, the existing Federation falls well short of satisfying everybody: true, those who do not approve of it need only stay out of it.

Emile Chapelier — Might I ask that addresses be shorter and more substantial? Since the address delivered by Malatesta yesterday, which exhausted the issue, not a single fresh argument has been adduced for or against organization. Before we talk about authority or liberty, it might be a good idea if we were to agree upon what the words imply. For instance, what is authority? If it is the influence that men of real ability exercise and will always exercise inside a grouping, I have nothing to say against it. But the authority which is to be avoided at all costs in our ranks is that which arises from the fact that certain comrades blindly follow such and such. That is a danger, and in order to pre-empt it, I ask that the organization which is to be set up should acknowledge no leaders or general committees.

Emma Goldman — As I have said already, I am for organization. Except that I should like the Dunois motion to explicitly affirm the legitimacy of individual action, alongside collective action. So I move an amendment to the Dunois motion.

Emma Goldman reads her amendment. Accepted by Dunois, it will be incorporated, in abridged form, into the latter's motion.

I.I. Samson — Here in Holland there is a Federation of libertarian communists, of which I am a member. Of course, as comrade Rinjnders has just stated, lots of comrades have refused to join it. On grounds of principle? No: for personality reasons only. We exclude no one and never have excluded anyone. We are not even opposed to affiliation by individualists. So let them join us, if they wish. To tell the truth, I have no illusions but that, whatever form the organization may take, they will always play the malcontents. They are malcontents by nature and not too much heed should be paid to their criticisms.

K. Vohryzek — As the Dunois motion has nothing to say about the character which the anarchist organization should assume, I move that it be complemented by a rider specifying that character, a rider to which Malatesta has been willing to put his signature alongside my own. (Vohyrzek reads out the rider which appears below).

The debate is wound up. Next the motions submitted are put to a vote. There are two: the first is Dunois's, amended by Emma Goldman and complemented by Vohryzek and Malatesta; the second one has been submitted by comrade Pierre Ramus.

The Dunois Motion

The anarchists assembled in Amsterdam on August 27, 1907, persuaded that the ideas of anarchy and organization, far from being incompatible as has sometimes been argued, are mutually complementary and illuminating, in that the very principle of anarchy resides in the free organization of the producers: that individual action, important though it may be, could not compensate for want of collective action and concerted movement **any more than collective action could compensate for the want of individual initiative**; that organization of militant forces would assure propaganda of a new fillip and could not but hasten the penetration into the working class of the ideas of federalism and revolution; that the workers' organization, founded upon identity of interests, does not exclude an organization founded upon identity of aspirations and ideas; are of the opinion that comrades of every country should add to their agenda the creation of anarchist groups and federation of groups already in existence.

The Vohyrzek-Malatesta Rider

The Anarchist Federation is an association of groups and individuals wherein no one may impose his will or curtail anyone else's initiative. Vis a vis the existing society, it has as its aim the changing of all moral and economic conditions and, to that end, it supports struggle by all appropriate means.

Pierre Ramus' Motion

The Amsterdam anarchist congress suggests to the groups in every country that they unite into local and regional federations, in accordance with the various geographical divisions.

We declare that our proposition is inspired by anarchism's very own principles, for we see no prospect for individual initiative and activity outside of the group, which, as we intend, will alone furnish a practical theater for the free expansion of each individual.

Federative organization is the formula best suited to the anarchist proletariat. It bands the existing groups into one organic whole which grows through the affiliation of further groups. It is anti-authoritarian, countenances no central legislative authority making decisions binding upon the groups and individuals, the latter having an acknowledged right to develop freely within our common movement and to act along anarchist and economic lines without let or hindrance. Federation excludes no group and each group is at liberty to withdraw and recover possession of funds invested, as it deems necessary.

Furthermore, we recommend the comrades to combine in accordance with the needs and requirements of their respective movement, and also that they keep it in mind that the strength of the anarchist movement, nationally and internationally, depends upon its being established upon international foundations, the means of emancipation being derived solely from concerted international action. Comrades from all countries, organize yourselves into autonomous groups and unite into an international federation: the anarchist International.

These motions having been read out in French, Dutch and German, a vote was held.

The Dunois motion obtained 46 votes; the Vohryzek rider obtained 48. Only one hand was raised against the motion, and none against the rider, which therefore secured unanimous backing.

The Ramus motion was then put to a vote: 13 votes were cast for it and 17 against. Many attending the congress stated that they were abstaining on the grounds that the Ramus motion added nothing to the motion just voted upon.

A report in the review *Pages libres* stressed the significance of the vote cast by the congress, in these terms:

> This Amsterdam resolution is not quite without significance: henceforth, our social democrat adversaries will no longer be able to invoke our old hatred of organization of any sort in order to exclude us from socialism without due process. The anarchists' legendary individualism has been put to death in public in Amsterdam by the anarchists themselves, and no amount of bad faith on the part of certain of our adversaries can succeed in breathing life back into it.

Friday, August 30

Emma Goldman rose to say that it was odd that an anarchist congress had not declared itself in favor of the right of rebellion, in the broadest sense of the term, and she read out the following declaration which bore her signature, along with that of comrade Baginsky:

> The international anarchist Congress declares itself in favor of the right of rebellion by the individual as well as by the mass as a whole.
> The congress is of the opinion that acts of rebellion, especially when directed against representatives of the State and of the plutocracy, should be interpreted in the light of psychology. They are the products of the profound impression made upon the individual's psychology by the awful pressures from our unjust society.
> As a rule, it could be said that only the noblest, most sensitive and most delicate mind is prey to deep impressions manifesting themselves as internal and external rebellion. Viewed in this light, acts of rebellion can be characterized as the socio-psychological consequences of an intolerable system: and as such, these acts, along with their causes and motives, are more to be understood rather than lauded or condemned.
> In times of revolution, as in Russia, the act of rebellion, leaving to one side its psychological character, serves a dual purpose: it undermines the very basis of tyranny and boosts the enthusiasm of the faint of heart. This is especially the case when terrorist activity is directed against despotism's most brutal, most despised agents.
> Congress, in accepting this resolution, expresses its support for the individual act of rebellion as well as its solidarity with collective insurrection.

Put to a vote, the Goldman-Baginsky declaration was carried unanimously.

Malatesta, the Anarchist International and War

The manifesto below was issued on February 15, 1915. It was signed by thirty-five well-known libertarians of various nationalities — among them Errico Malatesta, Alexander Schapiro, Alexander Berkman, Emma Goldman, Domela Nieuwenhuis, etc. Malatesta and Schapiro were two of the five secretaries of the International Bureau, elected at the international anarchist congress in 1907. Another of the secretaries, Rudolf Rocker,[1] had not been able to append his signature, in that he was an internee at the time — but he too was against the war.

Europe in flames, tens of millions of men at loggerheads in the most frightful butchery in recorded history, hundreds of millions of women and children in tears, the economic, intellectual and moral life of seven great peoples brutally suspended, with the daily more grave threat of further military complications — such, five months on, is the dismal, harrowing, odious spectacle offered by the civilized world.

But this spectacle was anticipated, by anarchists at any rate.

For there never has been and is no doubt — and today's horrific events reinforce this confidence — that war is permanently incubating within the existing body of society and that armed conflict, be it specific or general, in the colonies or in Europe, is the natural consequence and necessary, inescapable destiny of a regime founded upon the economic inequality of its citizens, relying upon the unbridled clash of interests, and placing the world of labor under the narrow, painful oversight of a minority of parasites who hold both political power and economic might. War was inevitable; from whatever quarter, it simply had to come. Not for nothing has the last half-century been spent on feverish preparation of the most formidable armaments and every passing day seen the death budgets swell. Continual refinement of war materials, every mind and every will kept constantly geared towards ever-better organization of the military machine — scarcely the way to work for peace.

So it is naive and puerile, once the causes and the occasions of strife have been multiplied, to try to define the degree of blame attaching to such and such a government. No distinction is possible between offensive wars and defensive wars. In the current conflict, the governments in Berlin and Vienna have justified themselves by producing documents every bit as authentic as those produced by the governments in Paris, London and Petrograd. It is for whoever on each side who will produce the most unchallengeable, most telling documentation to prove their bona fides and portray themselves as the unblemished defender of the right and of freedom, the champion of civilization.

Civilization? Who stands for that at the moment? Is it the German State with its redoubtable militarism, so powerful that it has stifled every vestige of rebellion? Or the Russian State, whose only methods of persuasion are the knout, the gibbet and Siberia? Or the French State with its Biribi, its bloody conquests in Tonkin, Madagascar, Morocco and forcible conscription of black troops; the France whose prisons have housed, for years past, comrades whose only crime was to have written and spoken out against war? Or England, as she exploits, divides, starves and oppresses the peoples of her huge colonial empire?

No. None of the belligerents has any right to lay claim to civilization, just as none of them is entitled to claim legitimate self-defense.

The truth is that the root of wars, of the war currently bloodying the plains of Europe, just like all the ones that went before it, is located exclusively in the existence of the State, which is the political form of privilege.

The State is born of military might; it has grown through recourse to military might, and, logically, it is upon military might that it must rely if it is to retain its omnipotence. Whatever the form it may assume, the State is merely oppression organized for the benefit of a privileged minority. The present conflict offers a striking illustration of this: all forms of the state are embroiled in the present war — absolutism is represented by Russia, absolutism mitigated by parliamentarism, by Germany, a State ruling over very different peoples, by Austria, constitutional democracy by England and the democratic republican system by France.

The misfortune of the peoples, who were nevertheless all deeply committed to peace, is that they trusted in the State with its scheming diplomats, in democracy and in the political parties (even the opposition parties, like the parliamentary socialists) to avert war. That trust was deliberately abused and continues to be abused when those in government, with the help of their whole press, persuade their respective peoples that this war is a war of liberation.

We are determinedly against any war between peoples, and, in the neutral countries, like Italy, where those in government are seeking once again to push more peoples into the inferno of war, our comrades have opposed, oppose and always will oppose war with every ounce of energy they possess.

No matter where they may find themselves, the anarchists' role in the current tragedy is to carry on proclaiming that there is but one war of liberation: the one waged in every country by the oppressed against the oppressor, by the exploited against the exploiter. Our task is to summon the slaves to revolt against their masters.

Anarchist propaganda and anarchist action should set about doggedly undermining and breaking up the various States, cultivating the spirit of rebellion and acting as midwife to the discontent in the peoples and in the armies.

To every soldier from every country convinced that he is fighting for justice and freedom, we must explain that their heroism and their valor will serve only to perpetuate hatred, tyranny and misery.

To the factory workers, we must be a reminder that the rifles they now hold in their hands have been used against them during strikes and legitimate revolts, and will again be deployed against them later to force them to submit to the employers' exploitation.

We have to show the peasants that after the war they will once again have to bend beneath the yoke and carry on working their masters' land and feeding the rich.

All of the outcasts must be shown that they should not lay down their weapons until such time as they have settled scores with their oppressors and taken the land and the factory for their own.

We will show mothers, sweethearts and daughters, the victims of overwhelming misery and deprivation, who bears the real responsibility for their grief and for the carnage of their fathers, sons and spouses.

We must capitalize upon every stirring of rebellion, every discontent in order to foment insurrection, to organize the revolution to which we look for the ending of all of society's iniquities.

No loss of heart, even in the face of a calamity such as war! It is in such troubled times, when thousands of men are heroically giving their lives for an idea, that we must show such men the generosity, grandeur and beauty of the anarchist ideal: social justice achieved through the free organization of producers: war and militarism eradicated forever, complete freedom won through the utter demolition of the State and its agencies of coercion.

Long live Anarchy!
(Followed by 35 signatures)

On a contrary note, in the spring of 1916, some other anarchists, including Kropotkin, Tcherkessoff, Jean Grave, Charles Malato, Christian Cornelissen, Paul Reclus (son of Elisee[2]), etc., issued a declaration approving the war. In France it was carried by *La Bataille Syndicaliste*, a news-sheet suspected of being subsidized by the French government. This declaration became famous as the "Manifesto of the Sixteen," although in fact it had only fifteen signatories. In May 1916, it elicited a protest from anarchist-communists, which concluded with these words:

> We declare that all propaganda in favor of continuance of the war between the peoples "to the bitter end," which is to say, "until victory" by one of the belligerent coalitions, is essentially nationalistic and reactionary propaganda; that the aims in terms of which

this propaganda attempts to justify and explain itself are quite ingenuous, profoundly mistaken and cannot withstand the slightest historical or logical scrutiny; that such propaganda, having nothing in common with anarchism, anti-militarism or internationalism, instead represents, in its very essence and in its practical consequences, a sort of propaganda on behalf of militarism and supposedly "democratic" nationalistic Statism; that it is the absolute duty of anarchist-communists to struggle firmly against such aberrations and against these currents of ideas which are utterly contrary to the workers' vital interests; and that, as a result, not only can we not, hereafter, regard the signatories to the "Declaration" as comrades in the struggle, but we find ourselves obliged to class them resolutely as enemies, unwitting enemies maybe, but real enemies of the working class for all that.

Notes to Malatesta, the Anarchist International and War

1. Rudolf Rocker (1873–1958), German anarchist historian and philosopher who died in the United States. Author, notably of *The Bankruptcy of Russian State Communism* (in German) 1921.
2. Charles Malato (1857–1938) anarchist writer, author, notably, of *The Philosophy of Anarchy* (1889): Paul Reclus, son of Elisee Reclus (on whom see Volume II of this anthology).

A Prophetic Letter to Luigi Fabbri[1]

London, July 30, 1919
Dearest Fabbri,

(...) It seems to me that we are in perfect agreement on the matters with which you are currently so preoccupied, to wit, the "dictatorship of the proletariat."

By my reckoning, on this score the opinion of anarchists cannot be called into question, and in fact, well before the Bolshevik revolution, it never was queried by anyone. Anarchy means no government, and thus, all the more emphatically, no dictatorship, meaning an absolute government, uncontrolled and without constitutional restraints. But whenever the Bolshevik revolution broke out, it appears that our friends may have confused what constitutes a revolution against an existing government with what was implied by a new government which had just dominated the revolution in order to apply the brakes to it and steer it in the direction of its party political purposes. And so our friends have all but declared themselves Bolsheviks.

Now, the Bolsheviks are merely marxists who have remained honest, conscientious marxists, unlike their teachers and models, the likes of Guesde, Plekhanov, Hyndman, Scheidemann, Noske, etc.,[2] whose fate you know. We respect their sincerity, we admire their energy, but, just as we have never seen eye to eye with them in theoretical matters, so we could not align ourselves with them when they make the transition from theory to practice.

But perhaps the truth is simply this: our pro-Bolshevik friends take the expression "dictatorship of the proletariat" to mean simply the revolutionary action of the workers in taking possession of the land and the instruments of labor, and trying to build a society and organize a way of life in which there will be no place for a class that exploits and oppresses the producers.

Thus construed, the "dictatorship of the proletariat" would be the effective power of all workers trying to bring down capitalist society and would thus turn into Anarchy as soon as resistance from reactionaries would have ceased and no one can any longer seek to compel the masses by violence to obey and work for him. In which case, the discrepancy between us would be nothing more than a question of semantics. Dictatorship of the proletariat would signify the dictatorship of everybody, which is to say, it would be a dictatorship no longer, just as government by everybody is no longer a government in the authoritarian, historical and practical sense of the word.

But the real supporters of "dictatorship of the proletariat" do not take that line, as they are making quite plain in Russia. Of course, the proletariat has a hand in this, just as the people has a part to play in democratic regimes, that is to say, to conceal the reality of things. In reality, what we have is the dictatorship of one party, or rather, of one party's leaders: a genuine dictatorship, with its decrees, its penal sanctions, its henchmen and above all its armed forces which are at present also deployed in the defense of the revolution against its external enemies, but which will tomorrow be used to impose the dictators' will upon the workers, to apply a brake on revolution, to consolidate the new interests in the process of emerging and protect a new privileged class against the masses.

General Bonaparte was another one who helped defend the French Revolution against the European reaction, but in defending it, he strangled the life out of it. Lenin, Trotsky and their comrades are assuredly sincere revolutionaries (. . .) and they will not be turning traitors — but they are preparing the governmental structures which those who will come after them will utilize to exploit the Revolution and do it to death. They will be the first victims of their methods and I am afraid that the Revolution will go under with them.

History repeats itself: *mutatis mutandis*, it was Robespierre's dictatorship that brought Robespierre to the guillotine and paved the way for Napoleon.

Such are my general thoughts on affairs in Russia. As for detailed news we have had, it is as yet too varied and too contradictory to merit risking an opinion. It may be, too, that lots of things that strike us as bad are the products of that situation, and, in Russia's particular circumstances, there was no option but to do what they have done. We would do better to wait, especially as anything we will say cannot have any influence upon the course of events in Russia and might be misinterpreted in Italy and appear to echo the reaction's partisan calumnies.

Notes to A Prophetic Letter to Luigi Fabbri

1. Luigi Fabbri (1877–1938), Italian anarchist writer and militant, author of *Dictatorship and Revolution*.
2. Jules Guesde (1845–1922) social democrat leader, after having been an anarchist and then pioneer of marxism in France. Georgi Plekhanov (1856–1918), a Russian populist turned marxist in exile: pioneered marxism in Russia: mentor and collaborator of Lenin, before breaking with him in order to condemn the Bolshevik seizure of power in 1917. Henry Hyndman (1842–1921) founder of laborism, after having been a pioneer of marxism in England, Philip Schedidemann (1864–1935), German Social Democrat chancellor in 1919. Gustav Noske (1868–1946) right-wing Social Democrat, governor of Kiel in 1918, joined the counter-revolutionary council of people's commissars at the start of 1919, then went on to become Army minister, organizing the repression of the post-war revolutionary movements.

EMILE HENRY
(1872-1894)

Unlike most of the terrorist anarchists, Emile Henry (1872–1894) was an intellectual. He was a brilliant scholarship student at the J.-B. Say school, where one of his teachers described him as "a perfect child, the most honest one could meet." It only remained for him to don the uniform of the Polytechnic student. But he declined to do so "lest I become a soldier and be compelled to fire on unfortunates as in Fourmies."[1]

His father, Fortuné Henry, had fought in the ranks of the Communards. Sentenced to death in absentia, he had successfully eluded the repression which followed the defeat, by fleeing to Spain, where his two children were born. He did not return to France until after the amnesty in 1882. He went on to be a contributor to *L'En-dehors*.

At 9:00 A.M. on February 12, 1894, a fair-haired youth entered the Terminus cafe in the Gare Saint-Lazare. Sitting at an unoccupied table, Henry abruptly drew from the pocket of his cardigan a small tin canister packed with explosives, and tossed it into the air. It struck a chandelier, exploded and shattered all of the windows as well as a few marble tables. A general scramble ensued. Around twenty people were injured, one of them succumbing to his wounds.

Emile Henry took to his heels, chased by a police officer and a waiter, who were joined by a railroad worker, at whom he fired a shot, but missed. A little further on, he seriously injured a police officer, before being caught.

During proceedings in the court of assizes, his repartee was scathing:

The president of the assize court. — You reached out that hand (...) which we see today covered in blood.

Emile Henry. — My hands are stained with blood, as are your red robes.

To the jury, he read out a statement, from which these are extracts:[2]

(...) I became an anarchist only recently. It was no longer ago than around mid–1891 that I threw myself into the revolutionary movement. Previously, I had lived in circles wholly permeated with the established morality. I had been accustomed to respecting and even cherishing the principles of nation, family, authority and property.

But those educating the present generation all too often forget one thing — that life, indiscreet, with its struggles and setbacks, its injustices and iniquities, sees to it that the scales are removed from the eyes of the ignorant and that they are opened to reality. Which was the case with me, as it is with everyone. I had been told that this life was easy and largely open to intelligent, vigorous people, and experience showed me that only cynics and lackeys can get a good seat at the banquet.

I had been told that society's institutions were founded on justice and equality, and all around me I could see nothing but lies and treachery. Every day I was disabused further. Everywhere I went, I witnessed the same pain in some, the same delights in others. It did not take me long to realize that the great words that I had been raised to venerate: honor, devotion, duty were merely a mask hiding the most shameful turpitude.

The factory-owner amassing a huge fortune on the back of the labor of his workers who lacked everything was an upright gentleman. The deputy, the minister whose hands were forever outstretched for bribes were committed to the public good. The officer testing his new model rifle on seven-year-old children had done his duty well, and in open parliament the premier offered him his congratulations. Everything I could see turned my stomach and my mind fastened upon criticism of social organization. That criticism has been voiced too often to need rehearsing by me. Suffice it to say that I turned into an enemy of a society which I held to be criminal.

Momentarily attracted by socialism, I wasted no time in distancing myself from that party. My love of liberty was too great, my regard for individual initiative too great, my repudiation of feathering one's nest too definite for me to enlist in the numbered army of the fourth estate. Also, I saw that, essentially, socialism changes the established order not one jot. It retains the authoritarian principle, and this principle, despite what supposed free-thinkers may say about it, is nothing but an ancient relic of the belief in a higher power.

(. . .) In the merciless war that we have declared on the bourgeoisie, we ask no mercy. We mete out death and we must face it. For that reason I await your verdict with indifference. I know that mine will not be the last head you will sever (. . .) You will add more names to the bloody roll call of our dead.

Hanged in Chicago, beheaded in Germany, garroted in Xerez, shot in Barcelona, guillotined in Montbrison and in Paris, our dead are many: but you have not been able to destroy anarchy. Its roots go deep: it sprouts from the bosom of a rotten society that is falling apart; it is a violent backlash against the established order; it stands for the aspirations to equality and liberty which have entered the lists against the current authoritarianism. It is everywhere. That is what makes it indomitable, and it will end by defeating you and killing you.

Notes to Emile Henry (1872-1894)

1. The reference is to May 1, 1891 when troops opened fire on a crowd of workers, leaving ten dead.
2. From Andre Salmon *La Terreur noire* 1959 and Jean Maitron *Ravachol et les anarchistes* 1964.

Letter to the Governor of the Conciergerie Prison[1]

February 27, 1894
Monsieur le Directeur,

During the visit which you paid to me in my cell on Sunday the 18th of this month, you had a rather amicable discussion with me on the subject of anarchist ideas.

You were greatly amazed, you told me, to see our theories in what was for you a new light, and you asked if I would prepare a written summary of what passed between us, so that you might familiarize yourself with what anarchist comrades want.

You will readily understand, Monsieur, that a theory that analyses every manifestation of existing social life, studying them the way a doctor sounds an ailing body, condemning them on the grounds that they are contrary to the happiness of humanity, and erects in their place a whole new life based on principles wholly contrary to those upon which the old society is built, can scarcely be explored in a few pages.

Moreover, persons other than myself have already done what you ask me to do. The Kropotkins, the Reclus and the Sebastien Faures[2] [have set out] their ideas and expanded upon them as far as possible.

Read Reclus's *Evolution and Revolution* or Peter Kropotkin's *Anarchist Morality, Paroles d'un Révolté*, or *The Conquest of Bread;* or Sebastien Faure's *Authority and Liberty* or *Machinism and its Consequences*; or Grave's *The Moribund Society and Anarchy;* or Malatesta's *Between Peasants;* or read the many pamphlets, or countless manifestoes which, over the past fifteen years, have appeared one by one, each of them expounding new ideas as suggested to their authors by study or circumstance. Read all that, and then you can formulate a fairly comprehensive opinion of Anarchy. And yet, beware of thinking that Anarchy is a dogma, an unassailable, incontrovertible doctrine, revered by its adepts the way Muslims venerate the Koran.

No: the absolute liberty which we demand is forever adding to our ideas, drawing them on towards new horizons (at the whim of the brains of various individuals) and making them overspill the narrow boundaries of any regimentation and codification.

We are not "believers," we bow the knee neither to Reclus, nor Kropotkin. We debate their ideas, accepting them when they elicit fellow-feeling in our minds, but rejecting them when they evoke no response from us.

We are far from having the blind faith of the collectivists, who believe in one thing, because Guesde has said that it must be believed, and who have a catechism whose contents it would be sacrilege to query.

Having established that, let me try to spell out for you briefly and quickly what Anarchy means to me, without thereby speaking for other comrades who may, on given matters, hold views differing from mine.

That the social system today is in a bad way you will not dispute, and the proof is that everyone suffers by it. From the wretched vagrant, breadless and homeless, forever hungry, to the billionaire who lives in constant fear of rebellion by the starvelings upsetting his digestion, the whole of mankind has its worries.

Well now! Upon what foundations does bourgeois society rest? Discounting the precepts of family, nation and faith, which are merely its corollaries, we can state that the two corner-stones, the two underlying principles of the existing State are authority and property.

I am loath to expound upon this point at greater length. It would be easy for me to show that all of the ills we suffer flow from property and authority.

Poverty, theft, crime, prostitution, wars and revolutions are merely the products of these principles.

So the twin foundations of society being evil, there are no grounds for hesitation. No need to try out a heap of palliatives (to wit, socialism) that serve only to relocate the evil: the twin seeds of vice must be destroyed and eradicated from the life of society.

Which is why we anarchists seek to replace individual ownership with Communism, and authority with liberty.

No more title deeds then, no more titles of ascendancy: rather, absolute equality.

When we say absolute equality, we are not claiming that all men are to have the same brains, the same physical make-up: we are very well aware that there will always be the widest variation in intellectual and bodily aptitudes. It is that variety in capabilities that will see to the production of everything that humanity needs, and we are also counting upon it to sustain emulation in an anarchist society.

Self-evidently, there will be engineers and there will be navvies, but the one will pretend to no superiority over the other: for the engineer's work would count for nothing without the assistance of the navvy and vice versa.

With everyone free to choose the trade he will follow, there will no longer be creatures completely in thrall to the inclinations naturally within them (a guarantee of productivity).

At which point a question is posed. What about the lazy? Will everyone be willing to work?

To which our answer is: yes, everyone will be willing to work, and here is the reason why: Today, the average working day is ten hours long.

Lots of workers are engaged in tasks of absolutely no use to society, particularly in the manufacture of military armaments for the land-based and marine services. Many, too, are stricken by unemployment. Add to these a considerable number of able-bodied men producing nothing: soldiers, priests, police, magistrates, civil servants, etc.

Thus we can argue, without fear of being accused of exaggeration, that out of every 100 persons capable of performing some work, only fifty turn in an effort of any real use to society. It is these fifty that produce the entire wealth of society.

From which it follows that if everyone were to work, the working day, instead of being ten hours, would fall to just five hours.

Bear in mind, too, that in the current situation, the total of manufactured products outweighs by four times, and the sum of agricultural produce by three times, the amount required to meet the needs of humanity — which is to say, that a human race three times as numerous could be clothed, housed, heated, fed, in short could have all its needs met, if the surplus production was not destroyed through waste and many other factors.

(These production figures can be found in a little pamphlet entitled *Les produits de la Terre et les produits de l'Industrie*).

So, from the foregoing we can deduce the following conclusion:

A society in which everyone would do his bit for production and which would be content with production not greatly in excess of its needs (the excess of the former over the latter should build up a small reserve), need require of each of its able-bodied members only two or three hours' labor, maybe even less.

So who would refuse to contribute such a tiny amount of labor? Who would be willing to live with the shame of being despised by everybody and regarded as a parasite?[3]

(. . .) Property and authority always march in step, the one supporting the other, to keep humanity enslaved!

What is property right? Is it a natural right? Can it be right that one should eat while the other starves? No. Nature, when she created us, made us similar creatures, and a laborer's stomach demands the same satisfactions as a financier's.

And yet, today, one class has appropriated everything, robbing the other class not just of the sustenance of the body but also of the sustenance of the mind.

Yes, in an age dubbed the age of progress and science, is it not painful to think that millions of minds thirsting for knowledge are denied the opportunity for improvement? How many children of the people, who might have made men of great value to humanity, will never know anything beyond the few rudiments drummed into them in primary school!

Property — that is the enemy of human happiness, for it gives rise to inequality, and thence to hatred, envy and bloody revolution.

Authority is merely property's sanction. Its function is to place force in the service of spoliation.

Well! Since labor is a call of nature, you will agree with me, Monsieur, that no one will shirk the requirement for such a paltry effort as we mentioned above.

(Labor is such a call of nature that History shows us statesmen happily dodging the cares of policy in order to toil like ordinary workmen. To cite only two well-known instances: Louis XVI dabbled in the locksmith's trade, and "the grand old man," Gladstone, spent his holidays chopping down oak trees in his woodland, like a common woodsman.)

So you can well see, Monsieur, that there will not be any need to have recourse to law to abolish laziness.

If, by some fluke, however, someone did want to deny his colleagues his contribution, it would still be cheaper to feed such a wretch, who cannot but be sick, than it is to maintain legislators, magistrates, police officers and warders in order to curb him.

Many other questions arise, but these are of secondary significance: the important thing was to establish that the abolition of property and taking from the common store would not lead to a halt in production as a result of an upsurge of idleness, and that the anarchist society could feed itself and provide for its every need.

Any other objections that might be raised will easily be rebutted on the basis that an anarchist setting will develop solidarity and love of his fellows in every one of its members, for man will know that in producing for others he will at the same time be working on his own behalf.

One objection which might appear to have more substance is this:

If there is no authority any more, if there is no more fear of the policeman to stay the hand of the criminals, do we not risk seeing offenses and crimes proliferating to a frightening extent?

The answer is simple:

The crime committed today can be classified under two main headings: crimes for gain and crimes of passion.

The former will vanish of their own accord, for there will no longer be any point to such offenses, trespasses against property, in a setting where property has been abolished.

As for the latter, no legislation can prevent them. Far from it. The existing law which frees the spouse who has murdered his adulterous wife, is merely an encouragement to such crimes.

By contrast, an anarchist environment will raise humanity's moral standards. Man will grasp that he has no rights over a woman who gives herself to someone else, because that woman is simply acting in conformity with her nature.

As a result, in the future society, crime will become rarer and rarer until it disappears completely.

Let me sum up for you, Monsieur, my ideal of an anarchist society.

No more authority, which is a lot more contrary to the happiness of humanity than the few excesses which might attend the birth of a free society.

Instead of the current authoritarian organization, individuals combined on the basis of sympathies and affinities, without laws or leaders.

No more private property: products held in common; everyone working in accordance with his needs, and everybody consuming according to his needs, which is to say, according to his whim.

No more selfish bourgeois family making man woman's property and woman the property of man; requiring two creatures who happen to have been in love for a moment to bind themselves one to the other until the end of their days.

Nature is capricious, forever questing after new sensations. She wants free love. Which is why we advocate the free union.

No more fatherlands, no more hatred between brothers, pitting, one against the other, men who have never even laid eyes on one another.

Replacement of the chauvinist's narrow, petty attachment to his homeland with the open, fertile love of the whole of humanity, without distinctions of race or color.

No more religions, forged by priests for the degradation of the masses and to afford them hope of a better life while they themselves savor this earthly life.

Instead, the continual pursuit of the sciences, made accessible to everyone who may be inclined to study them, nursing men gradually towards a materialist consciousness.

Special study of the hypnotic phenomena which science is even today beginning to take under its notice, in order to expose the charlatans who present the ignorant with purely physical feats in a marvelous, supernatural light.

In short, no further impediment to the free development of human nature. Unfettered exercise of all physical, intellectual and mental faculties.

I am not such an optimist as to expect that a society with such foundations should straight-away arrive at perfect harmony. But it is my profound conviction that two or three generations will prove enough to wrest man away from the influence of the artificial civilization to which he is subject today and return him to the state of nature, which is the state of kindness and love.

But if this ideal is to succeed, and an anarchist society is to be erected upon solid foundations, we must start with the work of destruction. The old, worm-eaten structure must be cast down.

Which is what we do.

The bourgeoisie claims that we shall never reach our goal.

The future, the very near future, will teach it differently.

Long live Anarchy!

Notes to Letter to the Governor of the Conciergerie Prison

1. This text is reprinted with the kind permission of Jean Maitron: taken from Jean Maitron *Histoire du mouvement anarchiste en France (1886–1914)*
2. Sebastien Faure (1858–1942) was initially schooled by Jesuits, before becoming a Guesdist socialist and standing in the October 1885 elections: after 1888 he was an anarchist: he launched the newspaper *Le Libertaire* in 1895: a brilliant public speaker and lecturer rather than a theoretician: he founded the libertarian school, La Ruche, in Rambouillet in 1904: he took over the supervision of the four-volume *Encyclopedie anarchiste:* author of, among other things, *La douleur universelle* (1895)
3. Jean Maitron mentions that there is a passage missing here.

THE FRENCH ANARCHISTS IN THE TRADE UNIONS

We come now to the penetration into the labor unions of anarchists, or to be more exact, certain anarchists. Indeed, libertarians' attitudes regarding the unions were not uniform. Some sectarians, clinging to doctrinal purity gauged, with undisguised diffidence, the risk of anarchists' being swallowed up by a mass proletarian movement preoccupied pretty well exclusively with short-term demands; others, the anarcho-syndicalists, had no hesitation in immersing themselves in the unions, albeit with the partisan and deliberate intention of "colonizing" them: still others entered the unions with utter lack of selfishness, intent only upon placing themselves in the service of the working class, and the latter were the ones who conjured into existence what has been labeled revolutionary syndicalism, a symbiosis of the libertarian federalist principle and corporative demands, through the day to day practice of the class struggle.

How are we to account for this anarchist entry into the trade unions?

Around 1880, anarchism in France was at an impasse. It had managed to cut itself off from the burgeoning workers' movement that was falling more and more under the sway of reformist social democratic politicians. It was walled up in a sort of ideological ivory tower, or else it had preached minority activity, in the shape of "propaganda by deed," a euphemism for terrorism and recourse to bombs.

Kropotkin must have been one of the first to set things to rights and urge anarchism to break out of its impotent insularity: "We have to be with the people, which is no longer calling for isolated acts but rather for men of action in its ranks," he wrote in one article. And to call for a resurrection of mass trade unionism along the lines of its First International fore-runner, but ten times stronger: "Monster unions embracing millions of proletarians."

Following Kropotkin's lead, a young anarchist journalist, Fernand Pelloutier, who came from Saint-Nazaire, published an article in the libertarian review *Les Temps nouveaux* in 1898, under the title of "Anarchism and the workers' unions," the text of which the reader will find below. According to him, the trade union was to be "a practical school of anarchism," much as it was supposed by communists of the Bolshevik school to be the ante-room to communism.

But another anarchist, Emile Pouget, was not quite of the same mind. He had no hesitation in arguing that trade unionism was self-sufficient and had no need of libertarian theoreticians acting as chaperones, and that the trade union should be regarded as the social combination 'par excellence'. So, after Pelloutier's article, we have included a particularly telling piece by Pouget.

The anarchists' entry into the unions was an event of some significance. It breathed new life into the movement, bringing it a mass base and, far from becoming bogged down in what Lenin was to term "economism," it was to afford it the opportunity to re-immerse itself and rediscover its bearings in a vibrant new synthesis.

Revolutionary syndicalism nevertheless carried with it an implicit risk, against which the die-hard anarchists had not been wrong to sound a note of caution. Might not corporative action in pursuit of short-term demands, in the long run, incubate a labor bureaucracy likely to sterilize the social struggle and reduce it to a conservatism comparable to that which the anarchists pointed to in the social democrats?

As we shall see, Fernand Pelloutier, to his credit, did not overlook this hypothesis in his argument. Far-sightedly, as early as 1895, he conceded that the trade union administrations could "turn into authorities," which is to say, spawn a bureaucracy. And, later, Malatesta, taking this objection further, was to sound the alarm at the Amsterdam international anarchist congress in 1907 when he opined:

"Inside the labor movement the official poses a threat comparable only with parliamentarism."

But Pierre Monatte, an overly optimistic supporter of "pure-syndicalism, was to reply that true, trade union bureaucracy was not without its dangers, but that syndicalism carried within it enough democratic antidotes to render its officials harmless.' Today, we know that they failed to work.

Note to Introduction to The French Anarchists in the Trade Unions

1. See Jean Maitron *Ravachol et les anarchistes*

Fernand Pelloutier (1867–1901)

Fernand Pelloutier (1867–1901), educated through the religious schools and then Saint-Nazaire College, had turned his back on the bourgeoisie to throw in his lot with the people. At a very early age he embarked upon a career in journalism. He joined the Parti ouvrier francais (French Workers' Party) and then, in 1892, he was sent by the Saint-Nazaire and Nantes Bourses du Travail as their delegate to a socialist congress at which — most unusually for such a setting — he won acceptance for the principle of the general strike.

At the beginning of 1893, he moved to Paris. It was not long before he had parted company from the marxists to embrace libertarian ideas. In a "Letter to the Anarchists," he wrote "We are (...) what they [the politicians] are not — full-time rebels, truly godless men, without master or homeland, incorrigible enemies of all despotism, moral or collective, that is to say, of laws and dictatorships, including that of the proletariat."

But at the same time, Pelloutier was urging anarchists to get actively involved in the labor movement. In 1895 he was appointed secretary of the Federation of Bourses du Travail and gave unstintingly of himself in that capacity. In 1897, he launched a monthly review of social economy *L'Ouvrier des Deux-Mondes,* seeing to the typesetting personally.

Pelloutier looked upon the Bourses du Travail as the very paragon of labor organization, the model closest to the people at the grassroots. He saw in them the embryo of the "free association of producers" to which Bakunin had looked forward, as well as the embryo of the workers' Commune, that essential structure of the coming society. Succumbing to an untimely death as a result of incurable illness, he left behind a posthumous volume, that classic work on revolutionary syndicalism, *Histoire des Bourses du Travail.*

Anarchism and the Workers' Union[1]

Just as some workers of my acquaintance, for all that they are fed up with parliamentary socialism, are loath to confess their libertarian socialism, because, as they see it, anarchy boils down to the individual recourse to dynamite, so I know a number of anarchists who, as a result of a once well-founded prejudice, steer well clear of the trade unions, and, if need be, oppose them, on the grounds that that institution has been, for a time, a downright nursery for would-be deputies. In Saint-Etienne, for example, (and I have this from a reliable source), the members of the trade unions venerate Ravachol; none of them, however, dares declare himself an anarchist, for fear that he might appear to be turning away from working towards collective rebellion and opting for isolated rebellion in its place. Elsewhere, by contrast, in Paris, Amiens, Marseilles, Roanne and a hundred other towns, anarchists admire the new spirit by which the trade unions have been moved these past two years, yet do not dare to venture into that revolutionary field to ensure that the good seed sown by harsh experience germinates. And, between these men, emancipated almost to the same extent, intellectually connected by a shared objective and by a perception here and a conviction there, regarding the necessity of a violent uprising, there is a lingering mistrust which keeps the former distant from comrades held to be systematically hostile to all concerted action, and the latter from a form of combination in which, they persist in believing, alienation of the freedom of the individual is still obligatory.

However, the rapprochement begun in a few large industrial or manufacturing centers is relentlessly spreading. A comrade from Roanne only recently indicated to readers of *Les Temps nouveaux* that not only have that city's anarchists at last joined the trades bodies, but that they have gained a moral authority there of real service to propaganda by virtue of the vigor and passion of their proselytization. What we have learned regarding the trade unions of Roanne, I might repeat relative to many trade unions in Algiers, Toulouse, Paris, Beauvais, Toulon, etc., where, worn down by libertarian propaganda, they are today studying teachings which yesterday, under marxist influence, they refused even to hear tell of. Now, analyzing the grounds behind this rapprochement, which would so recently have seemed impossible, and setting out the stages through which it has proceeded, amounts to dispelling the remains of the distrust that thwarts revolutionary unity and spells ruin for statist socialism, which has turned into the doctrinal form of inadmissible appetites. At one point the trade unions were ready (and — this is a guarantee against any back-sliding — ready because they had come to their own conclusion, in spite of counsels which previously they had so respectfully heeded) to withdraw from all truck with the so-called social laws; that point coincided with the implementation of the first of the reforms which they had been promised over a period of four years would work wonders.

So often had they been told: "Patience! We will see to it that your work hours are so regulated that you will have the leisure and study time without which you would be perpetually slaves" that they were transfixed in expectation of that reform, so to speak, over a period of several years and distracted from the aim of revolution. But once they had been awarded the law governing female and child labor, what did they find? That their wives' pay was cut, along with their children's and their own, in keeping with the cut in working hours, and there were strikes and lock-outs in Paris, Amiens and the Ardeche, out-work became more widespread, or the *sweating system,* or indeed industrialists' recourse to ingenious combinations (swing shifts, shift work) simultaneously circumvented the law and worsened working conditions. In the end, implementation of the law of November 2, 1892 had such an impact that female and male workers called and are calling still for it to be repealed.

What was the provenance of such a reversal? The trade unions hastened to look for an explanation, but, their faith in legislation being too recently acquired to be seriously stricken, too ignorant of social economy to probe beyond the tangible causes, they believed (in that the cuts in working hours had determined the cuts in pay) that the law would be flawless if regulation of labor costs could be added to regulation of hours.

But the hour of disappointment had finally come. The promises which had made for reformist socialism's power now yielded to the practice, which would spell its ruination. Fresh laws arose, designed either to see that the producer was paid better or to cater for his old age. But then the unions noticed (and it is primarily to the women that the credit for this discovery, crucial to socialism's evolution, must go) that the items for which they were paid most as producers were sold to them at increasingly high cost as consumers, and that as wage rates rose, so too the cost of bread, wine, meat, housing, furniture — in short, all of life's essential needs — rose too; and they noticed too (and this was spelled out formally at the recent Limoges congress) that in the last analysis, retirement pensions are still funded out of levies upon wages. And this lesson of experience, a lesson more instructive to them than the masterly analysis of the impact of taxation devised by Proudhon[2] or taught by the International and indeed accepted and incorporated into the collectivist programs of thirteen years ago — while it was not as yet enough to persuade them that attempts to reduce pauperism in an economic context where everything conspires to add to it are like trying to confine a liquid on a flat surface, at least impressed upon their minds a rough conclusion to the effect that social legislation may not be quite the panacea they had been told it would be.

However, that lesson would not have been enough to inspire the rapid evolution in them of which we speak, had not the socialist schools themselves been bent upon investing them with a distaste for politics. For a long time the trade unions reckoned that the socialist party's weakness, or rather, the weakness of the proletariat had been primarily, and maybe even exclusively attributable to divisions among the politicians. The moment that Citizen X fell out with Citizen Z, or the "bespectacled Torquemada," hitherto damned by Clovis

Hugues and Ferroul[3], and some prima donna from what Lafargue[4] has called the "Federation of Socialist Unreliables," the trade unions would be split down the middle, and if it came to the mounting of some concerted action like a May Day demonstration, say, they would find their members splitting into five, six or ten factions, pulling in different directions in obedience to their leaders' watchwords. This gave them pause for thought, and mistaking the effect for the cause, they expended what could be described as immeasurable-energy on efforts to resolve this insoluble problem of socialist unity.[5] Ah, no one who has not lived among the trade unions can have any conception of the efforts made to make a reality of that chimera! Agendas, deliberations, manifestoes: everything, but everything was tried, but found wanting: even as agreement seemed to have been reached, or when the discussions were being wound up, more as a result of weariness than of conviction, one word would fan the spark: Guesdists, Blanquists, die-hards and Broussists would jump angrily to their feet to exchange insults and take issue with this Guesde, Vaillant and Brousse, and this fresh outbreak of fighting would drag on for weeks, only to flare up again when scarcely it had finished.

In this world, everything comes to an end. Wearying of their growing weakness and their pointless endeavors to reconcile politics, which has to do primarily with individual interests, with economics, which has to do with the interests of society, the trade unions eventually came to understand (better late than never) that the divisions in their own ranks had a loftier cause than the division among the politicians, and that both of these proceeded from . . . politics. At which point, emboldened by the manifest ineffectuality of "social" legislation, by the treachery of certain elected socialists (some of whom gave their backing to the Bercy big business interest), by the lamentable results of interference by deputies or town councilors in strikes, notably the omnibus strike, by the hostility shown towards the general strike by newspapers and men whose entire policy consists of building or finding themselves a stepping stone towards their 25 francs and sash, the trade unions decided that from now on political agitations would be none of their concern, that all discussion, other than economic, would be ruthlessly excluded from their program of study and that they would devote themselves whole-heartedly to resisting capital. Recent instances have shown how quickly the trade unions have taken to this slant!

Yet the rumor of this about-turn had been vindicated. The new watchword "No more politicking!" had spread through the workshops. A number of union members deserted the churches devoted to the cult of electioneering. So the trade union terrain seemed to some anarchists ripe to receive and nurture their doctrine, and came to the aid of those who, freed at last of parliamentary tutelage, now strove to focus their attention and that of their comrades upon the study of economic laws.

This entry into the trade union of some libertarians made a considerable impact. For one thing, it taught the masses the true meaning of anarchism, a doctrine which, in order to make headway can very readily, let us say it again, manage without the individual dynamiter; and, through a natural linkage of ideas, it showed union members what this trades organization of which they had previously had only the narrowest conception is and may yet become.

Nobody believes or expects that the coming revolution, however formidable it should be, will realize unadulterated anarchist communism. By virtue of the fact that it will erupt, no doubt, before the work of anarchist education has been completed, men will not be quite mature enough to organize themselves absolutely without assistance, and for a long time yet the demands of caprice will stifle the voice of reason in them. As a result (and this seems a good time to spell it out), while we do preach perfect communism, it is not in the certainty or expectation of communism's being the social form of the future: it is in order to further men's education, and round it off as completely as possible, so that, by the time that the day of conflagration comes, they will have attained maximum emancipation. But must the transitional state to be endured necessarily or inevitably be the collectivist jail?[6] Might it not consist of libertarian organization confined to the needs of production and consumption alone, with all political institutions having been done away with? Such is the problem with which many minds have — rightly — been grappling for many a long year.

Now, what is the trade union? An association which one is free to join or quit, one without a president, with no officials other than a secretary and a treasurer subject to instant revocation, of men who study and debate kindred professional concerns. And who are these men? Producers, the very same who create all public wealth. Do they await the approval of the law before they come together, reach agreement and act? No: as far as they are concerned, lawful constitution is merely an amusing means of making revolutionary propaganda under government guarantee, and anyway, how many of them do not and will not ever figure in the unions' formal annual returns? Do they use the parliamentary mechanism in order to arrive at their resolutions? Not any more: they hold discussions and the most widely-held view has the force of law, but it is a law without sanction, observed precisely because it is subject to the endorsement of the individual, except, of course, when it comes to resisting the employers. Finally, while they appoint a chairman, a delegated supervisor, for every session, this is not now the result of habit, for, once appointed, that chairman is utterly overlooked and himself frequently forgets the powers vested in him by his comrades.

As a laboratory of economic struggles, detached from election contests, favoring the general strike with all that that implies, governing itself along anarchic lines, the trade union is thus the simultaneously revolutionary and libertarian organization that alone will be able to counter and successfully reduce the noxious influence of the collectivist politicians. Suppose now that, on the day the revolution breaks out, virtually every single producer is organized into the unions: will these not represent, ready to step into the shoes of the present organization, a quasi-libertarian organization, in fact suppressing all political power, an organization whose every part, being master of the instruments of production, would settle all of its affairs for itself, in sovereign fashion and through the freely given consent of its members? And would this not amount to the "free association of free producers?"

To be sure, there are many objections: the federal agencies may turn into authorities; wily persons may come to govern the trade unions just the way the parliamentary socialists govern the political groupings; but such objections are only partly valid. In keeping with the spirit of the trade unions, the federal councils are merely half-way houses generated by the need to spread and make economic struggles more and more formidable, but which the success of the revolution would make redundant, and which, also, the groups from which they emanate monitor with too jealous an eye for them ever to successfully win a directorial authority. On the other hand, the permanent revocability of officials reduces their function and their profile to very little, and often indeed having done their duty is not enough for them to retain their comrades' confidence. Then again, trades organization is still only in the embryonic stages. Once rid of politicians' tyranny, it can stride out freely and, like the child learning to take his first steps, toddle along the road of independence. But who can say where a softly-softly approach and, rather more, the fruits of freedom will have carried them in ten years' time? It is up to libertarian socialists to commit all of their efforts to getting them there.

"The Federal Committee of the Bourses du Travail" — say the official minutes carried by the *Bulletin de la Bourse de Narbonne* — "has as its task the instruction of the people regarding the pointlessness of a revolution that would make do with the substitution of one State for another, even should this be a socialist State." That committee, states another minute due to appear in the *Bulletin de la Bourse de Perpignan,* "should strive to prepare an organization which, in the event of a transformation of society, may see to the operation of the economy through the free grouping and render any political institution superfluous. Its goal being the abolition of authority in any of its forms, its task is to accustom the workers to shrug off tutelage."

Thus, on the one hand, the "unionized" are today in a position to understand, study and receive libertarian teachings; on the other, anarchists need not fear that, in taking part in the corporative movement, they will be required to forswear their independence. The former are ready to accept and the latter can strengthen an organization whose resolutions are the products of free agreement — which, to borrow Grave's words (*La Société future* p. 202) "has neither laws, not statutes, nor regulations to which each individual may be obliged to submit on pain of some pre-determined penalty"— which individuals are at liberty to quit as they see fit, except, let me repeat, when battle has been joined with the enemy; which, when all is said and done, may be a practical schooling in anarchism.

Let free men then enter the trade union, and let the propagation of their ideas prepare the workers, the artisans of wealth there to understand that they should regulate their affairs for themselves, and then, when the time comes, smash not only existing political forms, but any attempt to reconstitute a new power. That will show the authorities how well-founded was their fear, posing as disdain, of "syndicalism," and how ephemeral their teaching, evaporated before it was even able to put down roots!

Notes for Anarchism and the Workers' Union

1. Written on October 20, 1895: printed in *Les Temps nouveaux* of November 2-8, 1895.
2. The reference is probably to Chapter III1 of *Le Systéme des contradictions économiques* (1846) and perhaps also to Chapter III of *La Theorie de l'impôt* (1861).
3. Clovis Hugues (1851–1907), French politician and poet: Ernest Ferroul (1853–1921), physician, socialist mayor and deputy for Narbonne.
4. Paul Lafargue (1842–1911), born in Cuba of French parents, student of medicine, initially a Proudhonian libertarian, then disciple and son-in-law of Karl Marx, marrying his daughter Laura: member of the International: actively involved in the Commune: Karl Marx's delegate to Spain, designated to combat Bakunin's supporters there: amnestied in 1880: elected deputy in 1891, he joined Jules Guesde in the launching of the Parti Ouvrier francais: author of *The Right to be Lazy*, a pamphlet of somewhat libertarian panache. He committed suicide alongside his wife on November 26, 1911 "pre-empting a pitiless old age."
5. On socialist unity, see Daniel Guérin's introduction to a forthcoming edition of Rosa Luxemburg's *Le Socialisme en France (1898–1912):* Edouard Vaillant (1840–1915), one of the greatest of French revolutionaries, a Blanquist to begin with, a member of the Commune of 1971, condemned to death, then amnestied. Wound up supporting the "Sacred Union."
6. By this term, Pelloutier means State socialism.

Emile Pouget (1860–1931)

Emile Pouget's Life as an Activist by Paul Delesalle [1]

Youth

Emile Pouget was born in 1860 near Rodez in the department of the Aveyron. His notary father died young. His mother re-married and in this way his life was, in a sense, unbalanced. Nonetheless, his stepfather, a good republican in his day, and a fighter like his stepson, quickly lost his post as a petty official over something he wrote in a little campaigning journal which he had founded.

It was at the high school in Rodez, where he began his studies, that his passion for journalism was conceived. At the age of fifteen, he launched his first newspaper, *Le Lycéen républicain*. I need not say what sort of reception this little sheet received from his teachers.

In 1875, his stepfather died. Emile was obliged to leave the high school to earn his living. Paris attracted him (. . .) Working in a novelty store, he began, after work, to frequent public meetings and progressive groups and quickly became wholly committed to revolutionary propaganda.

But even then, merely speculative, idealist anarchism left his pronounced social sensibilities unsatisfied and, as early as 1879, he was involved in the foundation in Paris of the first shop assistants' union. Such was Pouget's single-mindedness as an activist that he soon got his trade union to publish the earliest of anti-militarist pamphlets. Needless to say, it had been penned by our syndicalist and let me add that it would be unpublishable today on account both of the vehemence of his text and of the advice with which it was punctuated.

In and around 1882–1883, unemployment was pretty bad in Paris, so much so that on March 8, 1883 the cabinet-makers' chamber of trade invited the unemployed to an open air meeting scheduled to be held on the Esplanade des Invalides.

Naturally, the meeting was quickly broken up by the police, but two sizable groups of demonstrators formed: one set off for the Elysee palace, only to be dispersed quickly; the other, which included Louise Michel[2] and Pouget, raced towards the Boulevard Saint-Germain. A bakery in the Rue du Four was pretty well stripped bare.

Nevertheless, the demonstration carried on and it was only on arrival in the Place Maubert that it confronted a significant force of police. When the police rushed forward to arrest Louise Michel, Pouget did what he could to free her: he in turn was arrested and marched off to the station.

A few days later, he was brought before the assizes on the incorrect charge of armed robbery. Louise was sentenced to twelve years in prison, and Pouget to eight years, a sentence he was to serve in the criminal prison in Melun. He remained there for fully three years and an amnesty granted after pressure from Rochefort[2a] ensured that he was then released. Prison, however, had not cowed the militant.

Le Père Peinard

February 24, 1889 saw the publication of the very first edition of *Le Père Peinard* in small pamphlet form, reminiscent of Rochefort's *La Lanterne* and written in the picturesque style of Hébert's *Père Duchêne*, but in a more proletarian style.

(...) Pouget's little pamphlets met with a success difficult to appreciate today. During the life-span of *Le Père Peinard* — and then *La Sociale* — there was real proletarian agitation in certain workers' centers and I could name ten or twenty workers' districts, like Trélazé or Fourchambault, where the whole movement dwindled to nothing once the pamphlets stopped coming out.

In Paris in particular, among the cabinet-makers in the Faubourg Saint-Antoine, the trade union movement lasted just as long as *Le Père Peinard* did. In the years 1891–1893, a little campaigning sheet called *Le Pot-à-Colle* was published there, imitating the style.

(...) Pouget's anarchism is above all primarily proletarian. Right from the earliest issues of *Le Père Peinard*, he was praising strike movements and the May 1st editions were wholly given over to encouragement to the "lads" to get involved: "May 1st is an occasion that can be put to good use. All that is required is that our brothers, the troopers, should disobey their orders as they did in February 1848 and March 18, 1871 and that would be that."

He was one of the first to grasp the potential of the idea of the general strike and as early as 1889 he was writing:

Yes, by God, there is nothing else for it today, but the general strike!

Look what would happen if the coal was to run out in a fortnight. Factories would grind to a halt, the big towns would run out of gas and the railways would be at a stand-still.

All of a sudden, virtually the whole population would be idle. Which would give it time to reflect; it would realize that it is being robbed blind by the employers and yes, it might shake them up in double quick order!

And again:

So once the miners are all out and the strike would be all but general, by God, let them set to beavering away on their own account: the mine is theirs, stolen from them by the moneybags: let them snatch back what is theirs, double-quick. Come the day when they've had enough arsing about, there'll be a crop of good guys who will raise a storm like this and then! by Père Peinard, we'll have the beginning of the end!

A Great Proletarian Pamphleteer

But while the labor movement occupies a prime position, Pouget subjects every other aspect of the social question to the fine scrutiny of his implacable censure: he overlooks none of the blights of bourgeois society: one huge bank, the Comptoir d'Escompte, had just gone bust: it is worth quoting his article "The gabbers" in its entirety:

Those in government, cake-guzzlers and financiers, blackguards and side-kicks they are! Take today: it has been decided that there will be an inquiry. Let me have the system of '89, which was better. Thus, in July '89, Berthier de Sauvigny was strung up on a street lamp and another of his cronies, Foullon[3], was massacred. When are we going to get around to reviving that system for popping the clogs of the whole Rothschild and Schneider clique?

The excitement on the streets never left him cold.

Thus: "At home with our pals next door"; "In addition to the lads from Germany who are strutting around with bravado, the Macaronis are socking it to their big landlords and the Serbian and Bulgarian peasants, whom our hack journalists describe as brigands, are pitching into the bigwigs. And even the Brits, for all their phlegm and namy-pamby airs, have had their little strike."

Next came the "military nincompoops," criticism directed at the army, the "dirty work in the barracks" and an all-out assault — and how! — against the army and militarism.

"In the Palace of Injustice" takes on the bench and class justice and all I can say is that it too gets the treatment it deserves.

But that is not all. Every murmur of public opinion triggered an article, a special edition, for Pouget, above all else, had a real talent for propaganda and what needed to be said to the crowd.

The drawing of lots was one good excuse, as were the anniversaries of the Commune or of July 14, and the relevant issue of *Le Père Peinard* often carried a pull-out poster.[4] Nothing that roused public opinion, however trivial, left him indifferent. Because Pouget was, above all, a born reporter.

But where his polemics took a more personal turn — which was not exclusive to him, for it was typical of all the anarchists of the day — was in his criticisms of parliamentarism and the whole machinery of State.

What Pouget and the anarchists of his day were reviving in fact were the old tussles of the First International, between libertarian socialism on the one hand, represented by Bakunin, and Marx's authoritarian socialism on the other.

Guesde, the best of the representatives of the authoritarian socialism of the day, Pouget's *bete noire*, who gave as good as he got, used to go around everywhere shouting: "You working class! Send half of the deputies to Parliament plus one and the Revolution will not be far off a fait accompli." To which Pouget and his friends retorted: "Band together into your trades societies, into your unions and take over the workshops."

Two approaches which then and now pitted libertarian and authoritarian socialists one against the other, sometimes violently.

And when Pouget turned to illustrating his argument, the polemics were mordant. Judge for yourself: "These blessed elections are scheduled for Sunday! Naturally there is no shortage of candidates — there is something for every taste and in every hue; a sow could not pick out her own farrow. But by God while the candidates' colors and labels may alter, one thing never changes: The patter! Reactionaries, republicans, Boulangists, socialists, etc. — they all promise the people that they'll work themselves to death!"

And there was a virulent poster to expand upon this line of argument.

Repression

But such propaganda, conducted with so much vigor, was certainly not without drawbacks. Prosecutions came hot and heavy and while his editors might escape, Pouget too served his time in Saint-Pelagie, the prison of the day, not that that stopped Le Père Peinard from appearing, as his colleagues took it in turns to collect his copy from inside prison itself.

A period of such intense agitation — and, it must be said, not just that — had driven a number of individuals over the edge; a series of attentats followed, culminating in the assassination of President Carnot[5] in Lyons.

Whipped up by its servile press, the bourgeoisie was so spooked that it could see no way of salvation other than the passing by Parliament of a series of repressive laws quite properly described, once the panic had subsided, as **lois scélérates**[6] (blackguardly laws).

Arrests followed the hundreds of house searches carried out across the country and a great trial, known as the "Trial of the Thirty" was mounted.

Pouget and quite a few other comrades put some distance between themselves and their would-be judges. For him, it was the start of his exile and February 21, 1894 saw the publication of the 253rd and final edition of the first run of *Le Père Peinard*.

He fled to London, where he found Louise Michel.[7] It would be a mistake to believe that our comrade was about to stop, and in September that very same year the first issue of the London run of *Le Père Peinard* appeared. Eight issues appeared, the last in January 1895. But exile was no solution. The bourgeoisie was feeling a little more reassured and Pouget went home to face the music, and was acquitted, as were all of his co-accused in the "Trial of the Thirty."

None of these adventures had changed the militant's fervor one iota; on May 11 the same year, *Le Père Peinard*'s successor *La Sociale* came out. For a number of reasons, its founder was unable for the time being to resurrect the former title (which reappeared only in October 1896).

What are we to say of Pouget's two newborn creations, except that in terms of the intensity of their propaganda they were the match of their older brother? There was the same courage, more than courage indeed, for the "blackguardly laws" made difficulties even worse, and there was the same effrontery. It is from this period that the celebrated *Almanachs du Père Peinard* date, as do numerous propaganda pamphlets, one of which, *Les Variations Guesdistes* (Guesdist Zig-zagging) under Pouget's own signature created something of a sensation in socialist political circles.

Come the Dreyfus Affair, Pouget again could not help commenting. He threw himself into the fray, but his goal was to demand justice also for anarchists deported for penal servitude and perishing on Devil's Island, which was a destination specially reserved for them. Through his many articles and the pamphlet *Les Lois scélérates* (co-written with Francis de Pressense), he successfully captured the attention of the masses, and the government of the day was obliged to release some of the survivors of a supposed revolt adroitly staged in advance by the prison administration.

"La Voix du Peuple"

We come now to the year 1898. The General Confederation of Labor (CGT) was growing and growing and assuming an ever greater significance in society.

At Pouget's instigation, the Toulouse Congress (1897) had adopted a significant report on *Boycotting and Sabotage* offering the working class a novel weapon of struggle.

Finally, and this was his most cherished idea, he had dreamt of equipping the working class with a fighting journal written entirely by interested parties. An initial commitment to this had been forthcoming at the Toulouse Congress, and had been reiterated by the Rennes Congress. What the comrades had in mind at that point was a daily newspaper, a project which they were later forced to abandon in the light of all sorts of financial difficulties.

No matter. The idea had been floated and we would do well to remember here that it was also thanks to Pouget's tenacity that the first edition of *La Voix du Peuple* appeared on December 1, 1900.

Pouget, who had been appointed assistant secretary of the CGT, Federations branch, was in charge of getting the newspaper out each week. Thanks to his dogged efforts and with the aid of Fernand Pelloutier, the working class for the first time ever had a newspaper all of its very own.

(...) It would be an easy matter for me, with the aid of a complete run of *La Voix du Peuple* to rehearse, one by one, the campaigns of all sorts, the struggle against the placement offices, the campaign for a weekly rest day, the eight hour day and the battles against all manner of iniquities, in which the name of Emile Pouget continually crops up in the forefront of the battle.

The entire working class fought through his pen.

However, I have to recall those splendid and unforgettable special editions on "Drawing lots" or "May the first," conceived and presented in such a way that it is no exaggeration to say that such intensity of propaganda has never been outdone.

Let me recall too the campaign for the eight hour working day, culminating in May 1, 1906: One has to have lived through those times alongside Pouget to appreciate what propagandistic science — and no, that does not strike me as too strong a word for it — he deployed then. With the aid of his alter ego Victor Griffuelhes,[8] over a period of nearly two years, he was able to come up with something new every time to hold spellbound a mass of workers occasionally overly inclined to self-doubt. So there is no exaggeration in saying that, wherever it was able to enforce its will entirely, the working class enjoyed the eight hour day and owes that, in no small part, to Emile Pouget.

One need only review the succession of CGT congresses between 1896 and 1907 to get the measure of the profound influence that he wielded over those labor gatherings. His reports, his speeches and above all his effective work on working parties are still the most reliable index of syndicalism's debt to him. Might I recall that in Amiens he wielded the pen and that the motion which to this day remains the charter of authentic syndicalism is partly his handiwork?[9]

Apart from the many brochures written by him, we ought also to remember his contributions to many little labor newspapers as well as his great articles in Hubert Lagardelle's *Le Mouvement socialiste*,[10] studies so substantial that they cannot be ignored in any future examination of the origins and methods of the syndicalist movement in France that may wish to probe beneath the surface.

"La Revolution," Villeneuve-Saint-Georges and Retirement

(...) Pouget had a life-long obsession with a daily newspaper, but it had to be a proletarian newspaper reflecting the aspirations of the working class only. This is what he had in mind when, with other comrades, he launched *La Révolution*. Griffuelhes had a hand in it, as did Monatte.[11] Unfortunately, it takes a lot of money to keep a daily newspaper afloat and the anticipated help was not forthcoming. After a few months, *La Révolution* was forced to shut down. It was one of the greatest disappointments he had in his life, watching the foundering of a creation for which he had yearned so fervently.

I might stop at this point, but I have to recall the Draveil-Villeneuve-Saint-Georges affair. Indeed, with hindsight, it really does appear that this miserable and dismal episode was desired by Clemenceau.[12] That moreover was Griffuelhes's view, as well as Pouget's. Prosecutions were mounted against a number of militants, of whom Pouget, of course, was one. But after more than two months spent in Corbeil prison, the charges had to be dropped and there is no exaggeration in saying that had it come to trial, the stigma would doubtless not have attached itself to those in the dock.

But even then the health of Pouget, who is a good ten years older than us, was beginning to leave something to be desired.

In the long run, the struggle — as he understood the term — consumed the man to some extent. For him rest consisted of starting back to working for a living and right up until the day when illness laid him low, he never stopped working, despite his seventy one years.[13]

Notes to Emile Pouget's Life as an Activist by Paul Delesalle

1. Paul Delesalle (1870–1948), former steel-worker, anarchist and revolutionary syndicalist: contributed to *Les Temps nouveaux*, then was elected secretary of the Federation of the Bourses du Travail until 1907: later publisher and revolutionary book-seller. This text has been taken from *Le Cri du Peuple* of July 29 and August 5, 1931.
2. On Louise Michel see note 7 below.
2a. Henri Rochefort (Marquis de Rochefort-Luzay, 1830–1913), journalist and pamphleteer: mounted lively opposition to the Empire from his weekly paper *La Lanterne*. Deputy of the Commune in 1871.

3. Joseph Foullon (1717-1789) comptroller-general of finances, hanged and then beheaded after the fall of the Bastille.

4. A number of placards and posters under the title of "Le Père Peinard au Populo" had a print run in excess of 20,000 copies, and I could cite more than thirty such. (Note by Paul Delesalle)

5. Sadi Carnot (1837–1894) President of the French Republic, assassinated in Lyons by the Italian anarchist Caserio.

6. The "blackguardly" laws, designed to stamp out anarchist terrorist activity were passed after Auguste Vaillant's outrage in 1894. Auguste Vaillant (1861–1894), anarchist, **enfant de la balle,** Jack of all trades, was guillotined after throwing a bomb into the benches of the Chamber of Deputies on December 9, 1893.

7. Louise Michel (1830–1905) teacher and indomitable anarchist militant: she participated in the Paris Commune of 1871, was deported and later pardoned.

8. Victor Griffuelhes (1874–1923) one-time cobbler: at first a Blanquist, he became a revolutionary syndicalist: general secretary of the CGT from 1902 to 1909.

9. The Charter of Amiens (1906), in which revolutionary syndicalism proclaimed itself independent of political parties.

10. Hubert Lagardelle (1875–1958), lawyer, began as a Guesdist, then became founder of *Le Mouvement socialiste* (1899–1914), a theoretical revolutionary syndicalist review: author of the remarkable book *Le socialisme francais*. He ended up a minister under Marshal Petain.

11. Pierre Monatte (1881–1960), proof-reader, contributed to the anarchist review *Les Temps nouveaux* then, having become a revolutionary syndicalist, joined the CGT's pre-1914 Confederal Committee: he founded the review *La Vie ouvriere* which lasted from 1909 to 1914. In 1923 he joined the French Communist Party and became editor of the social affairs page in *L'Humanite*. He was expelled from the Party in November 1924, whereupon he launched *La Revolution Proletarienne*, organ of the Ligue syndicaliste. See *Syndicalisme revolutionnaire et communisme, les archives de Pierre Monatte* (1969).

12. In 1908 strikes in Draveil and Villeneuve-Saint-Georges were crushed with bloodshed by the government of Georges Clemenceau (1841-1g29), after which the leaders of the CGT were arrested.

13. In 1920, in the village of Lozere (Palaiseau) a pauper's hearse, followed by Pierre Monatte, Maurice Chambelland and a few others, myself (Daniel Guérin) among them, bore Emile Pouget to his final resting place.

What is the Trade Union? by Emile Pouget[1]

Property and authority are merely differing manifestations and expressions of one and the same "principle" which boils down to the enforcement and enshrinement of the servitude of man. Consequently, the only difference between them is one of vantage point: viewed from one angle, slavery appears as a **property crime**, whereas, viewed from a different angle, it constitutes an **authority crime**.

In life, these "principles" whereby the peoples are muzzled are erected into oppressive institutions of which only the facade had changed over the ages. At present and in spite of all the tinkering carried out on the ownership system and the adjustments made to the exercise of authority, quite superficial tinkerings and adjustments, submission, constraint, forced labor, hunger, etc. are the lot of the laboring classes.

This is why the Hell of Wage-Slavery is a lightless Gehenna: the vast majority of human beings languish there, bereft of well-being and liberty. And in that Gehenna, for all its cosmetic trappings of democracy, a rich harvest of misery and grief grows.

Essential Association

The trade association is, in fact, the only focal point which, in its very composition, reflects the aspirations by which the wage slave is driven: being the sole agglomeration of human beings that grows out of an absolute identity of interests, in that it derives its raison d'être from the form of production, upon which it models itself and of which it is merely the extension.

What in fact is the trade union? An association of workers bound together by corporative ties. Depending on the setting, this corporative combination may assume the form of the narrower trade connection or, in the context of the massive industrialization of the 19th century, may embrace proletarians drawn from several trades but whose efforts contribute towards a common endeavor.

However, whatever the format preferred by its members or imposed by circumstance, whether the trade union combination is restricted to the "trade" or encompasses the "industry," there is still the very same objective. To wit:

1. The offering of constant resistance to the exploiter: forcing him to honor the improvements won; deterring any attempt to revert to past practice; and also seeking to minimize the exploitation through pressure for partial improvements such as reduction of working hours, increased pay, improved hygiene etc., changes which, although they may reside in the details, are nonetheless effective trespasses against capitalist privileges and attenuation of them.

2. The trade union aims to cultivate increasing coordination of relations of solidarity, in such a way as to facilitate, within the shortest time possible, the expropriation of capital, that being the sole basis which could possibly mark the commencement of a thoroughgoing transformation of society. Only once that legitimate social restitution has been made can any possibility of parasitism be excluded. Only then, when no one is any longer obliged to work for someone else, wage-slavery having been done away with, can production become social in terms of its destination as well as of its provenance: at which time, economic life being a genuine sum of reciprocal efforts, all exploitation can be, not just abolished, but rendered impossible.

Thus, thanks to the trade union, the social question looms with such clarity and starkness as to force itself upon the attention of even the least clear-sighted persons; without possibility of error, the trade association marks out a dividing line between wage slaves and masters. Thanks to which society stands exposed as it truly is: on one side, the workers, the robbed; on the other, the exploiters, the robbers.

Trade Union Autonomy

However superior the trade union may be to every other form of association, it does not follow that it has any intrinsic existence, independent of that breathed into it by its membership. Which is why the latter, if they are to conduct themselves as conscious union members, owe it to themselves to participate in the work of the trade union. And, for their part, they would have no conception of what constitutes the strength of this association, were they to imagine that they come to it as perfect union members, simply by doing their duty by the union financially.

Of course, it is a good thing to pay one's dues on a regular basis, but that is only the merest fragment of the duty a loyal member owes to himself, and thus to his trade union; indeed, he ought to be aware that the union's value resides, not so much in the sum of their monetary contributions as in multiplication of its members' coherent endeavors.

The constituent part of the trade union is the individual. Except that the union member is spared the depressing phenomenon manifest in democratic circles where, thanks to the veneration of universal suffrage, the trend is towards the crushing and diminution of the human personality. In a democratic setting, the elector can avail of his will only in order to perform an act of abdication: his role is to "award" his "vote" to the candidate whom he wishes to have as his "representative."

Affiliation to the trade union has no such implications and even the greatest stickler could not discover the slightest trespass against the human personality in it: after, as well as before, the union member is what he used to be. Autonomous he was and autonomous he remains.

In joining the union, the worker merely enters into a contract — which he may at any time abjure — with comrades who are his equals in will and potential, and at no time will any of the views he may be induced to utter or actions in which he may happen to participate, imply any of the suspension or abdication of personality which is the distinguishing characteristic and badge of the ballot paper.

In the union, say, should it come to the appointment of a trade union council to take charge of administrative matters, such "selection" is not to be compared with "election": the form of voting customarily employed in such circumstances is merely a means whereby the labor can be divided and is not accompanied by any delegation of authority. The strictly prescribed duties of the trade union council are merely administrative. The council performs the task entrusted to it, without ever overruling its principals, without supplanting them or acting in their place.

The same might be said of all decisions reached in the union: all are restricted to a definite and specific act, whereas in democracy, election implies that the elected candidate has been issued by his elector with a carte blanche empowering him to decide and do as he pleases, in and on everything, without even the hindrance of the quite possibly contrary wishes of his principals, whose opposition, in any case, no matter how pronounced, is of no consequence until such time as the elected candidate's mandate has run its course.

So there cannot be any possible parallels, let alone confusion, between trade union activity and participation in the disappointing chores of politics.

The Trade Union as School for the Will

Socrates's dictum "Know thyself!" is, in the trade union context, complemented by the maxim: "Shift for yourself!"

Thus, the trade union offers itself as a school for the will: its preponderant role is the result of its members' wishes, and, if it is the highest form of association, the reason is that it is the condensation of workers' strengths made effective through their direct action, the sublime form of the deliberate enactment of the wishes of the proletarian class.

The bourgeoisie has contrived to preach resignation and patience to the people by holding out the hope that progress might be achieved miraculously and without effort on their part, through the State's intervention from without. This is nothing more than an extension, in less inane form, of millenarian and crude religious beliefs. Now, while the leaders were trying to substitute this disappointing illusion for the no less disappointing religious mirage, the workers, toiling in the shadows, with indomitable and unfailing tenacity, were building the organ of liberation to which the trade union amounts.

That organ, a veritable school for the will, was formed and developed over the 19th century. It is thanks to it, thanks to its economic character that the workers have been able to survive inoculation with the virus of politics and defy every attempt to divide them.

It was in the first half of the 19th century that trades associations were established, in spite of the interdicts placed upon them. The persecution of those who had the effrontery to unionize was ruthless, so it took ingenuity to give repression the slip. So, in order to band together without undue danger, the workers disguised their resistance associations behind anodyne exteriors, such as mutual societies.

The bourgeoisie has never taken umbrage with charitable bodies, knowing very well that, being mere palliatives, they cannot ever offer a remedy for the curse of poverty. The placing of hope in charity is a soporific good only for preventing the exploited from reflecting upon their dismal lot and searching for a solution to it. This is why mutual associations have always been tolerated, if not, encouraged, by those in charge.

Workers were able to profit from the tolerance shown these groups: under the pretext of helping one another in the event of illness, of setting up retirement homes, etc., they were able to get together, but in pursuit of a more manly objective: they were preoccupied with bettering their living conditions and aimed to resist the employers' demands. Their tactics were not always successful in escaping the attentions of the authorities which, having been alerted by complaints from employers, often kept these dubious mutual aid societies under surveillance.

Later, by which time the workers, by dint of experience and acting for themselves, felt strong enough to defy the law, they discarded the mutualist disguise and boldly called their associations resistance societies.

A splendid name! expressive and plain. A program of action in itself. It is proof of the extent to which workers, even though their trades associations were still in the very early stages, sensed that had no need to trot along behind the politicians nor amalgamate their interests with the interests of the bourgeoisie, but instead should be taking a stand against and in opposition to the bourgeoisie.

Here we had an instinctive incipient class struggle which the International Working Men's Association was to provide with a clear and definitive formulation, with its announcement that "the emancipation of the workers must be the workers' own doing."

That formula, a dazzling affirmation of workers' strength, purged of all remnants of democratism, was to furnish the entire proletarian movement with its key-note idea. It was, moreover, merely an open and categorical affirmation of tendencies germinating among the people. This is abundantly demonstrated by the theoretical and tactical concordance between the hitherto vague, underground "trade unionist" movement and the International's opening declaration.

After stating as a principle that the workers should rely upon their own unaided efforts, the International's declaration married the assertion of the necessity of the proletariat's enjoying autonomy to an indication that it is only through direct action that it can obtain tangible results: and it went on to say:

Given,

That the economic subjection of the worker to those who hold the means of labor, which is to say, the wherewithal of life, is the prime cause of political, moral and material servitude;

The economic emancipation of workers is, consequently, the great goal towards which every political movement should be striving (...)

Thus, the International did not confine itself to plain proclamation of workers' autonomy, but married that to the assertion that political agitations and adjustments to the form of the government ought not to make such an impression upon workers as to make them lose sight of the economic realities.

The current trade unionist movement is only a logical sequel to the movement of the International — there is absolute identity between them and it is on the same plane that we carry on the endeavors of our predecessors.

Except that when the International was setting out its premises, the workers' will was still much too clouded and the proletariat's class consciousness too under-developed for the economic approach to prevail without the possibility of deviation.

The working class had to contend with the distracting influence of seedy politicians who, regarding the people merely as a stepping-stone, flatter it, hypnotize it and betray it. Moreover, the people also let itself be carried away by loyal, disinterested men who, being imbued with democratism, placed too great a store by a redundant State.

It is thanks to the dual action of these elements that in recent times (beginning with the hecatomb of 1871) the trade union movement vegetated for a long time, being torn in several directions at once. On the one hand, the crooked politicians strove to bridle the unions so as to tie them to the government's apron strings: on the other, the socialists of various schools beavered away at ensuring that their faction would prevail. Thus, one and all intended to turn the trade unions into "interest groups" and "affinity groups."

The trade union movement had roots too vigorous, and too ineluctable a need for such divergent efforts to be able to stunt its development. Today, it carries on the work of the International, the work of the pioneers of "resistance societies" and of the earliest combinations. To be sure, tendencies have come to the surface and theories have been clarified, but there is an absolute concordance between the 19th century trade union movement and that of the 20th century: the one being an outgrowth of the other. In this there is a logical extension, a climb towards an ever more conscious will and a display of the increasingly coordinated strength of the proletariat, blossoming into a growing unity of aspirations and action.

The Task in Hand

Trade union endeavor has a double aim: with tireless persistence, it must pursue betterment of the working class's current conditions. But, without letting themselves become obsessed with this passing concern, the workers should take care to make possible and imminent the essential act of comprehensive emancipation: the expropriation of capital.

At present, trade union action is designed to win partial and gradual improvements which, far from constituting a goal, can only be considered as a means of stepping up demands and wresting further improvements from capitalism.

The trade union offers employers a degree of resistance in geometric proportion with the resistance put up by its members: it is a brake upon the appetites of the exploiter: it enforces his respect for less draconian working conditions than those entailed by the individual bargaining of the wage slave operating in isolation. For one-sided bargaining between the employer with his breast-plate of capital, and the defenseless proletarian, it substitutes collective bargaining.

So, in opposition to the employer there stands the trade union, which mitigates the despicable "labor market" and labor supply, by relieving, to some extent, the irksome consequences of a pool of unemployed workers: exacting from the employer respect for workers and also, to a degree proportionate with its strength, the union requires of him that he desist from offering privileges as bribes.

This question of partial improvements served as the pretext for attempts to sow discord in the trades associations. Politicians, who can only make a living out of a confusion of ideas and who are irritated by the unions' growing distaste for their persons and their dangerous interference, have tried to carry into economic circles the semantic squabbling with which they gull the electors. They have striven to stir up ill-feeling and to split the unions into two camps, by categorizing workers as reformists and as revolutionaries. The better to discredit the latter, they have dubbed them "the advocates of all or nothing" and they have falsely represented them as supposed adversaries of improvements achievable right now.

The most that can be said about such nonsense is that it is witless. There is not a worker, whatever his mentality or his aspirations, who, on grounds of principle or for reasons of tactics, would insist upon working ten hours for an employer instead of eight hours, while earning six francs instead of seven. It is, however, by peddling such inane twaddle that politicians hope to alienate the working class from its economic movement and dissuade it from shifting for itself and endeavoring to secure ever greater well-being and liberty. They are counting upon the poison in such calumnies to break up the trade unions by reviving inside them the pointless and divisive squabbles which have evaporated ever since politics was banished from them.

What appears to afford some credence to such chicanery is the fact that the unions, cured by the cruel lessons of experience from all hope in government intervention, are justifiably mistrustful of it. They know that the State, whose function is to act as capital's gendarme, is, by its very nature, inclined to tip the scales in favor of the employer side. So, whenever a reform is brought about by legal avenues, they do not fall upon it with the relish of a frog devouring the red rag that conceals the hook, they greet it with all due caution, especially as this reform is made effective only if the workers are organized to insist forcefully upon its implementation.

The trade unions are even more wary of gifts from the government because they have often found these to be poison gifts. Thus, they have a very poor opinion of "gifts" like the Higher Labor Council and the labor councils, agencies devised for the sole purpose of counter-balancing and frustrating the work of the trades associations. Similarly, they have not waxed enthusiastic about mandatory arbitration and regulation of strikes, the plainest consequence of which would be to exhaust the workers' capacity for resistance. Likewise, the legal and commercial status granted to the workers' organizations have nothing worthwhile to offer them, for they see in these a desire to get them to desert the terrain of social struggle, in order to lure them on to the capitalist terrain where the antagonism of the social struggle would give way to wrangling over money.

But, given that the trade unions look askance at the government's benevolence towards them, it follows that they are loath to go after partial improvements. Wanting real improvements only. This is why, instead of waiting until the government is generous enough to bestow them, they wrest them in open battle, through direct action.

If, as sometimes is the case, the improvement they seek is subject to the law, the trade unions strive to obtain it through outside pressure brought to bear upon the authorities and not by trying to return specially mandated deputies to Parliament, a puerile pursuit that might drag on for centuries before there was a majority in favor of the yearned-for reform.

When the desired improvement is to be wrested directly from the capitalist, the trades associations resort to vigorous pressure to convey their wishes. Their methods may well vary, although the direct action principle underlies them all: depending on the circumstances, they may use the strike, sabotage, the boycott, or the union label.

But, whatever the improvement won, it must always represent a reduction in capitalist privileges and be a partial expropriation. So, whenever one is not satisfied with the politician's bombast, whenever one analyzes the methods and the value of trade union action, the fine distinction between "reformist" and "revolutionary" evaporates and one is led to the conclusion that the only really reformist workers are the revolutionary syndicalists.

Building the Future

Aside from day to day defense, the task of the trade unions is to lay the groundwork for the future. The producer group should be the cell of the new society. Social transformation on any other basis is inconceivable. So it is essential that the producers make preparations for the task of assuming possession and of reorganization which ought to fall to them and which they alone are equipped to carry out. It is a social revolution and not a political revolution that we aim to make. They are two distinct phenomena and the tactics leading to the one are a diversion away from the other.

Notes to What is the Trade Union? by Emile Pouget

1. Taken from *Le Syndicat* 1905.

THE SPANISH COLLECTIVES

Given that most of the preceding texts have had to with plans for an anarchist society, it strikes us that it might be useful to add, by way of contrast and complement, some documents telling of an actual experiment in libertarian construction: the experiment of the Spanish **collectives** of 1936. The anarchists' political and military role in the Spanish Revolution and Civil War will, of course have to wait until Volume IV of this anthology. But we believe a leap forward in time may be useful at this point: after the speculation comes the practice of self-management. In any case, there is a direct link between the speculators and the practitioners: the latter had very specifically heeded the lessons of the former. Thus, the reader will be better placed to appreciate anarchism's constructive, rather than destructive, potential.

Collectivization in Spain by Augustin Souchy[1]

What occurred in Spain [in the wake of July 19] was something quite unprecedented. In fact, the commandeering of land and factories by the Spanish workers was not designed merely to bring pressure to bear upon the proprietors, managers and public authorities in order to secure improved working conditions and pay: instead, it was well and truly aimed at vesting direct management of the means of production and exchange in all who operated them — and, in the case of lands left fallow or inefficient firms, this "taking charge" was in the nature of an authentic social rescue measure. Handicapped on the world market for farm produce and industrial products by a parasitical administration as well as competition from new countries, bourgeois Spain had not the ability to help its unemployed nor to make proper use of its own soil and grow its own food.

The response of the Spain of the workers and peasants to that was an act of fairness and responsibility performed by the rank and file, eschewing all bureaucracy and party political dictatorship, enabling the country to feed itself.

On July 19 and the days that followed every large undertaking was abandoned by its directors. The directors of the railway companies, urban transport companies, shipping lines, heavy steel industries, the textile industry, and the chairmen and representatives of the employers' associations had all vanished. The general strike which the working class had unleashed by way of defending itself against the rebels brought the entire economic life of the country to a standstill for eight days.

Once the back of the rebellion had been broken, the workers' organizations resolved to call off the strike. The CNT members in Barcelona were convinced that work could not be resumed on the same conditions as before. The general strike had not been a strike designed to protect or secure improvements in pay or better working conditions. None of the entrepreneurs had stuck around. The workers had not just to return to their jobs in the plant, on the locomotive or tram or in the office. They also had to take over the overall direction of factories, workshops, firms, etc. In other words, the management of industry and the entire economy was now in the hands of workers and clerical staff employed in every segment of the country's economy.

In Spain, especially in Catalonia, the socialization process started with collectivization. This should not be construed as the implementation of some preconceived scheme. It was spontaneous. In any case, the influence of anarchist teachings upon this change-over cannot be questioned. For many a long year, Spain's anarchists and syndicalists had regarded the social transformation of society as their ultimate objective. In their trade union assemblies and groups, in their newspapers, pamphlets and books, the issue of social revolution was endlessly and systematically discussed. What should happen once the proletariat had won? The machinery of government had to be dismantled. The workers had to operate their firms for themselves, administer themselves and the unions should oversee all economic activity. The industrial federations had to run production: local federations would see to consumption. Such were the ideas of the anarcho-syndicalists, ideas to which the FAI subscribed also. In its conferences and congresses, the latter had continually reiterated that economic life should be run by the trade unions.

(...) After 19 July 1936, the CNT unions took charge of production and supply. At first the unions strove to resolve the most pressing problem: keeping the population supplied. In every district, canteens were set up on the union premises. Supply committees took it upon themselves to seek out provisions in the central depots in the towns, or in the countryside. These provisions were paid for with vouchers whose value was guaranteed by the unions. Every union member and the wives and children of militians, as well as the general populace were all fed free of charge. During strikes, workers got no wages. The Antifascist Militias Committee decided to pay workers and staff however much they would have earned had they worked those days.

COLLECTIVIZATION OF INDUSTRY[2]

(...) Stage one of collectivization began when the workers took charge of running their firms. In every workshop, office, bureau or retail outlet trade union delegates were appointed to act as the managers. Often, these new directors lacked grounding in theory and lacked expertise in national economics. However, they had a thorough grounding in their personal needs and the demands of the moment.

(...) They knew their trade, their industry's production process and could offer advice. What they lacked in training they made up for in initiative and inventiveness.

In some textile plants, red and black silk neckerchiefs were produced, over-printed with antifascist slogans. These neckerchiefs were put on sale. "How did you come to set the price? How did you work out the profit margin?" asked one foreign, marxist reporter. "I don't know anything about profit margin," answered the worker to whom these questions had been put. "We looked up the raw material costs in books, worked out running costs, added on a supplement by way of reserve funds, tacked on wage costs, added on a 10 percent supplement for the Antifascist Militias Committee, and the price was set." The neckerchiefs were sold cheaper than they would have been under the old regime. Wages had been increased and the profit margin — sacrosanct in bourgeois economics — was put towards the fight against fascism.

In this way, in most firms the management of production was assumed by the workers. As long as they resisted the new economic management the bosses were shown the door. They were allowed in as workers if they agreed to the new arrangements. In which case, they would be taken on as technicians, business directors or indeed as simple workmen. They received a wage equivalent to that earned by a worker or technician following that trade.

That start and these changes were comparatively rather straightforward. Difficulties emerged later. After rather a short time, raw materials ran out. In the first few days after the Revolution, raw materials had been requisitioned. Later they had to be paid for, which is to say, entered in the accounts. Very few raw materials arrived from abroad, leading to an escalation in the prices of raw materials and finished goods. Wages were increased, but not across the board. In some industries, the increase was considerable. During the first phase of collectivization, the wages of workers or staff differed, even within the same industry.

(. . .) The unions decided to look to the control of firms themselves. Factory unions turned into industrial enterprises. The Barcelona construction union took charge of work on different building sites in the city. Barber shops were collectivized. In every barber shop, there was a trade union delegate. Each week, he brought all of the takings to the union's economic committee. The costs of the barber shops were defrayed by the trade union, as was the wage bill.

(. . .) However, certain sectors of the economy worked better than others. There were rich industries and poor ones, high wages and low ones. The collectivization process could not (. . .) stop at this point. At the Barcelona Local Federation of (CNT) Unions, there were discussions about the creation of a liaison committee. The latter was to embrace all of the economic committees from the various unions, funds were to be concentrated in a single place, and an equalization fund would ensure that funds were properly allocated. In certain industries, this liaison committee and equalization fund had been in existence from the outset. The Barcelona Bus Company, a profitable undertaking run by its workforce had excess revenues. A portion of that revenue was set aside for the purchase of materials abroad. A further portion was set aside for the upkeep of the Tram Company whose revenues were lower than those of the Bus Company.

When petrol became scarce, 4,000 taxi drivers became unemployed. Their wages still had to be paid by the union. This was a heavy burden upon the Transport Union. It was forced to seek assistance from two other unions and from Barcelona corporation.

In the textile industry, because of the dearth of raw materials, working hours had to be reduced. In certain plants, they were down to a three-day week. However, the workers had to have their pay. As the Textile Union did not have the funds at its disposal, the Generalidad had to pay the wages instead.

The collectivization process could not rest there. Trade unionists pressed for socialization. But socialization does not, to them, signify nationalization, or State direction of the economy. Socialization is to be generalized collectivization. It is a matter of gathering the capital from various unions into one central fund: concentration at local federation level turned into a sort of communal economic enterprise. It boils down to a bottom-up socialization of workers' activities at commune level.

Collectivization in Agriculture

Not just in Catalonia, but also in every other part of Spain, collectivist traditions went deep. Once the power of the generals had been defeated, there was a discernible general aspiration favoring collectivization of the existing large estates. The trade union organizations and anarchist groups placed themselves at the head of this campaign for collectivization. They kept faith with their traditions.

Collectivization of the land in Spain proceeded along different lines from the ones in Russia. Agricultural property, at commune level, was collectivized if it had previously belonged to a large landowner. The latter had sided with the clerical-military clique and against the people. Those landowners who had agreed to the economic changes were able to go on working under the supervision of the union which spear-headed the collectivization. Exporters also went over to the union and, in several places, so too did the small-holders.

The land and property were worked in common by the rural workers, all produce being handed over to the union which paid the wages and marketed the produce. Those small-holders unwilling to join the trade union operate on the outside of the collectivization. They have a hard struggle to make a living. No pressure was brought to bear on them, but the advantages of collective production were not extended to them either. Inside the union, on the other hand, work is organized along rational lines. The principle of "all for one and one for all" really does apply there. So the small-holder lives apart from the commune (or community). When it comes to the sharing out of farm machinery, food produce, etc., the small-holder is at the back of the queue.[3]

The farmworkers' union today constitutes an economic enterprise. The cleaning and packaging of different fruits destined for shipment were entrusted to union supervision. Workers get their wages from the union. In certain communes, economic life as a whole is in the unions' hands. The union has appointed several committees to organize work, oversee consumption and distribution and the fight against fascism. Insofar as they exist, cafes and cinemas are under trade union control. In small localities there is no difference between the various trades unions or crafts sections. They are all amalgamated into a local federation which represents the economic nerve center as well as the political and cultural hub of the commune.

In one sector there was no collectivization: banking.

So how come the banks were not organized? The bank staffs were barely organized. They belonged, not to the CNT unions, but to the unions of the UGT which is against collectivization. The socialist UGT in fact has a different tradition. Its ideology is social democratic and it aims at State ownership. According to that outlook, socialization has to be implemented by the State through decrees. The government failed to order the banks collectivized (...) The seizure of bank assets would have made possible a central, single reallocation of funding and the drafting of a financial plan. A regulating body might have been established. At the instigation of representatives from the industrial unions, the bank employees could have drawn up a scheme for the financing of essential sectors of the country's economy. The country's mighty financial power could have been placed immediately in the service of collectivization. Collectivization would not have stayed partial but could have been extended into the whole of economic life.

After seven months of collectivizations, the unions, in the light of their experiences, observed that all of the collectivized undertakings across a range of industries stood in need of coordination. So they worked on the basis of first hand experience. The central directory, which has been established today, need not bother itself with the creation of subordinate bodies, as these already exist. The edifice of collectivization rests on a solid foundation, based on the industrial union, its trades sections in firms and the workshops themselves.

The unions also entertained the notion of regulating supply, without, however, intending to claim a monopoly there. The Foodstuffs Union took over the operation of the bakeries. (In Barcelona, there are no large bakeries, no bread factories.)

Alongside the latter there are still little bakers' shops operating as before. The ferrying of milk from the countryside into the towns is also handled by the unions who likewise see to the running of most of the dairies. The Foodstuffs Union oversees agricultural concerns and works hand in glove with the collectivized farms.

(...) In Russia, during the early days of the revolution, the shops were shut down. This was not the case in Spain. The larger outlets were taken over by the unions. The smaller shops obtained their goods from the union. In the case of small shops, prices were fixed across the board. Organized internal commerce was controlled. The supply monopoly was headed by a Supply Council. The aim was to organize and orchestrate supply generally right across Catalonia, in such a way that every area's needs might be met. A uniform price was set by the collectivized communes, the fishermen's unions and other food suppliers, in accordance with availability. The object of this economic policy was to prevent rises in food prices. In which case speculators and hoarders could be eliminated.

In mid-December, this policy was set aside. December 16 saw the formation of a new Catalan government. The communists managed to have the POUM (Workers' Party for Marxist Unification) excluded from the government. In the allocation of ministries, the supply ministry was awarded to Comorera,[4] a member of the (Third International-affiliated) Unified Socialist Party (PSUC). Another ministry was assigned to Domenech, representing the members of the CNT. Comorera did away with the monopoly on supply. Freedom of trade was reintroduced. The gates were opened for price rises. In that area, collectivization was set aside.

In the transport sector, the felicitous results of collectivization are striking. Despite a general rise in costs, the fares of the Barcelona transport companies were not increased. Brand-new and freshly painted trams as well as new buses appeared on Barcelona's streets. Lots of taxi cabs were overhauled.

The position in the textile industry is not so good. Because of the dearth of raw materials, many plants are down to a two- or three-day week, but four days' pay is issued. Persistence of this situation undermines these undertakings. The income of workers in receipt of only four days' pay is inadequate. This is not a result of collectivization, but rather a product of the war. Catalonia's textile industry has lost its main outlets. Part of Andalusia, Extremadura, Old Castile and the whole of northern Spain, along with the teeming industrial region of Asturias are in fascist hands. There is no way to locate fresh markets.

(. . .) During the first month of 1937, the position improved a little, thanks to army contracts. In Sabadell, a textile town with a population of 60,000 people, all of the workforce is in employment. In Barcelona, some spinning mills are still on reduced hours.

(...) Collectivization opens up new prospects and leads down new roads. In Russia, the Revolution followed the path of State controls. (. . .) In Spain (...) the people itself, the peasants in the countryside and the workers in the towns, have assumed control of the use of the land and the means of production. Amid great difficulties, groping their way and learning by trial and error, they press ever forwards, striving to build up an equitable economic system in which the workers themselves are the beneficiaries of the fruits of their labors.

Notes to Collectivization in Spain by Augustin Souchy

1. Augustin Souchy, a German anarcho-syndicalist who placed himself in the service of the Spanish Revolution. These extracts are from his *Collectivization, l'oeuvre constructive de la révolution espagnole* of April 1937 (republished 1965): The abbreviations used are: CNT – National Confederation of Labor (anarcho-syndicalist); FAI – Iberian Anarchist Federation; UGT – General Workers' Union.
2. The sub-titles have been added (Daniel Guérin's note).
3. In the province of Valencia, I witnessed an assembly of the farmworkers, at which the smallholders were also represented. These were also free to take part in the discussions. They complained that they did not have such and such. They were invited to join the union. A commission submitted a report on potential improvements to the working of the soil. It was very educational to see the workers there present fleshing out the commission's proposals with their own experiences. (Note by Augustin Souchy).
4. Juan Comorera, a Catalan socialist turned Communist in 1936 and a councilor in the Generalidad of Catalonia: he was later expelled from the party: fearing that he was marked for assassination, he entered Spain clandestinely and was sentenced to a lengthy term of imprisonment: he died in prison.

The Program of the Aragonese Federation of Collectives (March 14, 1937)

I. Structure of the Regional Federation of Agricultural Collectives

1. The regional federation of collectives is hereby constituted, for the purpose of coordinating the region's economic potential, and in order to afford solidary backing to that federation, in accordance with the principles of autonomy and federalism which are ours.

2. In the constitution of this federation, the following rules must be observed: a) collectives must federate with one another at cantonal level; b) in order to ensure that the cantonal committees achieve cohesion and mutual control, a **Regional Committee of Collectives** is to be established.

3. The collectives are to make precise inventory of their output and their consumption, which they are to forward to their respective cantonal committee — which is to forward it to the regional committee.

4. The abolition of money in the collectives and its replacement by ration card will make it possible for the requisite amounts of basic necessities to be made available to each collective.

5. So that the regional committee may see that the collectives are supplied with imported goods, the collectives or the cantonal committees shall furnish the regional committee with a quantity of products reflecting the wealth of each locality or canton, so as to build up the regional fund for external trade.

II. The New Organizational Schema for Land Administration

We embrace the municipality or commune as the future agency to oversee the administration of the people's assets. However, as **cantonally federated collectives**, we intend to do away with the local boundaries of the property which we farm and, in our view, the congress will have to tackle the following items:

1. As the collectives are organized as cantonal federations, it is to be understood that the local holdings administered by these federations shall henceforth constitute a single estate without internal boundaries. And, with regard to anything having to do with tilled lands, working tools, farm machinery and the raw materials set aside for them, these are to be made available to collectives which may be lacking in them.

2. An appeal is to be issued to those collectives with a surplus of manpower or which, at certain times in the year, are not using all of their producers because their services may not yet be required, and the available teams may be put to work, under the supervision of the cantonal committee, to bolster those collectives which are short of man-power.

III. Policy with Regard to Local Councils and Small-holders

1. Relations with local councils: a) Local councils made up of representatives from the various antifascist organizations have a specific, wholly lawful function, as acknowledged by the Aragon Regional Defense Committee. b) The administrative councils of collectives perform a function clearly distinct from that of the local and cantonal councils. c) But as the trade unions are called upon to appoint and monitor the delegates to the two aforementioned functions, they can be performed by the same comrade, it being understood that he ought not to mix them up in any way.

2. Relations with small-holders: a) Be it understood that small-holders who, of their own volition, hold aloof from the collectives, have no right to require labor services or services in kind from it, since they claim that they can meet their own needs for themselves. b) All real estate, rural and urban, and other assets which belonged to seditious personnel at the moment of expropriation and which are incorporated into the collective, become collective property. In addition, all of the land which has thus far not been put to work by its owner, farmer or sharecropper, passes into the ownership of the collective. c) No small-holder holding aloof from the collective will be allowed to possess more land than he will have farmed for himself, the understanding being that such possession will not entitle him to receipt of any of the benefits of the new society. d) In the eyes of the combined workers, he shall be deemed a free and responsible individual as long as his person and his possessions shall cause no upset to the collective order.

Some Local Examples of Collectivization[1]

Lecera (Aragon)

Lecera is the premier village in the province of Zaragoza and within the jurisdiction of Belchite, from which it lies twelve kilometers distant.

It has a population of 2,400 and has a few industries, notably the plaster industry. Agriculture accounts for the remainder, and the most important crops are wheat, vines, saffron and a few other cereals, albeit on a small scale.

Upon arrival in these places which have today been turned into camps servicing the militias, the first thing we do is to discover the whereabouts of the people's committee. Here, we discover it in the former mayor's office.

Comrade Pedro Navarro Jarque, a national school-teacher and native of Lecera, answers our queries: — The Committee was known as the antifascist revolutionary committee and was made up of seven members, all drawn from the CNT-affiliated Amalgamated Trades union. It has a completely free hand and no political party can stay its hand or influence it. We were appointed at an assembly and we reflect the aspirations of the whole village. We have the same powers as a mayor's office as far as anything to do with administration and the life of the population are concerned. There is a local administrative council made up of five members who are also drawn from the CNT trade union and it oversees work in the fields and in the industries in Lecera. We have appointed a labor delegate who, in conjunction with twelve sub-delegates, looks after the requirements of the column fighting on the front and looks after collective labor. All of them, of course, are in agreement with the revolutionary committee.

— Have you collectivized the lands?

— That was a very thorny issue, or, to be more exact, the problem is still there, for we want people to come to us out of belief in the excellence and advantages of our ideas. We have collectivized the big estates and have thus far not touched the small-holdings. If circumstances work in our favor, we hope to see the small-holder throw in his lot with the collective voluntarily, because Lecera people are intelligent, as they proved to us by offering the collective much of the produce they harvest.

At present we are harvesting saffron from all the small-holdings, holding it as collective property and placing it in storage to meet consumer requirements and for use in trade.

The small-holders who, in times gone by, could scarcely feed themselves, in that the harvest was virtually wholly taken away by the big landowners in payment of debts incurred, at first wanted to hold on to their lands: but, at a general assembly, the need to pool their harvests was explained to them and they agreed unanimously. We have to respect people's wishes and win them over without pressure by the power of example. The Revolutionary Committee wants to make known the tremendous work of comrade Manuel Martinez, the social sub-delegate from the Lecera front. The whole village is indebted to him.

— Has he been serving on the Committee for long?

— Nearly three months. On August 25, he took up office, introducing the libertarian communist system since then and doing away with money in the village.

We have traded various products with Tortosa and Reus. Five thousand sheep have been butchered for the militias on this front and 280,000 kilos of wheat turned over for consumption. The Committee in charge of supply, issues all sorts of items to the civilian population in return.

— With no money in circulation, how do the small-holders contrive to meet their various needs?

— As we said before, we preach by example. There are neither classes nor differentials here. As far as we are concerned, the small-holder who will of course have ceased to be that tomorrow is a producer.

Through the good offices of the labor sub-delegates who are also delegates from the city districts, we are perfectly familiar with the workers in work and the supply delegate who keeps a family register in the food store issues every family with whatever it needs. Distribution is effected as fairly as possible — Navarro, the Committee's chairman concluded — and we shall ensure that we demonstrate the superiority of our system in every regard.

(...) A short way away from the Revolutionary Committee's offices stands Lecera's warehouse. It occupies a huge hall and the separate rooms of a building that was to have seen use as a dance hall. The shops are filled with foodstuffs, churns of milk, sacks of vegetables, drums of oil, stacked tins of beef, etc. and upstairs are the stores of clothing and farming tools. So provisions are plentiful.

Amposta (Catalonia)

(...) Amposta is a village with ten thousand inhabitants, the economy of which is dependent on agriculture. The chief crop is rice, in the production of which it leads Catalonia.

In the last rice harvest, in September, 36 million kilos were harvested. It has to be noted that one hundred kilos of unrefined rice produces sixty kilos of white rice.

The lands collectivized by workers will produce a larger return thanks to the good conditions in which they will be put to work. And, irrigated by the rushing waters of the Ebro, they will afford a hardworking, free people like the people of Amposta a greater abundance of produce.

There are twelve hundred farmworkers in the district. With an eye to giving a boost to agriculture, some old olive groves and carob trees have been pulled up to make room for a more needed irrigated area. The poultry farm which the comrades have set up with every modern feature is worthy of attention. Its value is estimated at two hundred thousand pesetas. For this year, as soon as installation is completed, five thousand hens will be housed there, and it is estimated that in the coming year, with the aid of incubators, production will be a potential two thousand chicks per week.

Besides the poultry projects, every other project has been collectivized: one huge farm has been set up for the rearing of cattle, pigs and sheep: there are already seventy dairy cattle on the farm, production from which will provide the basis for a modern dairy.

The collective has no problem carrying out its work, for it already has fourteen tractors, fifteen threshing machines and seventy horses. The land has been taken into municipal control and those who, not being members of the farming collective, wish to acquire a few plots to farm for themselves, have to apply to the municipality which grants them — in this way the hateful wage system, a remnant of slavery which has endured into our own times will be done away with. The building workers have collectivized — their sector includes the manufacture of mosaic tiles and a firing kiln. Entertainments and other trades bodies have also been collectivized.

As far as education goes, Amposta was very backward; at present there are thirty eight schools in the town, a figure representing an increase of fifteen schools on pre-revolutionary days. Schooling is compulsory.. (. . .)

To house the new schools, the municipality has commandeered a number of premises. It also has the requisite equipment and need not turn to the Generalidad of Catalonia. (. . .) Six adult classes have been started. Within a short time an Arts and Crafts School and a school canteen are to be founded.

The municipality already has a library which is to be developed in order to meet the wishes of a populace generally eager for self-improvement.

In the educational area, some social lectures have been given and a choir and a theater troupe are to be set up, with the object of nurturing a taste for the arts in children. Teachers have already been found.

(. . .) Amposta has experienced no shortages, thanks to the bartering of rice against other products. And there are still many tons of that nutritious foodstuff left. They have introduced a family ration card for the distribution of basic necessities, with three days' supply being issued at a time.

In the former church the consumers' cooperative has been installed and it is curious to see the use to which the various outbuildings have been put. Much of the population obtains its provisions from this cooperative, which sells eleven to twelve thousand pesetas' worth of goods per week.

In the village there are some forty five households unable to work on grounds of age or illness. The municipality has seen to it that they want for nothing.

In short, the provisioning of the commune is entirely provided for.

— All we lack, we were told by the smiling secretary of the municipality, are wine and alcohol. But that is because we are concerned that as little as possible should get into Amposta.

The municipality wants to carry out significant improvements, and in particular demolition of the dilapidated old housing located at the entrance to the town, the completion of sewage systems and extension of water supply.

In Amposta there is a water-works, one of Spain's first and most important. The water serving the town's needs and which is drawn from the Ebro is purified by liquid chlorine.

Thanks to the sanitary work which has been carried out, epidemics like typhoid fever and certain ailments which have sorely afflicted workers have been eradicated.

A hospital has been set up to cater for the needs of the population. And as an after-thought, a dispensary has been added for the very first time. Now they can care for everyone wanting treatment. Finally, a sanitarium has been built outside the town to treat TB sufferers effectively.

Although the Confederation dominates in Amposta, the various posts in the municipality have been shared among personnel from the CNT and the UGT, and there is absolute harmony between them.

(. . .) All urban property has been collectivized, rents have been reduced and the revenues from them service the municipality. The municipality has requisitioned some saltworks which can bring in around five hundred thousand pesetas a year and there is a plan to set up a lye factory. (. . .) There is a plan to set a family wage and the best means of implementing this is being looked into, and the understanding is that the municipality will call a meeting of the people once a year to examine the best way of utilizing profits, after deductions for expenses (. . .)

Note for Some Local Examples of Collectivization

1. Taken from CNT documents.

IN THE PROVINCE OF LEVANTE BY GASTON LEVAL[1]

The Levante Regional Federation set up by CNT comrades, which has served as a basis for the establishment of the parallel federation of agrarian collectives, embraced five provinces: Castellón de la Plana, Valencia, Alicante, Murcia and Albacete. The significance of agriculture in the first four of these provinces, all of which border the Mediterranean and are among the richest provinces in Spain, and the size of their population (almost 3,300,000 people) add to the profile of the social experiments which have been carried out there. In our view, it is in Levante, on account of its natural resources and the creativity of our comrades, that the work of the agrarian collectives has been conducted on the largest scale and been handled best. (...)

(...) Of the five provinces, the movement has been most extensive in Valencia.

This can be explained, first, in terms of its great importance: it had a population of 1,650,000 when the revolution came. Next in descending order came the province of Murcia, with its 622,000 inhabitants, Alicante with 470,000, Castellón de la Plana with 312,000, and finally, Albacete with 238,000. The number of collectives reflected the size of the population. But it was in Valencia province that the socializations proceeded at the most consistent and accelerated rate.

(...) At the time of the congress of the Levante Peasant Federation on November 21-23, 1937, the collectives numbered 430. Five months on, there were five hundred. To get the measure of these figures, we ought to point out that the five provinces together had a total of 1,172 municipalities, ranging from the largest city down to the tiniest village. Which means that in 43 percent of the settlements in Spain's wealthiest farming region, where, in the huerta[2] of Valencia, the population density was the world's highest at 450 people per square kilometer, five hundred agrarian collectives sprouted in twenty months.

Broadly speaking, such collectives were not of the same character as the collectives in Aragon. In the latter region, the virtually unchallenged ascendancy of the CNT and FAI troops has for long deterred the police, the State administration and political parties using the lever of governmental authority from placing obstacles in the way of their growth. In Levante, as in the remainder of Spain's regions, the authorities had remained in place, as had the Assault Guards, the Carabineros and troops commanded by officers who displayed no revolutionary mentality at all.

Thus, right from the beginning, it was hard to carry out collectivization at the same dogged rate as in Aragon. Also, in the Levante region, the size of villages which were often like small towns also made it hard to win the unanimous backing of the populace: political and social divisions there were more plainly marked and the different tendencies better organized.

In Levante, the collectives were almost always launched at the instigation of the local peasants' unions: but it did not take them long to become an autonomous organization. An external link to the trade union, which represented the necessary meeting place between collectivists and individualists was all that was retained. In fact, the individualists used to bring along their produce for exchange against something else. In practice, therefore, their isolationism was entirely dissolved into the intermediary activity of the union, which had been overhauled structurally to cope with this new mission. Commissions had been set up under it aegis — rice commissions, orange commissions, horticultural commissions, potato commissions, etc. — each with its harvest and distribution depot. The collective itself had its own depot and commissions. Later, this pointless duplication was done away with. The depots were amalgamated: the commissions were manned by collectivists and by individualists who were union members. Other collectives set up mixed commissions: such as purchasing commissions buying machinery, seed, fertilizers, insecticides, veterinary products, etc. They used the same trucks. Solidarity was extended. And the collectivist mentality was increasingly attractive to those who had misgivings.

(...) This network quickly tended to amalgamate and rationalize everything. Rationing and the family wage were introduced at cantonal level, with the richest villages helping the poorest through go-between cantonal committees. A corps of technicians was established in each cantonal center; it comprised book-keepers, an agronomist, a veterinarian, an expert in combating plant diseases, an engineer, an architect and an expert in commercial affairs.

(...) Every collective had its vet. Most of the engineers and vets joined the CNT trade union. There was also a large number of agronomists. Nearly every specialist in viticulture and wine-making belonged. The engineers and vets employed by other undertakings, and not the collective, also worked for the collective, indeed did so disinterestedly, devoting themselves to the drafting of plans and implementation of projects. The revolution's creative mentality had won over the progressively minded.

Agronomists tabled undertakings that were necessary and feasible: agricultural planning, introduction of crops which individual ownership could not always allow to adapt to more favorable geological and climatic conditions. The vet would scientifically organize stock-rearing. If need be he would consult with the agronomist concerning resources which might be available. And, in concert with the peasant commissions, the latter switched cultivation insofar as was necessary.

But the vet also consulted the architect and the engineer over the construction of piggeries, stables, byres and collective poultry houses. Work was planned spontaneously. The planning took place at grassroots level, from the bottom up, in accordance with libertarian principles.

Thanks to the engineers, a huge number of canals and artesian wells had been constructed, the better either to irrigate the soil, which was scarce, or to transform waterless soil. By means of vacuum pumps, water was captured and distributed. This was scarcely a new technique, but it was in fact a novelty for many of the region's villages. The highly porous nature of the soil and the meager rainfall 400 mms. on average — had always made it very hard to bring up water for which one had to go down 50, 100 or 200 meters below the surface. The greatest ventures were made in the Murcia region and Cartagena. On the outskirts of Villajoyosa, the building of a dam made it possible to irrigate a million almond trees which had hitherto been drought stricken.

Not that the architects concerned themselves only with housing for livestock. Touring the region, they offered advice on human accommodations, apropos of architecture, materials, foundations, position, sanitation, etc., (...) The adjacent situation of the villages which were a lot less widely scattered than in Aragon, encouraged this active solidarity. Work was an inter-communal venture. A team was set up to fight plant diseases, carry out sulfate spraying, poll trees, and work in the fields and orchards. There was another squad involved in repairing and laying roads.

(...) The five hundred collectives and branches in the Levante region were sub-divided into fifty four cantonal federations collected into five provincial federations, which built up to a Regional Committee that oversaw everything.

The Committee appointed by the annual congresses and answerable to them — peasants in smocks and clogs — comprised twenty six technical sections: commissions dealing with fruits in general, with citrus fruits, vines, olive trees, horticulture, rice, sheep and goats, pigs and cattle; then came the industrial sections; wine-making, alcohol production, liqueurs, conserves, oil, sugar, fruits, essences and perfumes as well as their derivatives; in addition, miscellaneous produce sections, sections for import-export, machinery, transport and fertilizers were set up; then there was the construction section, overseeing and encouraging local construction of all manner of buildings; and, finally, the health and educational section.

(...) Half of the orange production — nearly four million quintals — was in the hands of the Levante Peasant Federation and 70 percent of the whole yield was shipped away and marketed by its commercial organization — thanks to its depot warehouses, trucks, and ships — and to its export branch which had opened marketing outlets in France (in Marseilles, Perpignan, Bordeaux, Sete, Cherbourg and Paris) at the beginning of 1938.

The same situation obtained where rice was concerned. There were 30,000 hectares given over to rice in the province of Valencia alone, out of the 47,000 hectares under rice in the whole of Spain. This was true also of fresh vegetables — the huerta of Valencia and the gardens of Murcia produced two or three crops each year.

(. . .) When a district's collectives thought fit to set up a factory producing liqueurs, fruit syrups, conserves, etc., they passed the idea on to the appropriate section of the central committee in Valencia. The latter would look into the proposal and, depending on the circumstances, would invite a delegation from the proposers to see it. If there were enough factories in existence to cope with the available raw materials, the proposal was turned down and that decision explained. If the initiative was a viable one, the proposal was endorsed. But the work was not left to the local collectives unaided. All five hundred collectives had to do their bit, through the regional committee.

(. . .) Hitherto, a huge amount of fruit has been written off because it spoiled on the spot for want of national and international markets. This was particularly true of oranges eaten whole in their natural state, which had to face competition on the English market from Palestinian and South African produce, forcing a reduction in price and a cut-back in production. The closure of many of the markets in Europe, and the loss of the domestic markets occupied or cut off by Franco's troops, and the obstacles placed in the way of socialization by the government, exacerbated the problem. And this crisis affected not just oranges, but potatoes and tomatoes as well. Once again there appeared to be a call for initiative on the part of the collectives.

The latter set up drying plants for potatoes, tomatoes and oranges. And so dried vegetables started to be used all year round; starch and flour were extracted from potatoes. But the innovations applied mostly to oranges. They were used as a source of zest extracted in greater quantities than ever from the peel, orange syrup, pulp for the preservation of blood in abattoirs with an eye to turning it into nourishing poultry feed, orange wine from which alcohol was extracted for medicinal use.

The most important concentrate factories were set up in Olive and in Burriana. Factories producing pickled canned vegetables, primarily in Murcia, Alfasar, Castellon and Paterna were also run by the Federation.

In most cases the premises of the cantonal federations were deliberately located near to rail or road connections, making the shipment of goods all the easier. The collectives in each canton would send their surplus produce there. This was valued, classified, stored and the relevant figures were passed on to the different sections of the regional federation in Valencia, so that the Federation always knew exactly what stocks were available for trade, export and distribution.

The spirit of invention was also displayed in the intensified rearing of livestock. Every day brought more henhouses, hutches and pens. New breeds of rabbits or hens unknown to the ordinary peasant became more and more widespread and the collectives which had led the way helped the others. Finally, essays in economic organization were not the only motives for action. Every collective set up one or two schools. [They were able] to offer schooling to all children. After the revolution, the collectives in Levante, as well as the ones in Aragon, Castile, Andalusia and Extremadura, had stamped out illiteracy. And let it not be forgotten that around 70 percent of the people in the Spanish countryside were uneducated.

By way of complementing this effort and for immediate practical purposes, a school for secretaries and book-keepers was opened, to which the collectives sent upwards of a hundred students. The most recent venture was the University of Moncada. A creation of the Levante Regional Federation, it was placed by the latter at the disposal of National Peasant Federation of Spain. It offers training in stock-breeding and the rearing of livestock, animal husbandry, breeding methods, breed identification, agriculture, arboriculture, etc. It had 300 students from the collectives.

Notes for In the Province of Levante

1. Gaston Leval, a French anarcho-syndicalist closely connected with Spanish anarcho-syndicalism from well before the Revolution of 1936, as will be seen in Volume IV of this anthology. This extract is from his Italian book *Né Franco Né Stalin*.
2. **huerta** = an expanse of irrigated orchard.

The Decree on Collectivization of the Catalan Economy

Reproduced below, virtually in its entirety, is the Decree of Collectivization of Catalonia's industries which, as we would say today, institutionalized self-management which had been introduced, in anticipation of any legislation, by the workers themselves when, following the Revolution of July 19, they had taken over their firms and elected workers' councils.

Even at the time of its appearance, the Decree was regarded by one of its authors, Terradellas, as an "historic document." Indeed, it can be regarded as the prototype of the legislative texts which, nearer our own day, have certainly and more or less satisfactorily codified self-management in Yugoslavia in the first place and later in Algeria. From a strictly libertarian point of view, it displays both the merits and the shortcomings of these last-named documents. In fact, self-management was not universal. It had emerged from a compromise between Terradellas, a left-leaning petit bourgeois, representing Catalonia's Republican Left (Esquerra), and the CNT'S representative, Jose Xena. That compromise was worked out only after bitter wrangling between the two men over several days. It was another anarchist, Juan P. Fabregas, Economy councilor in the Generalidad of Catalonia, who countersigned the document on the CNT's behalf.

Under the Decree, self-management was regimented. It was incorporated into the frame-work of a State and power at factory level was split between the workers' elected council, the director appointed by the workers' council, — but whose appointment, in the case of the larger concerns, required the endorsement of the Economy council (or ministry) of the Generalidad of Catalonia, — and, lastly, an auditor from the Generalidad, appointed by the councilor for Economy.

Moreover, the Decree was careful to link the workers' council on the one hand, and on the other, the trade union organization — two elements which certain contemporary advocates of the "councils system" today regard as mutually exclusive. In fact, Article 10 stipulated that, within the council "if need be, there will be equal representation for the various trade union denominations to which workers are affiliated, representation proportionate with their numbers." And Article 24 states that "eight representatives from the different trade union associations, appointed on a basis of proportionality, are to join the industry's general councils."

Thus defined, collectivization was not universal because it applied only to one category of firms, to wit, the most important, with the private sector subsisting elsewhere. In fact, collectivization palpably went further than the letter of the decree, in that a number of indebted concerns, even though they failed to meet the specifications for collectivization as set out in Article 2 were socialized anyway.

The rules set out with regard to the operation of the workers' council in the private sector were devised in a spirit of extreme solicitude for the small employers, since the workers' control committee's remit included supervision of strict discipline at work.

The Decree of October 24, 1936, and particularly this last-mentioned provision, have been quite perceptively glossed by certain anarchist authors like Vernon Richards in his *Lessons of the Spanish Revolution* (1953). But the decree was the inevitable consequence of the anarchists' deliberate decision, on the morrow of the Francoist putsch, to forswear, in the interests of antifascist unity of action, the immediate introduction of libertarian communism and to take their place in the appendages of the petit bourgeois republican State which was intent upon exercising its rights of supervision while simultaneously safe-guarding small proprietors. (See Volume IV on this point.)

As to "State" interference in the economic power of the workers, that was obvious, but the National Confederation of Labor (CNT) itself wielded great influence in the Generalidad of Catalonia and the Decree was, in part at least, the handiwork of anarchists. It should be added that it was prompted by a concern for economic integration and a remarkable sensibility to socialist planning. It was anticipated that in every industry there would be an industrial council made up of workers, trade unionists, and technicians, whose task it would be to "lay down the industry's work plans and regularize production in their sector"(Article 25). In every firm, output would have to "conform to the overall plan laid down by the industrial council" (Article 12).

For all its shortcomings and limitations, the Decree of October 24, 1936 represents the first legislative document since the Russian Revolution of October 1917, to attempt to define, with an eye to socialist planning, how workers' power in the larger concerns and workers' control in the smaller workshops or craft shops might be exercised democratically. The Decree, of course, is open to criticisms, but it does not deserve, perhaps, all of the onslaughts which it has suffered from anarchist sticklers and "councilists" (supporters of workers' councils) today.

DECREE

Article the first. — In accordance with the rules laid down by the present decree, Catalonia's commercial and industrial ventures are classified into:
a) Collectivized ventures wherein the responsibility for management devolves upon the workforce of the concern as represented by a works council;
b) Private enterprises in which management is vested in the owner or manager, with the assistance and supervision of the workers' control committee.

a) Collectivized firms

Article 2. — All industrial or commercial undertakings which, as of June 30, 1936, employed a workforce in excess of one hundred, as well as those with a smaller workforce but whose owners have been found to be seditious or who have deserted the firm, shall be compulsorily collectivized. In exceptional circumstances, firms with a workforce of less than one hundred may be collectivized after agreement is reached between the majority of the workforce and the owner or owners. Concerns with more than fifty workers and less than one hundred can be collectivized upon approval by three fourths of their workforce.

The Council of Economy may also decide upon collectivization of other industries which, by virtue of their importance to the national economy or on other grounds, will have to be removed from private control.

Article 3. — By way of complementing the preceding article, it shall be left to the popular tribunals alone to determine what constitutes a seditious employer.

Article 4. — Any person whose name shall be so listed, regardless of opinions, provided that he performs intellectual or manual labor, is to be regarded as part of the workforce and included in the total number of workers making up the firm.

Article 5. — The credits and debits ascribed to the firm prior to implementation of this present Decree shall pass in their entirety to the collectivized venture.

Article 6. — Ventures represented by autonomous production and sale agencies and those which, in the same way, embrace within the same undertaking, several shops or factories, shall continue to operate under the guise of a single collectivized organization. They shall not be allowed to sub-divide without express permission from the Councilor for Economy, after he has brought the matter to the attention of the Economy Council of Catalonia.

Article 7. — Within the framework of the collectivized undertaking, erstwhile owners or managers shall be assigned to posts where their technical or administrative expertise shall have been found indispensable.

Article 8. — During the transitional period while collectivization is being implemented, no worker may be dismissed from the enterprise, but he may be reassigned within the same category, should circumstances so require.

Article 9. — In every instance where the interests of foreign investors are represented in the firm, the councils of said firms or the workers' control committees shall be obliged to bring this to the attention of the Council of Economy. The latter shall summon the interested parties or their representatives, with an eye to discussing litigious matters and ensuring that the interests in question are safeguarded.

b) Enterprise councils

Article 10. — The management of collectivized enterprises shall be handled by an enterprise council appointed by the workers, selected from among their own number in general assembly. That assembly will determine the number of the members of the enterprise council, a number that shall never be less than five nor more than fifteen. Its make-up should contain representatives of the various services: production, administration, technical services and marketing services. If need be, there shall also be representatives of the various trade union denominations to which the workers are affiliated, in proportion to their numbers.

The duration of their mandate is set at two years, with a half of the council coming up for replacement every year. Enterprise council members shall be eligible for re-election.

Article 11. — The enterprise councils shall enjoy the same powers as the former management councils in limited companies and firms placed under the control of a board of management.

They shall be answerable for their management to the workers of their own firm and to the general council of the relevant industry.

Article 12. — In the performance of their duties, the enterprise councils shall take account of the fact that production must conform to the overall plan laid down by the industry's general council and shall match their efforts to the principles laid down for the development of the sector to which they belong. In the setting of profit margins, prescription of general sale conditions, purchasing of raw materials, and everything having to do with rules governing depreciation of materials, the extent of liquid capital, reserve funds or profit-sharing, the dispositions taken by the industry's general councils shall be adhered to.

In social terms, the enterprise councils shall ensure that the rules laid down in this respect are strictly observed and that such others are suggested as they may deem appropriate. They shall take all necessary steps to ensure the preservation of workers' physical and moral well-being; they shall engage in intense cultural and educational endeavor, sponsoring the creation of clubs, recreation centers, sports centers, cultural centers, etc.

Article 13. — The enterprise councils of firms confiscated prior to publication of the present Decree and those of industries which will have been collectivized subsequent to such publication, will, within the compass of fifteen days, forward to the general secretariat of the Council of Economy a record of their constitution, in conformity with the model that will be issued to them from the appropriate offices.

Article 14. — For the purposes of ongoing monitoring of the proper operation of the enterprise, the council shall appoint a director, upon whom it shall bestow all or part of its functions.

In firms with a workforce of more than five hundred, in those with capital assets in excess of a million pesetas, in those which manufacture, convert or market materials bearing upon national defense, the appointment of the director will require the approval of the Council of Economy.

Article 15. — In all collectivized enterprises, it is obligatory that there will be a Generalidad auditor who will be part of the enterprise council and will be appointed by the councilor for Economy, by agreement with the workers.

Article 16. — The lawful representation of the firm will be assured by the director and his signature will be counter-signed by those of two members of the enterprise council elected by that council. The appointments of the director and the two consultants are to be notified to the Council of Economy which will provide them with accreditation for presentation to banks and various official bodies.

Article 17. — The enterprise councils will keep minutes of their meetings and will forward a certified copy of decisions which they may adopt to the relevant general councils of the industry. When these decisions require it, the general council of the industry will intervene as it deems appropriate.

Article 18. — The councils will be under obligation to attend to the demands or proposals advanced by the workers. They are to record these and, if need be, bring them to the attention of the general council of the industry.

Article 19. — At the end of their period in office, the enterprise councils will have to render an account of their stewardship to the workers gathered in a general assembly.

Likewise, they are to provide the general council of the industry with a half-yearly or annual balance sheet or report which will set out in detail the state of progress of the business, its plans and its future projects.

Article 20. — The enterprise councils may be revoked in part or in whole by the workers meeting in general assembly, and by the general council of the relevant industry, in the event of manifest incompetence or default from the prescribed norms. Once they are pronounced revoked by the general council of the industry, they may, with the agreement of the firm's workers meeting in general assembly, appeal that decision to the Councilor of Economy, but the latter's decision, once he has reported to the Council of Economy, shall be final.

c) The control committees in private firms

Article 21. — In non-collectivized industries or businesses, it will be compulsory that a workers' control committee be established and all the services, productive, technical and administrative, making up the firm, be represented on that committee. The number of personnel on the committee will be left to the free choice of the workers. Each union's representation will be in proportion with the respective numbers of their members in the firm.

Article 22. — The functions of the control committee shall be: a) The monitoring of working conditions and strict implementation of applicable norms with regard to pay, hours, social assurance, health and security, etc., as well as ensuring strict discipline in work. All warnings and notices which the manager may feel obliged to issue to the workforce shall be passed on through the committee. b) Administrative oversight, collections and payments in kind as well as through banks and tailoring these transactions to the size of the firm, oversight of other commercial transactions. c) Overseeing production, in close collaboration with the owner of the firm, so as to perfect the expansion of production. The workers' control committees will maintain the best of relations with technicians, with the object of ensuring that work proceeds smoothly.

Article 23. — The owners will be required to present the workers' control committees with annual balance sheets and reports which they will forward to the relevant general council of industry.

d) The General councils of industry

Article 24. — The general councils of industry are to comprise: four representatives from the enterprise council of that industry; eight representatives from the various trade union associations appointed on a basis of proportionality; four technicians appointed by the Council of Economy. Each of these councils is to be chaired by the sector's representative on the Council of Economy.

Article 25. — The general councils of industry are to set the industry's work plans, prescribe production targets for their sector and rule on all matters of concern to it.

Article 26. — The decisions adopted by the general councils of industry are to be binding. No enterprise council and no private enterprise will be able to oppose implementation of them. At best, they will be able to submit an appeal to the councilor of Economy, against whose decision there will be no appeal.

Article 27. — The general councils of industry are to liaise with Catalonia's Council of Economy and will monitor its operations closely so as to be in agreement with it every time that matters requiring concerted action may arise.

Article 28. — The general councils of industry will be required to forward to Catalonia's Council of Economy, within the prescribed time-limit in each instance, a detailed document in which the overall progress of the industry in question will be set out and analyzed, and where fresh plans will be advanced for its consideration.

e) Industrial Groupings

Article 29. — In order to promote establishment and organization of general councils of industry, the general Council of Economy shall, within a period of fifteen days from publication of the present Decree, propose that different industries be classed and grouped together in accordance with their respective specialty and coordination of the sections into which each of them is sub-divided.

Article 30. — In such grouping, account shall be taken of raw materials and of the different industrial operations right through to the point of sale, of the technical unit, of the business management and, whenever possible, steps will be taken to arrive at comprehensive concentration.

Article 31. — At the same time, the Council of Economy is to propose the regulation which will govern the establishment and operation of said industries (. . .)

> Barcelona October 24, 1936
> The Prime Councilor: Jose Terradellas
> The Councilor for Economy: Juan P. Fàbregas

The Writings of Diego Abad de Santillán [1]

A Libertarian Planning Blue-Print

The organization of labor — From factory council to Council of Economy

The trade unions are organizations charged with the operation of the economy at grassroots level. We can condense their functions into eighteen councils, to wit:

> Essential needs: a Council overseeing Foodstuffs, accommodation and clothing.
> Raw Materials: Councils to oversee agricultural production, livestock, forestry, mines and fisheries.
> A Liaison Council: Councils for transport, communications, press and publishing, credit and exchange.
> Manufacturing Industry: Councils for the metal-working, chemical, glass and ceramics industries.
> Councils for electricity, power and water.
> A Health Council.
> A Cultural Council.

These various councils together make up each local council of Economy.

These same councils will provide the basis for the formation of regional councils, and, at national level, of the Federal Council of Economy.

With the economic organism superimposed upon the existing organization of labor, we achieve maximum coordination. Neither capitalism nor the so-called socialist State can attain such identification.

There is the added advantage that the individual's autonomy within the group, that of the group within the union and that of the union within each council is not affected.

This is a federative arrangement which can, if need be, bring pressure to bear upon the individual in respect of his libertarian development, but which may equally provide a guarantee of liberty and foster communication between individuals, which is impossible with an essentially authoritarian organism.

Regional councils of economy

The local councils of economy in the towns and municipal councils or district councils in the countryside coalesce to form regional councils of economy which perform the same functions as the local councils, albeit on a larger scale. Each zone will have its political autonomy. There are no independent regions in Spain which can be self-sufficient although some regions are wealthier than others.

The regional council of economy, through its credit and exchange council, compiles statistics on production, population, consumption in its own territory, the labor force and raw materials. The regional councils of economy regularly hold congresses at which they re-elect their members and outline the program they are to implement. Delegations from the regional councils are elected either through the local councils or through congresses in order to fill the federal council of economy, the most important economic body in the land.

The federal council of economy

Finally we come to the federal council of Economy, the country's main coordinating agency.

The federal council of economy, elected from the bottom up by the workers, coordinates the entire economy of the country with the same aim in mind: producing more and improving distribution.

With the aid of statistics forwarded to it, the council will at all times know the exact economic position throughout the country.

It will know which is the most blessed region, the one which has a surplus, and it will appreciate where there are shortcomings in transport and communications, where new roads, new crops and new factories will be needed. Regions with few assets will be helped by the country in the completion of useful projects.

Two Views of "Libertarian Communism": Utopia or Economic Integration[2]

Buenos Aires, July 10, 1965

[My book] *El organizmo económico de la revolución* was part and parcel of the propaganda which I had been peddling in our reviews and newspapers for some years past. I wanted to set out a practical scheme for immediate implementation, and not some paradisical utopia. The network of trade union interconnections, as I saw it, made it possible to replace the capitalist proprietor of industry and land advantageously, and I wanted to make a contribution towards the out-growing of the puerility of a libertarian communism based on supposedly free independent communes, as peddled by Kropotkin and others and presented as being more perfect than schemes deriving from Bakunin's collectivism or Proudhon's collectivism. Indeed, I hold the latter to be closer to man's true nature, in that man is generous and full of self-sacrifice, but selfish with it.

I understand and I argue in favor of local autonomy in a host of particular matters, but a commune is a focus for communal living and work is a duty which requires the creation of bonds, whether these be bonds of affinity or not, at local, regional, national and international levels. Consequently, in work and in economics, my preoccupation is not with family affinities or close friendship, but with efficiency. I cannot call for independence but rather advocate inter-dependence, transcending all borders. The trade union organizations, the local federations of industry and the national federations in Spain held in their hands concrete opportunities to introduce improvements to the system of production and distribution, beyond anything that private, competing, anachronistic enterprises had to offer. In 1936, we were able to give a powerful fillip to Spain's economic development, because we added the fervor of belief and intensification of effort to the existing plant. And the point was, as a first step, to raise the industrial and agricultural levels of the country; we felt able to give it that boost, albeit through the instrument that we had at our disposal, the trade union organization, and not through the idyllic libertarian communes of nudists and practitioners of free love.[3]

What is more, I was uneasy about the widespread tendency to take the line that ownership of the instruments of labor and of the land would devolve upon the workers and peasants, and I issued warnings against that tendency, which is to say, against the prospective new class, the class of administrators and managers of these undertakings. Land, factories and the means of transportation belong to the community and must perform social functions. If, in our hands, they fail to perform those functions, the new form of ownership would be as unacceptable as its predecessor. The slogan "The land to the peasants, the factories to the workers" struck me as legitimate, on condition that it does not lead to thoughts of novel private ownership, vested in a larger number rather than in a minority. The society, the community take precedence over the interests of minorities and majorities. Ownership of the land is a social asset, just as ownership of the other instruments of production ought to be. It is not my belief that we need pass through a phase of new owners before we arrive at a new world which is neither capitalist nor monopolistic.

At the Zaragoza Congress, which I myself did not attend, approval was given to an outline future organization that mirrored the Kropotkinist view. A schema inspired by the ideas in my book was put to the Congress by the Graphic Arts and Paper Federation, at my instigation. But as we were not present in Zaragoza, the one drafted by Federica Montseny on the basis of a pamphlet by Isaac Puente which I had published in *Tierra y Libertad* was adopted. In contradiction of these simplistic views, I had argued in favor of the ideas set out in *El organismo económico de la revolución* in the pages of the review *Tiempos Nuevos* at the time. And as it so happened that shortly afterwards, our forecasts and predictions had to be put into practice, we generally set about it in the manner which I had anticipated, because we were working on the basis of an instrument of action and achievement, to wit, the trade union, the federation of industry, etc.

Notes to The Writings of Diego Abad de Santillán

1. Diego Abad de Santillán, who was to become minister of Economy with the Generalidad in Catalonia, published this outline prior to the revolution of July 1936: (this extract is from his book *El organismo económico de la revolución* 1936)
2. Unpublished letter from Diego Abad de Santillán.
3. The reference is to certain utopian articles in the program adopted at CNT congress in Zaragoza in May 1936.

VOLINE
(1882–1945)

Vsevolod Mikhailovitch Eichenbaum, better known by his pseudonym Voline, was born on August 11, 1882.[1] Having enrolled as a student in the Saint Petersburg Faculty of Law, he promptly dropped out, attracted even then by the ideas of the Social Revolutionary Party. Which led to his being an active participant in the 1905 revolution. He was along on the workers' march on the Winter Palace, led by Father Gapon. A little later, he was present at the birth of the first soviet in Saint Petersburg. Arrested by the tsarist police and imprisoned and finally deported to Siberia, he managed to escape in 1907, making his way to France.

It was in Paris that Voline became an anarchist. As a member since 1913 of the International Anti-War Action Committee, his activities led to his being placed under arrest in 1915. Threatened with internment in a concentration camp, Voline successfully sailed aboard a steamship, as a coaltrimmer, for the United States. For several months past, he had been sending correspondence from Paris to a Russian anarcho-syndicalist weekly *Golos Truda* ("The Voice of Labor") in America. In 1917, its editors — and with them, Voline — arrived in revolutionary Russia, intent upon transferring the weekly to Saint Petersburg.

Around this time Russian anarchists who had stayed behind in Europe (and who were under the sway of Peter Kropotkin's ideas) and those who had spent some time in America were reconciled with one another, as manifested in a declaration, followed up by an organization which then took as its name: the Petrograd Anarcho-Syndicalist Propaganda Union and decided to bring out *Golos Truda,* which was regarded as the continuation of the American publication. Voline was selected to edit it. After the October revolution, *Golos Truda* turned to daily publication and Voline had the help of an editorial panel which included, among others, Alexander Schapiro.

At a time when the proletarian revolution was only a few months old, Voline was already issuing terribly prophetic warnings in that paper: "Once their power has been consolidated and legalized, the Bolsheviks [...] will set about husbanding the country's life and the people's with governmental and dictatorial means. [...] Your soviets will gradually turn into mere executive organs of the will of the central government. We shall witness the installation of an authoritarian political and State apparatus that will operate from above and will set about crushing everything with its mailed fist (...) Woe betide anyone who does not see eye to eye with the central government!"

Later, after he had left the paper, Voline traveled to Bobrov, where he worked on the staff of the town's soviet. A little later, he joined the newspaper *Nabat* ("The Tocsin") and became one of the prime movers behind a Ukrainian anarchist conference in Kursk on November 18, 1918. At that conference, he was commissioned to draft the resolutions passed and to draw up a declaration agreeable to every one of the schools of anarchism, so that they all might work together inside a common framework. The drafting of a program led Voline to articulate the idea of an "anarchist synthesis" which could embrace all three schools of anarchism: the anarcho-syndicalist, the libertarian communist and the individualist.

A second *Nabat* congress was held in March-April 1919. Participants declared themselves to be "categorically and irreversibly opposed to all participation in the soviets, which have become purely political bodies, organized on authoritarian, centralist and Statist foundations." This declaration was very poorly received by the Bolshevik authorities.

After the congress, Voline left Moscow and went back to work with *Nabat* in Kursk, with the central body (for *Nabat* had regional bodies too). This was still a time of relative political tolerance, but it was fated not to last for much longer. Soon, the Bolshevik authorities did away with the free press, harassing and arresting the anarchists. It was at that point, July 1919, that Voline managed to link up with the headquarters of the Ukrainian anarchist guerrilla, Nestor Makhno. The intellectual with the ever-ready pen and the comparatively uncouth warrior-peasant, by virtue of the very fact that they were profoundly dissimilar, complemented each other, not that they did not clash on more than one occasion.

As the *Makhnovshchina* had established a cultural and educational department, Voline, In conjunction with one of Makhno's erstwhile prison acquaintances, Piotr Arshinov, took charge of it and was placed in charge of organizing meetings, conferences, lectures, popular briefings, the publication of tracts, posters and all the rest of the Makhnovists' printed output. He chaired a congress of the insurgent movement, the one held in October 1919, in Alexandrovsk. It saw the adoption of *General Theses*[2] which spelled out the doctrine of "free soviets" (See Volume IV of this anthology).

For six months, as a member of the military council, Voline beavered away unstintingly. But he was arrested by the 14th Red Army, taken to Moscow and placed in the care of the political police (Cheka). Not until October 1920 would he regain his freedom under a military agreement between the Bolshevik government and Makhno. Whereupon he traveled to Kharkov where, in concert with the *Nabat* Confederation, he laid the preparations for an anarchist congress scheduled for December 25. On the eve of the congress, the Bolsheviks had Voline arrested once again, along with any anarchists who had served with Makhno.

From Kharkov, the prisoners were removed to Moscow and placed in the Butyrky prison. There they mounted a hunger strike which was called off following unexpected intervention: European revolutionary syndicalist delegates who had come to attend the first congress of the Red International of Labor Unions[3], secured the release of ten of them, including Voline, on condition that they leave the country for good (under threat of execution should they breach this agreement).

Moving to Germany where he had help from the Frei Arbeiter Union based in Berlin, Voline worked on the FAU's behalf, bringing out a damning pamphlet entitled *The Persecution of Anarchism in the Soviet Union,* translating Piotr Arshinov's book *History of the Makhnovist Movement* into French and also launching and editing the leading Russian-language weekly *The Anarchist Worker,* an anarchist synthesis review.

At the suggestion of Sebastien Faure, who urged him to move to France, Voline contributed to the *Encyclopédie anarchiste*. For it, he wrote essays which have frequently been reprinted as propaganda pamphlets or in the foreign press, notably the Spanish. The Spanish CNT invited him to edit its French language paper *L'Espagne antifasciste* on its behalf.

In 1938, Voline left Paris for Nîmes, at the invitation of his friend Andre Prudhommeaux[4] who ran a cooperative printing-works there. For a time he helped with the editing of the weekly review *Terre libre* and above all he had the peace to write, with the maturity of hindsight, *The Unknown Revolution*, the libertarian classic on the Russian revolution and one of anarchism's most significant texts. Later, in Marseilles, from 1940 on, Voline was able to finish off the book. Stricken by tuberculosis, he died in Paris on September 18, 1945. *The Unknown Revolution*, in its French edition was published at the expense of friends of Voline in 1947. For a long time it was ignored or buried by "authoritarian" revolutionaries. It was not until 1969, thanks to re-publication in French, that it was at last able to reach what is conventionally referred to as the wider public.

Notes to the Introduction to Voline

1. This introductory essay on Voline is based upon the biography published by "The Friends of Voline," with which *La Revolution inconnue* opens. An essay on Nestor Makhno appears at the beginning of Volume IV of this anthology.
2. This precious document, which appeared in print and which Voline intended later to translate into French, has never been relocated: all that we have of it are short quotations.
3. See Volume IV of this anthology.
4. For more about Prudhommeaux, see Volume IV.

The Unknown Revolution[1]

Voline and Trotsky[2]

In April 1917 I happened to be in New York with Trotsky[3], in a printworks which worked primarily for various left wing Russian bodies. At the time, he was in charge of a left marxist daily paper, *Novy Mir*. As for me, the Federation of Russian Workers' Unions had entrusted me with the editing of the final editions of its weekly, the anarcho-syndicalist *Golos Truda*, before its removal to Russia. I spent one night each week at the printworks, on the eve of the newspaper's coming out. And that is how I came to meet Trotsky on my first night on duty.

Naturally, we talked of the revolution. We were both making preparations to quit America shortly in order to move "over yonder."

One time I said to Trotsky: "On balance, I am absolutely sure that you left marxists will end up by taking power in Russia. It is inevitable, for the resuscitated soviets will unfailingly come into conflict with the bourgeois government. The latter will not be able to stamp them out because all of the country's toilers, workers, peasants, etc., and pretty well all of the army as well, will of course wind up siding with the soviets against the bourgeoisie and its government. Now, as soon as the people and the army support the soviets, the latter will be the winners in the struggle begun. And as soon as they win, you left marxists will inevitably be swept into power. For the toilers will assuredly carry through the revolution to its bitter end. As syndicalists and anarchists are too weak in Russia to focus the toilers' attention quickly upon their ideas, the masses will place their trust in you and you will become 'the masters of the country.' Whereupon woe betide us anarchists! It is inevitable that you and we should come into conflict. You will begin to persecute us just as soon as your power has been consolidated. And you will end by having us shot down like partridges..."

"—Come, come, comrade," Trotsky replied. "You people are pig-headed and incorrigible fantasists. Look, as things now stand, what is the difference between us? A little question of methodology, quite secondary. You, like us, are revolutionaries. Like you, we are anarchists, in the final analysis. The only thing is that you want to introduce your anarchism straight away, without transition or preparation. Whereas we marxists believe that one cannot "leap" into the libertarian realm in a single bound. We anticipate a transitional stage during which the ground can be cleared and smoothed for the anarchist society with the aid of an anti-bourgeois political power: the dictatorship of the proletariat exercised by the proletarian party in power. In short, it is only a difference of "degree," nothing more. Essentially, we are very close to one another. Brothers in arms. Think of it: we will have a common foe to fight. Will it even occur to us to fight one another? And anyway, I have no doubt but that you will quickly be persuaded of the necessity for a provisional socialist proletarian dictatorship. So I really cannot see any reason for warfare between you and us. We will assuredly march hand in hand. And then, even if we do not see eye to eye, you are overstating things a bit to suggest that we socialists will use brute force against anarchists! Life itself and the views of the masses will be enough to resolve the matter and bring us into agreement. No! Can you really, for a single instant, entertain such a nonsense: left-wing socialists in power turning their guns on the anarchists! Come, come, what do you take us for? Anyway, we are socialists, comrade Voline! So we are not your enemies …"

In December 1919, gravely wounded, I was arrested by the Bolshevik military authorities in the Makhnovist region. Deeming me a militant "of some standing," the authorities notified Trotsky of my arrest by means of a special telegram asking his view of how I should be handled. His answer arrived snappily and tersely and plainly — also by telegram: "Shoot out of hand. — Trotsky." I was not shot, thanks solely to a set of particularly felicitous and quite fortuitous circumstances.

BOLSHEVISM IN THE DOCK[4]

The working class dispossessed

[...] The working class was weak. Unorganized (in the proper sense of the word), inexperienced and, essentially, unwitting of its real task, it soon proved incapable of acting for itself and on its own behalf. This it left to the Bolshevik party, which hogged the action.

(...) Instead of simply rallying to the workers' aid in their efforts to carry through the Revolution and emancipate themselves; instead of helping them in their fight, the role which the workers had in mind for them, a role which, normally, should be the role of all revolutionary ideologues and which does not at all require the seizure nor the exercise of "political power" — instead of fulfilling that role, the Bolshevik party, once in power, ensconced itself there, of course, as absolute master; there, it was quickly corrupted; it organized itself into a privileged caste and thereafter it crushed and subjugated the working class so as to exploit it in new ways for its own benefit.

In light of which, the whole Revolution will be warped, diverted and led astray. For, by the time that the masses of the people realize this mistake, this danger, it will be too late: after a tussle between them and these new masters who are solidly organized and can call upon adequate material, administrative, military and police powers — a bitter, but unequal tussle that will drag on for about three years and will long remain unknown outside of

Russia — the people will succumb. And the authentic liberating Revolution will once again be smothered, by the "revolutionaries" themselves.

(...) From October 1917 on, the Russian revolution entered quite new terrain: that of the great social revolution. Thus it proceeded along a very specific route, virgin territory. From which it follows that the subsequent progress of the Revolution was of a quite novel and original sort.

[...] Through all of the crises and failures that followed one upon another up until the Revolution of October 1917, Bolshevism alone put the case for a social revolution to be carried out. Not counting the (Left) Social Revolutionary doctrine with its similarities to Bolshevism in terms of its political, authoritarian, Statist and centralistic outlook, and a few other small kindred currents, a second fundamental idea, which also envisaged a frank, thoroughgoing social revolution emerged and spread through revolutionary ranks and made headway among the laboring masses also: this was the anarchist idea.

Its influence, initially very slight, grew as events broadened their scope. By the end of 1918, this influence had become such that the Bolsheviks, who would brook no criticism, let alone contradiction or opposition, were seriously worried. From 1919 on and up until the end of 1921, they were to wage a very savage struggle against this idea's onward march: a struggle at least as long and as bitter as the struggle against the reaction had been.

On this score, let us stress a third factor which is not sufficiently appreciated: Bolshevism, once in power, fought against the anarchist and anarcho-syndicalist ideas and movements, not at the level of ideological or practical experimentation, not by means of open, above board struggle, but with the same methods of repression that it employed against reactionaries, unadulteratedly violent methods. It began by brutally shutting down all the libertarian organizations' premises in order to bar the anarchists from carrying out any propaganda or activity. It doomed the masses to not hearing the anarchist voice or to misconstruing it. And since, in spite of these impediments, the idea gained ground, the Bolsheviks quickly moved on to more violent measures: imprisonment, proscription and death sentences. So the unequal struggle between the two tendencies, one of them in power and the other opposed to power, escalated and spread and in certain regions resulted in full-scale civil war. In the Ukraine in particular, this state of war dragged out for more than two years, obliging the Bolsheviks to mobilize all their resources in order to smother the anarchist idea and crush the popular movements drawing their inspiration from it.

So the strife between the two approaches to social revolution and, by the same token, between the Bolshevik authorities and certain movements of the toiling masses occupied a very important place in the events of the years between 1919 and 1921.

Two conflicting ideas

(...) The Bolshevik idea was to erect upon the ruins of the bourgeois State a new "workers' State," to establish a "worker and peasant government" and introduce the "dictatorship of the proletariat."

The anarchist idea was to overhaul the economic and social foundations of society without resorting to a political State, government or "dictatorship" of any description, which is to say to carry out the Revolution and resolve its difficulties, not by political and State means, but by means of the natural, unforced economic and social activity of the workers' very own associations, once the last capitalist government had been overthrown.

In order to coordinate activity, the first of these outlooks envisaged a central political authority, orchestrating the life of the State to abet the government and its agents, in accordance with formal directives emanating from the "center."

The alternative approach implied jettisoning political and State organization once and for all; direct and federative arrangements between economic, social, technical or other bodies (trade unions, cooperatives, various associations, etc.) at local, regional, national and international levels; signifying not a political, statist centralization reaching out from the government at the center to the periphery controlled by it, but rather an economic and technical centralization, dictated by real needs and interests, moving from the periphery towards the centers and established naturally and logically in accordance with actual needs, with no domination and no commands.

Note the absurdity, or partisanship of the reproach leveled at anarchists to the effect that they know only "how to destroy" and have no "positive" ideas [...] especially when that reproach emanates from "leftists." Discussions between the far left political parties and the anarchists had always centered upon what [...] had to be done once the bourgeois State had been destroyed — a destruction upon which all are agreed. Along what lines should the construction of the new society proceed: statist, centralist and political, or federalist, apolitical and merely social? This was as ever the subject of disputations between the two sides: irrefutable evidence that the anarchists' central preoccupation was always nothing less than building the future.

In place of the parties' thesis that there should be a "transitional" political, centralized State, anarchists offered their own: that there should be ongoing but immediate progress towards real economic and federative community. The political parties rely upon the social structure bequeathed by bygone ages and regimes and argue that there are constructive ideas implicit in this model. Anarchists reckon that, from the outset, fresh construction requires fresh methods and they advocate such methods. Whether their contention be right or wrong, it proves at any rate that they are perfectly clear as to what they want and that they have clear-cut constructive ideas.

Generally speaking, a wrong-headed, or, most often, knowingly incorrect interpretation argues that the libertarian approach signifies absence of all organization. Nothing could be further from the truth. It is not a question of "organization" or of "non-organization," but rather of two different organizing principles.

Of necessity, every revolution begins in a more or less spontaneous — and thus confused and chaotic fashion. It goes without saying, and libertarians understand this as well as anybody else, that if a revolution remains at that stage, the primitive stage, it founders. Immediately following the spontaneous eruption, the organizing principle has to intervene in a revolution, as in any other human undertaking. And it is at that point that the serious question arises: what are the tenor and the basis of that organization to be?

Some contend that a central leadership group, an "elite" group, should be formed in order to take the whole endeavor in hand and see it through in accordance with its lights, imposing the latter upon the entire collectivity, establishing a government and organizing a State, dictating its wishes to the population, imposing its "laws" through force and violence and combating, eliminating and even annihilating those in disagreement with it.

Others reckon that such a view is absurd, contrary to the underlying trends in human evolution and, in the last analysis, more than sterile: downright damaging to the whole undertaking. Of course, the anarchists say, society must be organized. But that new, normal and henceforth feasible organizing ought to proceed freely and socially and, above all, from the grassroots up. The organizing principle should emanate, not from some center ready-made for the purpose of capturing the whole and overruling it, but the very opposite, from all points, arriving at coordinating centers, natural centers designed to service all these points.

Of course, the organizing spirit, men with a capacity for organization, "elites," must play their part. But everywhere and in all circumstances, all such human resources must participate freely in the common undertaking as true collaborators and not as dictators. Everywhere, they should set an example and set about marshaling, coordinating and organizing people's goodwill, initiative, expertise, talents and aptitudes, without dominating, subjugating or oppressing them. Such men would be true organizers and their handiwork would amount to authentic, fruitful, solid organization precisely because it would be natural, humane and genuinely progressive. Whereas the other sort of "organization," modeled upon that of an old society rooted in oppression and exploitation, and consequently tailored to those two purposes, would be sterile and unstable, because incongruent with the new targets and thus in no way progressive. Indeed, it would contribute nothing to the new society: instead, it would take all of the blights of the old society to extremes in that only their appearance would have altered.

Belonging to an obsolete society overtaken in every respect and thus impossible as a natural, free and truly human institution, it could not survive other than with the aid of some new artifice, some new trickery, some new violence, fresh oppressions and exploitations. Which would, of necessity, sidetrack, mislead and jeopardize the entire revolution. Self-evidently, such organization would remain stalled as a locomotive of the social revolution. In no way could it serve as a "transitional society" (as the "communists" contend) for such a society would necessarily have to carry at least a few of the seeds of the one towards which it would be evolving — now, every authoritarian and Statist society would possess only residues from the overthrown society.

According to the libertarian case, it was the toiling masses themselves who, through their various class agencies (factory committees, industrial and agricultural unions, cooperatives, etc.), federated and centralized in reponse to real needs, were everywhere to busy themselves on the spot with resolving the problems (...) of the Revolution. Through their activity which would be powerful and fruitful in that it would be free and deliberate they were to coordinate their efforts right across the length and breadth of the land. As for the "elites," their role, as libertarians saw it, was to assist the masses; to enlighten and instruct them, to offer them the requisite advice and nudge them towards such and such an initiative, setting an example and supporting them in their activity, but not directing them government style.

According to libertarians, happy resolution of the problems of the social revolution could only come about through the freely and consciously collective, solidary efforts of millions of men, contributing and reconciling the whole diversity of their needs and interests as well as of their ideas, strengths and capabilities, their talents, aptitudes, dispositions, professional know-how and expertise etc. Through the natural inter-play of their economic, technical and social bodies, with the aid of the "elites" and, if need be, under the umbrella of their freely organized armed forces, the toiling masses, according to libertarians, ought to have been able to move the social revolution forward and arrive progressively at the practical accomplishment of all its tasks.

The Bolshevik line was diametrically the opposite. According to the Bolsheviks, it was the elite — their elite — which, by forming a government (a so-called "workers" government enforcing the so-called "dictatorship of the proletariat") was to carry through the transformation of society and resolve its immense problems. The masses were to assist this elite (the converse of the libertarians' line, whereby the elite was to assist the masses) by faithfully, blindly and "mechanically" implementing its plans, decisions, orders and "laws." And the armed forces, likewise modeled upon those of the capitalist countries, had to be blindly obedient to the "elite."

Such was and is the essential difference between the two outlooks.

Such also were the two contrary notions of social revolution at the time of the Russian overthrow in 1917.

The Bolsheviks, as we have stated, were unwilling even to listen to the anarchists, much less allow them to put their thesis to the masses. Believing themselves to be possessed of an absolute incontrovertible and "scientific" truth, arguing that they had a duty to impose and apply it as a matter of urgency, they fought and eliminated the libertarian movement through recourse to violence as soon as the latter began to awaken the interest of the masses: the customary practice of all overlords, exploiters and inquisitors.

What, then, is the State?

(. . .) The Bolshevik State, broadly established in 1918–1921, has been in existence for twenty years.

What, precisely, is that State?

It calls itself: the Union of Soviet Socialist Republics (USSR). It purports to be a "proletarian" State, or even a "worker and peasant" State. It claims to exercise a "dictatorship of the proletariat." It flatters itself that it is "the workers' homeland," the bulwark of revolution and socialism.

What truth is there in all this? Do the facts and deeds justify such declarations and claims?

(. . .) The Bolshevik Party's prime concern in power was to bring all activity, the whole life of the country, under State control: everything that could was to come under the State. The aim was to create the regime which modern terminology describes as "totalitarian."

Once possessed of enough coercive power, the Bolshevik Party and government set to that task as best they could.

It was in carrying this out that the Communist authorities spawned their vast bureaucratic apparatus. It has finished up fashioning a multitudinous, mighty caste of "accountable" officials which today accounts for a highly privileged caste of some two million individuals. Effectively master of the country, the army and the police, it upholds, protects, venerates and flatters Stalin: its idol, its "tsar," the only man it holds capable of maintaining "order" and safe-guarding its privileges.

Little by little, the Bolsheviks slickly and quickly brought under the State, monopolized and "totalitarianized . . ." the entire administration, the labor organizations, peasant organizations and the rest, finance, the means of transport and communications, the sub-soil and mining output, foreign trade and large-scale domestic trade, heavy industry, the land and agriculture, culture, teaching and education, the press and literature, art, science, sports, recreations and even thought, or, at any rate, all its manifestations.

State takeover of workers' agencies — soviets, trade unions, factory committees, etc. — was the easiest and quickest course. Their independence was done away with. They became simple administrative and executive cogs of the Party and the government.

The game was played skillfully. The workers even failed to notice that they were being placed in fetters. Since the State and the government were now "theirs," it struck them as natural that they should not stand apart from them. They saw nothing out of the ordinary in their organizations performing certain functions in the "workers'" State and implementing the decisions of the "comrade commissars."

Soon these organizations found all autonomous action, all unsolicited deeds forbidden to them.

In the end they realized their mistake. But by then it was too late. When certain worker agencies, hampered in their operation and uneasy about it, sensing that "something was rotten in the kingdom of soviets," indicated a degree of dissatisfaction and sought to recoup a little of their independence, the government resisted this with all of its energy and guile. For one thing, it immediately took steps and imposed sanctions. For another, it tried reason, telling the workers, as casually as possible, "Since we now have a workers' State wherein the workers exercise their dictatorship and where everything belongs to them, this State and its agencies are yours. So how can 'independence' possibly come into it? Independence from whom? From yourselves? For you are the State now. Failure to understand that signifies a failure to understand the revolution that has been carried through. Opposition to this state of affairs means opposition to the Revolution as such. Such ideas and movements are intolerable, for they can receive their inspiration only from the enemies of the Revolution, of the working class, its State, its dictatorship and workers' power. Those among you who are still sufficiently unenlightened to listen to the whispering of those enemies and heed their poisonous suggestions simply because not everything is going swimmingly in your young State, are engaged in an outright act of counter-revolution."

The Bolshevik system

(. . .) The Bolshevik system wants the boss-State also to be the drill-sergeant, the moral guide, the judge and the dispenser of rewards and punishments for every citizen. The State supplies that citizen with work and assigns him a job, the State feeds and pays him, the State monitors him, the State uses and handles him howsoever it pleases, the State educates and molds him, the State sits in judgment of him,: the State rewards or punishes him; prosecutor, judge, jailer, executioner — absolutely all, rolled into one, one

State that, with the aid of its officials, aims to be omnipresent, omniscient and omnipotent. Woe to him who dares try to escape from it!

Let us emphasize that the Bolshevik State (government) has seized not just all existing material and moral assets, but, more seriously, perhaps, has also asserted its eternal title to all truth, in every realm: truths historical, economic, political, social, scientific, philosophical or whatever. In every sphere the Bolshevik government regards itself as infallible and destined to give a lead to humanity. It alone is possessed of the truth. It alone knows where and how to proceed. It alone has the capacity to bring off the Revolution. And so, logically and inevitably, it argues that the 175 million people populating this country must also regard it as the sole bearer of truth; a bearer infallible, unassailable, sacrosanct. And as a matter of logic, inevitably, any person or group daring, not to fight that government, but merely to question its infallibility, criticize it, contradict it or in any way rebuke it, is deemed its enemy and, parting company, as an enemy of truth, from the Revolution, a "counter-revolutionary!"

What this amounts to is an outright monopoly upon opinion and thought. Any opinion, any thought other than that of the State (or government) is deemed heretical; dangerously, intolerably, criminally heretical. And, logically, heretics must inevitably suffer punishment: imprisonment, exile, execution.

Syndicalists and anarchists, savagely persecuted solely because they dare entertain an independent opinion with regard to the Revolution, know something of that.

As the reader can see, this system is indeed a system for the complete and absolute enslavement of the people: physical and moral enslavement. If you like, it represents a ghastly new Inquisition in social terms. Such has been the Bolshevik Party's handiwork. Did it intend this outcome? Did it knowingly pursue it? Certainly not. Without doubt, its finest representatives aspired to an arrangement that would have made it possible to build real socialism and open the way to full-blooded communism. They were certain that the methods advocated by their great ideologues would surely lead there. Moreover, they believed any means valid and justified, just as long as they brought that goal nearer.

These honest men were deceived. They took the wrong road.

Which is why certain of them, having realized their irreparable mistake and loath to outlive their evaporated hopes, took their own lives.

The conformists and parvenus of course simply adapted.

Here I must place on record an admission made to me some years ago by an eminent, sincere Bolshevik during a heated, impassioned argument. He said to me: "Sure we have gone astray and have become bogged down where we neither wanted nor expected to wind up. But we will strive to repair our mistakes, overcome the impasse and get back on the right track. And we will succeed in that."

Instead, we may be absolutely certain that they will not succeed, that they will never overcome. Because, in the final analysis, the logical sequence of things, human psychology generally, the interconnection of material facts and the predictable impact of causes and effects are mightier than the intent of a few individuals, no matter how strong and sincere these may be.

Ah, if only millions of free men had gone astray, if it were a case of mighty collectivities operating with a free hand, with all candor and in complete agreement — then we might, by a common effort of will, have made good the mistakes and redressed the situation. But such an undertaking is beyond a group of individuals placed outside of and above a subjugated mass of humanity passive towards the mammoth forces lording over it.

The Bolshevik Party seeks to build socialism through a State, a government and centralized, authoritarian political activity. All it has managed is a monstrous and murderous State capitalism, rooted in odious exploitation of "mechanized," unseeing, unenlightened masses.

The more proof is garnered that the Party's leaders were sincere, vigorous and competent and that they had an enormous mass following, the starker the historical conclusion that must be drawn from their handiwork. That conclusion is this:

Any attempt to carry out the social Revolution with the aid of a State, a government and political action, even should that attempt be very sincere, very vigorous, attended by favorable circumstances and buttressed by the masses, will necessarily result in State capitalism, the worst sort of capitalism, which has absolutely nothing to do with humanity's march towards a socialist society.

Such is the lesson which the world must draw from the formidable and crucial Bolshevik experiment; a lesson that offers mighty backing to the libertarian contention and which will shortly, in the light of these events, be grasped by all who labor, suffer, think and struggle.

Notes to **The Unknown Revolution**

1. Extracts taken from *La Révolution inconnue, 1917–1921* republished in 1969 by Pierre Belfond.
2. Voline's own testimony, taken from his unpublished "Conclusions" to *La Révolution inconnue*.
3. "We had known each other in Russia and later in France from where he, like me, was deported in 1916" (Voline's note).
4. The sub-headings have been added by us (Daniel Guérin's note).

Proceedings of *Nabat*

Here now are three important documents relating to the conferences or congresses of the Ukrainian anarchist *Nabat* movement, of which Voline was one of the leading lights. These texts have been taken from the anarchist historian Ugo Fedeli's important work *Dalla insurrezione dei contadini in Ucrania all Rivolta de Cronstadt* (Milan, 1950).[1]

The First Congress of the Anarchist Organizations of the Ukraine (Nabat) November 18, 1918

The conference which assembled and which was very important prescribed as its primary duty "organizing all of the life forces of anarchism; uniting the various strands of anarchism; bringing together through a common endeavor all anarchists seriously desirous of playing an active part in the social revolution which is defined as a process (of greater or lesser duration) giving rise to a new form of social existence for the organized masses."

Another one of the most important items on the agenda of the get-together was item number three, dealing with the [Makhnovist] "insurgent movement." The final decision was clear and plain.

It stipulated:

a) The need to step up the struggle against reactionary forces of every sort, against all who have laid hands upon the Ukraine and are using it as a bridge-head.

b) The need to inject the anarchist spirit into that struggle, thereby bolstering anarchist power for an imminent victory and for the organizing of the forces of revolution. Conference acknowledges the need for anarchists to be broadly and actively participants in the Ukraine's insurgent movement.

Given the lack of success and the negative results of purely anarchist formations, as demonstrated by experience, conference takes note of the ineffectuality of the latter.

As for anarchists' participation in all sorts of insurgent units and in non-anarchist organizations, conference states:

1. That anarchists' participation in insurgent organizations of all sorts and most especially in non-party (worker and peasant) insurgent units organized by anarchists is vital.
2. Anarchist participation in each sort of insurgent organization (revolutionary war committees, staffs, etc.) is feasible on the following conditions:

a) The revolutionary war committees and like organizations must be regarded by anarchists exclusively as technical-executive bodies (overseeing exclusively military operational matters), but should on no account be regarded as administrative or executive bodies posing, in any form, the problem of authority or assuming the latter.

b) Anarchists should not participate in organizations (revolutionary war committees, staffs, etc.) which are of the nature of party political or authoritarian institutions. Wheresoever this may be the case, anarchists must do all in their power to establish analogous organizations above party.

c) Anarchists may work with organizations that are not of the political or party sort, and not authoritarian in nature. In the event of the organizations with which anarchists work becoming political and party organizations, anarchists should quit them and launch separate but analogous organizations.

d) Anarchists are to create revolutionary war committees, where none exist. In exceptional cases, such as, say, critical times of decisive struggle, and when the salvation of the revolution depends upon it, anarchists' provisional participation in military organizations is allowed, even should the latter be of a party political nature: this, however, is permissible for information purposes only.

Conference draws the attention of militants in a particular way to the inescapable need:

1. Not to mass in military formation organizations and not to be content to be mere combatants, but rather to devote all available time to propaganda activity, striving to develop and reinforce ideas and practices of an anarchist nature among the members of such organizations and formations. We must arouse their spirit of initiative and activities of their own, inculcating the moral and cultural principles and underlying ideas of anarchism.

2. Not to restrict ourselves to the narrow confines of organizations and formations, but to strive at all times to join the life and activities of these formations and organizations to the life of the populace, doing what we can, by word and deed, to cultivate the populace's sympathy with the insurgents, engaging in active and deliberate revolutionary effort, thereby inducing the populace to render effective support to the insurgents.

Third Congress of the Anarchist Organizations of the Ukraine (Nabat) (September 3-8, 1920)

The third congress of the full members of the Nabat confederation took place in particularly difficult circumstances. After the second congress in March-April of 1919] a further congress had been scheduled for August that year, but it was unable to proceed because of the sweeping offensive unleashed in June by the White general, Denikin.

That offensive and the ensuing advance by Denikin's troops necessarily had to smash all possible liaison between the organizations. In the end, the Nabat's own secretariat was scattered and its members put to flight. One of them was captured by the White Guards in the autumn of 1919, two other joined the ranks of the **makhnovitsi** and fought with them against Denikin, while the fourth [Voline] was arrested in Moscow.

Against this backdrop, work had to be resumed clandestinely and confronted enormous difficulties, with very limited results.

So, the third congress met a year and a half later, after numerous occurrences had altered previous situations and positions.

At this congress, which assembled under the control and in the presence of the Cheka (the Bolshevik police), discussion focused upon three main items 1. principles; 2. organization; 3. tactics.

Important and grave resolutions were passed.

With regard to principles, one of those taking part in the congress asked for a specific answer to the question: "Might not anarchism's fundamental principles be in need of a modicum of revision, in the light of the lessons of the Revolution?"

The mere fact that such questions were raised demonstrated that explanations were needed. Certain people's preoccupation with leading anarchism down a road closer to the road taken by the Bolsheviks, and also the preoccupation with prosecuting and defending the revolution, made this congress one of the most important ones held thus far. Among the issues dealt with, pride of place went to the issue of the "transitional period," with all that it necessarily implied, as well as to the matter of the "dictatorship of labor." These matters provoked such an animated and stormy debate that it seemed at one point that the various tendencies would never come to an agreement and that a split was inevitable.

But the final resolution, upon which there was majority agreement, spelled out the anarchist viewpoint on all these many issues. Here are the essential points of that text:

Resolution

Passed at the Ukrainian Anarchists' Nabat Federation Congress, meeting from September 3 to 8, 1920.

We need scarcely stress the significance of the following resolution, wherein the grave ideological differences dividing Russian anarchists from the Bolsheviks are clearly and firmly set out. This resolution was adopted in the absence of Voline, he being captive in Moscow at the time.

1. Anarchy's deserters may argue that the revolution has demonstrated the flimsiness of anarchist theory, but this is without foundation. On the contrary; the underlying principles of the anarchist teaching remain unbelievably solid and have been further confirmed by the experience of the Russian revolution.

These facts demonstrate the necessity of standing firm in the struggle against all forms of authority.

2. Anarchists deny that, between the libertarian-inclining first days of the Revolution and the ultimate goal of anarchy, an anarchist Commune must interpose itself for a time, during which the remnants of the old slavery would be mopped up and new forms of free association effectively devised. That interval, fraught with uncertainties and errors but also filled with unceasing amelioration, might instead be described as a "period for accumulation of anti-authoritarian experiences, or a "period of deepening of the social revolution," or indeed, "the launching of the anarchic Commune."

Describing that transitional period in the conventional manner, one might even dub it "the change-over to the perfect form of social coexistence." But we do not recommend use of that description, because it has a precise and very special meaning inherited from the socialist movement over the past fifty years.

The notion of the "transitional period" suggests something final, fixed and rigid.

The term "transitional period" has become so much part and parcel of the international social democracy and so heavily impregnated with the historical marxist mentality as to have become unacceptable to an anarchist.

3. We likewise refuse to employ the term "dictatorship of labor," despite the efforts of some comrades eager to see it adopted. This "dictatorship of labor" is nothing but that so-called "dictatorship of the proletariat" that has been such a resounding and protracted failure; ultimately it leads, of necessity, to the dictatorship of one fraction of the proletariat, and more especially of the party, of its officials and a few condottieri, over the mass of the proletariat.

There is no reconciling anarchy with any dictatorship, even with that of workers possessed of class consciousness, over other workers and even should it have the interests of the latter in mind.

(...) Once the notion of "dictatorship" is embraced, it would lead on to acceptance (...) of the brutal domination and unrestrained force of the State. Introducing the notion of dictatorship into the anarchist program would sow unforgivable confusion in minds.

4. The revolution advocated by anarchism, one in which the principle of communism and of non-recourse to violence occupy pride of place, faces lots of difficulties in its development. The forces of active resistance, which have an interest in the preservation of the authoritarian capitalist regime, and the passivity and ignorance of the toiling masses can give rise to circumstances that would force the anarchist Commune, free and organized, to deviate from its ideal. It is an impossibility to define in hard and fast terms the various social forms of the future, given that we are ignorant of the qualitative and quantitative content of various forces which, taken together, make up reality. For that reason we regard the writing of prescriptions for an unknown future as pointless.

We draft no "minimum program." We act directly upon actual events with utter faith and in open view of the toiling masses, in order to show them the ideal of anarchism and communism clearly and in its entirety.

Following that first part, and the essential business of the resolutions passed, attentions turned to other business; the matter "of the situation in Russia generally and on the Ukraine in particular", and finally, to conclude, "relations with soviet authority."

Regarding these latter deliberations, it is important that the following points be made:

In their ongoing struggle against every form of the State, the anarchists of the Nabat confederation would countenance no compromise and no concession.

For a time, we conducted ourselves differently with regard to "soviet power."

The October Revolution's outpouring of energy (...) the anarchist phraseology of the Bolshevik "leaders" and the urgency of the struggle against worldwide imperialism, enclosing the revolution, born amid torment, in a circle of iron... all of these tempered our opposition to soviet power.

We invited the peasant and worker masses to consolidate the Revolution, and offered our advice to the new rulers, offering them comradely criticisms.

But when the soviet power born of the revolution turned, over a three year period, into a mighty machinery of rule, the revolution was strangled.

The "dictatorship of the proletariat" (without the bourgeoisie) has replaced the bourgeoisie with the dictatorship of one party and one minuscule fragment of the proletariat over the whole toiling people. That dictatorship has stifled the will of the broad masses of the toilers. Thereby dissipating the only creative force that could have resolved the various problems of the Revolution.

Note to **Proceedings of** *Nabat*

1. Ugo Fedeli (1898–1964), an Italian anarchist who also used the pen-name of Ugo Treni, was a disciple of Malatesta. Exiled from Italy until 1945, he was a countryman and collaborator with Camillo Berneri (for whom see Volume IV): in 1936 he placed himself in the service of antifascist Spain and helped Berneri publish the newspaper *Guerra di classe*. On his return to Italy, he published historical works.

NO GODS, NO MASTERS: VOLUME 4

NESTOR MAKHNO (1889–1935)

NESTOR MAKHNO, ANARCHIST GUERRILLA

In the wake of the October Revolution, the young anarchist son of poor peasants, Nestor Makhno, had taken it upon himself to organize the peasant masses of the southern Ukraine socially and militarily, on a basis of autonomy. It had all started with the establishment in the Ukraine of a right-wing regime imposed by the German and Austrian armies of occupation — a regime that had wasted no time in restoring to the former landlords estates which the revolutionary peasants had just wrested from them. The farm laborers took up arms in defense of what they had so recently won and defended it against the reactionaries, as well as against the ill-timed intrusions into the countryside of Bolshevik commissars and their unduly onerous requisitioning.

This mammoth Jacquerie, married to a guerrilla war, was enlivened by an avenger, a sort of anarchist Robin Hood whom the peasants nicknamed *Batko* (Little Father) Makhno. The armistice on November 11, 1918 led to a withdrawal of the German-Austrian armies of occupation, as well as offering Makhno a unique opportunity to accumulate weapons reserves and stock-pile.

The congress of the *Makhnovshchina* embraced both peasants' delegates and delegates from the guerrillas. Indeed, civilian organization was an extension of a peasant insurgent army prosecuting a guerrilla war. It was remarkably mobile, capable of covering up to a hundred kilometers a day, not just because it had cavalry but thanks also to its infantry who traveled aboard light horse-drawn and spring-loaded carts. This army was organized on the specifically libertarian foundations of volunteer service, the elective principle applicable to all ranks, and freely accepted discipline; the rules of the latter, drawn up by teams of partisans and then endorsed by general assemblies, were strictly observed by all.

"The honor of having eradicated Denikin's counter-revolution in the autumn of 1919 belongs chiefly to the anarchist insurgents," writes Piotr Arshinov, the chronicler of the *Makhnovshchina*.

But Makhno refused to place his army under the supreme command of the Red Army chief, Trotsky. Inventing a ploy that the Spanish Stalinists were to deploy against the anarchist brigades some eighteen years later, the Bolsheviks withheld arms from Makhno's partisans. They defaulted upon their duty to afford them aid, only to accuse them later of "treachery" and of letting themselves be beaten by White troops.

However, the two armies twice came to another accommodation, when the gravity of the interventionist threat required that they act in concert — action which came, first, against Denikin in March 1919 and then, in the summer of 1920, when Wrangel's White troops threatened before Makhno put them to flight. But once the dire threat had receded, the Red Army resumed military operations against Makhno's guerrillas, who matched them blow for blow.

At the end of November 1920, the Bolshevik authorities had no hesitation in laying an ambush. The officers of Makhno's Crimean army were invited to participate in a military council. Whereupon they were promptly arrested by the political police, the Cheka, and shot out of hand, or stripped of their weapons. At the same time, an all-out offensive was launched against the partisans. The struggle — an increasingly one-sided struggle — between libertarians and "authoritarians," between a conventional army and a guerrilla force, dragged on for a further nine months. In the end, thwarted by forces far outnumbering him and better equipped, Makhno was obliged to give up. He managed to flee into Rumania in August 1921, before moving on to Paris, where he was to die much later, in July 1935, ailing and impoverished.

With Piotr Arshinov, we may regard the *Makhnovshchina* as the prototype of an independent mass peasant movement, while it can also be viewed as a foretaste of 20th century revolutionary guerrilla warfare, as practiced by the Chinese, the Cubans, the Algerians and heroic Vietnam.

Makhno's Visit to the Kremlin

In June 1918, Makhno went to Moscow for consultations with some anarchist militants regarding methods and approaches to the revolutionary libertarian work needing to be done among the Ukrainian peasantry. He availed of the occasion to present himself at the Kremlin and meet with Yakov Mikhailovitch Sverdlov, the then secretary of the Bolshevik Party's Central Committee, and then with Lenin himself. Here, from his as yet unpublished *Memoirs*,* is Makhno's account of these two meetings.

My Audience with Sverdlov

I arrived at the gates of the Kremlin resolved to see Lenin and, if possible, Sverdlov, and to have an audience with them. A trooper sat behind a counter. I handed him the credentials with which I had been issued at the Moscow soviet. After a careful reading of them, he issued me with a pass which he himself clipped to my credentials and I crossed the porch to the inner Kremlin. There a Latvian rifleman was marching up and down. I slipped past him and entered a courtyard where I came face to face with another sentry whom one could ask to point out the building one was looking for. After that, one was at liberty to stroll around, look at the cannons and cannonballs of various caliber, dating from before or after Peter the Great, to loiter in front of the Tsar-Bell (a monumental bell) and other celebrated sights or to make straight for one of the palaces.

I turned to my left and disappeared inside one of these (I cannot recall its name), climbed a staircase, as far as the third floor, I think, then wandered down a long, empty corridor where there were placards attached to doors reading "Party Central Committee" or indeed "Library," but, being after neither of those, I continued on my way. In any case, I was unsure what lay behind those doors.

---

* In addition to reprinting the first volume of Makhno's Memoirs, under the title of *La Révolution russe en Ukraine*, which first appeared in French in 1927, the "Changer la vie" collection from the Pierre Belfond publishing house publishes a French translation of Volumes I and II, which were printed later, albeit in Russian, for they were never translated.
AK Press will be publishing Paul Sharkey's translation of Alexander Skirda's biography of Makhno: *Nestor Makhno, Anarchy's Cossack: The Struggle for Free Soviets in the Ukraine 1917–1921 (Nestor Makhno — Le Cosaque de l'Anarchie: La Lutte pour les sovies libres en Ukraine 1917-1921)*

As the other placards carried no name either, I doubled back and stopped before the one which read "Party Central Committee;" I knocked on the door. "Enter," a voice answered. There were three people seated inside the office. Of these, I thought I recognized Zagorski, whom I had seen two or three days before in one of the Bolshevik Party's clubs. I asked these people, who were busy with something amid a deadly silence, if they could let me know where the Central Executive Committee's offices were.

One of the trio (Bukharin[1], if I am not mistaken) stood up and, tucking his briefcase under his arm, said to his colleagues, but loud enough for me to hear: "I'm off," and, gesturing in my direction, "I'll point out the CEC's offices to this comrade." Whereupon he walked towards the door. I thanked those present and walked out with what I took to be Bukharin. A sepulchral silence still prevailed in the corridor.

My guide asked me where I was from. "The Ukraine," I replied. Then he asked me several questions about the terror to which the Ukraine was prey and was keen to know how I had managed to reach Moscow. Reaching the staircase, we stopped in order to pursue our conversation. Finally, my informal guide pointed to a door on the right hand side of the corridor, where, he claimed, I would be given the information I needed. And, after shaking my hand, he descended the staircase and left the palace.

I stepped up to the door, knocked and entered. A young girl asked what I wanted.

- I would like to see the chairman of the Executive Committee of the Soviet of Worker, Peasant, Soldier and Cossack Deputies, Comrade Sverdlov, I answered.

Without a word, the young girl sat behind a table, took my credentials and my pass, scanned them, scribbled a few words and issued me with a fresh pass showing the number of the office to which I had to go.

At the office to which the young girl had directed me, I found the secretary of the CEC, a thickset, dapper man who looked weary. He asked what I wanted. I explained. He asked to see my papers. I handed them over. They piqued his interest and he asked me:

- So, comrade, you've come from Southern Russia?
- Yes, from the Ukraine, I replied.
- I see you were chairman of the Committee for the Defense of the Revolution even in Kerensky's day?
- Yes.
- You're a Social Revolutionary then?
- No!
- What links have you or have you had with the Communist Party in your region?

– I am on personal terms with several Bolshevik Party militants, I replied. And I mentioned the name of the chairman of the Alexandrovsk Revolutionary Committee, Comrade Mikhailevitch, a few other militants from Ekaterinoslav.

The secretary said nothing for a moment, then questioned me about the state of mind of the peasants of "Southern Russia," their behavior towards the German troops and the Central Rada's[2] soldiers, their attitude to the soviet authorities, etc.

I made some short replies which manifestly satisfied him: personally, I regretted that I did not have the time to answer more fully.

Then he made a telephone call to somewhere and promptly invited me to enter the office of the CEC chairman, Comrade Sverdlov.

En route my thoughts turned to the tales peddled by the counter-revolutionaries as well as by revolutionaries, by my own friends indeed, who were against the policies of Lenin, Sverdlov and Trotsky, tales to the effect that it was impossible to gain access to these earthly gods. They were, talk had it, surrounded by bodyguards and the leader of the latter only granted admission to those of whom he liked the look.

Now, with only the CEC secretary for company, I realized the absurdity of these rumors. Sverdlov himself opened the door to us with a wide grin, tinged, it seemed to me, with comradeship, offered me his hand and steered me to an armchair. After which the CEC secretary returned to his desk.

Comrade Sverdlov struck me as being in better form than his secretary. He also gave me the impression that he had more interest than him in what had been happening in the Ukraine over the past two or three months. Straight out, he said:

– So, comrade, you've come from our tortured South; what work did you do down there?

– The same as was done by the broad masses of the revolutionary toilers of the Ukrainian countryside. The latter, having been active participants in the Revolution, strove to secure their complete emancipation. I was, you might say, always the first among them to go down that road. Today, following the collapse of the Ukrainian revolutionary front, I find myself momentarily stranded in Moscow.

– What's that you say? shouted Comrade Sverdlov, interrupting me. The peasants in the South are, for the most part, kulaks or supporters of the Central Rada.

I burst out laughing and at no great length but sticking to the essentials, I described for him the operations of the anarchist-organized peasants of the Gulyai-Polye region against the Austro-German occupation troops and the soldiers of the Central Rada.

Seemingly shaken, Comrade Sverdlov was nonetheless unable to stop repeating: Why then have they not supported our Red Guards? According to our intelligence, the South's peasants are infected by the worst Ukrainian chauvinism and have everywhere rapturously welcomed the German troops and Rada soldiers as liberators.

I could feel myself getting irritable as I set about strenuously rebutting Sverdlov's information about the Ukrainian countryside. I admitted to him that I myself had been the organizer and leader of several battalions of peasant volunteers who waged a revolutionary fight against the Germans and the Rada and I was sure that the peasants could recruit a mighty army from among their ranks to fight them, but they could not see the Revolution's battle-front clearly. The Red Guard units which, with their armored trains, had fought along the railway lines without ever straying far from them, withdrawing at the first set-back, very often without taking care to load up their own fighters and surrendering dozens of versts to the enemy, whether the latter advanced or not... these units, I told him, inspired no confidence in the peasants who realized that, being isolated in their villages and unarmed, they were the ones at the mercy of the Revolution's foes. Indeed, the Red Guards' armored trains never sent detachments out into the villages located within a ten or twenty kilometer radius, not merely to issue them with weapons but also to stimulate the peasants and urge them into mounting daring strikes against the Revolution's enemies by taking a hand in the action themselves.

Sverdlov heard me out attentively and from time to time exclaimed: Can that be possible? I named several units of Red Guards attached to the groups of Bogdanov, Svirski or Sablin and others; very calmly, I pointed out that Red Guards charged with protecting the railroads for armored trains thanks to which they could switch rapidly on to the offensive, but more often beat a retreat, could scarcely inspire much confidence in the peasant masses. Now, those masses saw the Revolution as the means of getting rid of the oppression not just of the big landowners and rich kulaks but also of their hirelings and of escaping from the political and administrative power of the State official, and that consequently they were ready to defend themselves and their gains against summary executions and mass destruction, whether these emanated from the Prussian Junkers[3] or from the hetman [Skoropadsky's] troops.

- Yes, said Sverdlov, I believe that you are right as far as the Red Guards are concerned... but we have now reorganized them into a Red Army, which is building up its strength and if the peasants in the South are, as you describe, driven by such revolutionary commitment, there is every chance of the Germans' being flattened and the hetman's biting the dust shortly — in which case soviet power will triumph in the Ukraine also.

- That will depend upon the clandestine action carried out in the Ukraine. For my own part, I reckon that such action is more necessary today than ever, provided that it be organized and whipped into fighting shape, which would inspire the masses to open revolt in town and countryside against the Germans and the hetman. In the absence of an essentially revolutionary uprising inside the Ukraine, the Germans and Austrians will not be forced to evacuate and we will not be able to get our hands on the hetman and those supporting him or to force them to flee with their protectors. Do not forget that on account of the Brest-Litovsk treaty and international political factors with which our Revolution has to contend a Red Army offensive is out of the question.

While I was putting this to him, Comrade Sverdlov was making notes.

- As it happens, he told me, I am entirely of the same view as yourself. But what are you, a Communist or a Left[4] Social Revolutionary? It is plain from the way you talk that you are Ukrainian, but it is unclear to which of those two parties you belong.

While it did not bother me (the CEC secretary having put it to me already) that question did place me in a bit of a quandary. What was I to do? Tell Sverdlov bluntly that I was an anarcho-communist, the comrade and friend of those whom his party and the State system created by it had crushed in Moscow and several other cities just two months previously, or should I fly some other flag of convenience?

I was of two minds and Sverdlov noticed it. I was loath to spell out my conception of the social revolution and my political affiliation in the middle of our interview. But I also found it repugnant to conceal them. That is why, after a few moments' deliberation, I told Sverdlov:

- Why so much interest in my political affiliation? Are my papers which show you who I am, whence I come and the part I have played in a certain region in the organizing of the toilers of town and country as well as partisan bands and volunteer battalions to fight the counter-revolution which has fastened on the Ukraine, not enough for you?

Comrade Sverdlov offered his apologies and begged me not to doubt his revolutionary honor or suspect him of lacking confidence in me. His pleas struck me as so heartfelt that they made me uneasy and without further ado I declared to him that I was an anarcho-communist of the Bakunin-Kropotkin stripe.

What manner of anarcho-communist are you, comrade, since you accept organization of the toiling masses and their direction in the struggle against the power of capital? Sverdlov exclaimed with a comradely grin.

To his amazement, I told the CEC chairman:

- Anarchism is too realistic an ideal not to understand the modern world and current events, and the part that its exponents play in one way or another in those events is there to be seen, and not to pay attention to the guide-lines by which its action must be governed and the means that have to be used to that end. ...

- Glad to hear it, but you are not at all like these anarchists who, here in Moscow, had set up their headquarters in Malaia Dmitrovka, Sverdlov told me, and he was about to add something else, but I interjected:

- Your Party's crushing of the Malaia Dmitrovka anarchists[5] must be regarded as a painful episode of which, for the sake of the Revolution, there must be no repetition in the future ...

Sverdlov mumbled something into his beard and, rising from his armchair, came up to me, placed his hands on my shoulders and told me:

- I see that you are very well-briefed about what happened during our withdrawal from the Ukraine and, above all, about the peasants' state of mind. Ilitch, our comrade Lenin, would certainly be glad to hear you. Do you want me to telephone him?

My answer was that there was not a lot more for me to tell Comrade Lenin, but Sverdlov was already holding the telephone and was telling Lenin that he had with him a comrade with very important intelligence on the peasants of Southern Russia and their feelings towards the German invasion troops. And, right there and then, he asked Lenin when he could grant me an audience.

A second later, Sverdlov replaced the telephone and scribbled me a pass making it possible for me to return. As he handed it to me, he said:

- Tomorrow, at one in the afternoon, come straight here: we will go see Comrade Lenin together. Can I rely upon you?

- Rely on it, was my reply.

My Audience with Lenin

The next day, at one o' clock, I was back in the Kremlin where I met Comrade Sverdlov who promptly took me to Lenin. The latter welcomed me like a brother. He took me by the arm and tapping my shoulder lightly with his other hand, had me sit in an easy chair. Having invited Sverdlov to settle into another armchair, he went over to his secretary and told him.

- Be so kind as to finish that job by two o'clock.

Whereupon he sat facing me and began to question me.

His first question was: What region do you come from? Then: How have the peasants of the area taken to the watchword **All power to the soviets in the villages** and what has the reaction been from the enemies of that watchword, and the Central Rada's reaction in particular?. Then: Have the peasants of your area risen up against the Austro-German invaders? If so, what prevented the peasant revolts from turning into a general uprising and linking up with the actions of the Red Guard units which have so courageously been defending our revolutionary gains?

I gave Lenin brief answers to all of these questions. With that talent that was all his own, he strove to put the questions in such a way that I could answer them point by point. Take, for instance, the question: How have the peasants of the area taken to the watchword **All power to the soviets in the villages?** Lenin put it to me three times, and was astonished at my reply: The peasants have welcomed it after their fashion, which is to say that, as they understand it, all power should, in every sphere, mirror the consciousness and wishes of the toilers; that the soviets of worker-peasant deputies, at village, cantonal or district levels are nothing more nor less than offshoots of the revolutionary organization and economic self-management of the toilers struggling against the bourgeoisie and its lackeys, the Right Social Revolutionaries and their coalition government.

- Do you think that that is a proper construction to place upon our watchword? asked Lenin.

- Yes, I replied.

- In that case, the peasants of your region have been infected with anarchism, he told me.

- Is that such a bad thing? I asked.

- That is not what I mean. On the contrary, it is to be celebrated for it would hasten communism's victory over capitalism and its power.

- I find that flattering, I told Lenin, straining not to laugh.

- No, no, I am very seriously arguing that this social phenomenon in the life of the peasant masses would hasten communism's victory over capitalism, Lenin reiterated, adding: But I think that this phenomenon has not come about spontaneously; it is a consequence of anarchist propaganda and will not take long to evaporate. I am even inclined to believe that this mentality, cornered by the triumphant counter-revolution before it had the time to spawn an organization, has already perished.

I pointed out to Lenin that a political leader ought never to display pessimism or skepticism.

- So, according to you, Sverdlov interrupted, these anarchist tendencies in the life of the peasant masses ought to be given encouragement?

- Oh, your party is not going to encourage them, I replied. Whereupon Lenin interjected:

- And why should we encourage them? In order to divide the proletariat's revolutionary forces, clear a path for the counter-revolution and, when all is said and done, mount the scaffold ourselves along with the proletariat?

I could scarcely contain myself, and with my voice betraying my irritation, I pointed out to Lenin that anarchism and anarchists did not aspire to counter-revolution and would not lead the proletariat there.

- Did I really say that? Lenin asked me, and he added: I meant to say that anarchists, lacking mass organizations, are not in a position to organize the proletariat and the poor peasants and, as a result, incite them to defend, in the broadest sense of the term, what has been won by us all and which we hold dear."

The conversation then turned to other matters raised by Lenin. To one query, regarding "The Red Guard units and the revolutionary courage with which they defended our common gains" Lenin forced me to give as complete an answer as possible. Plainly the question bothered him or else reminded him of what the Red Guard units had recently accomplished in the Ukraine in achieving, so they claimed, the objectives which Lenin and his party had set themselves and in the name of which they had despatched them from Petrograd and other far-off great cities in Russia. I remember Lenin's emotion, the emotion that could only be displayed by a man who passionately lived the struggle against the social order which he despised and wanted to see beaten, when I told him:

- Having been involved in the disarming of dozens of Cossacks withdrawn from the German front at the end of December 1917 and the start of 1918, I am well-informed about the 'revolutionary bravado' of Red Army units and especially their commanders. Now it strikes me, Comrade Lenin, that, taking second- and third-hand intelligence as your basis, you are exaggerating it.

- How so? Are you questioning it? Lenin asked.

- The Red Guard units have displayed revolutionary spirit and courage, but not to the extent you describe. The Red Guards' struggle against the Central Rada's 'haidamaks'[6] and above all against the German troops have seen times when revolutionary spirit and bravery, as well as the Red Guards' and their commanders' actions, have proved very flimsy. To be sure, in many instances, there are, as I see it, grounds for putting this down to the fact that the Red Guard detachments had been hastily put together and employed against the enemy tactics that resembled neither the tactics of partisan bands nor those of regulars. You must know that the Red Guards, whatever their numerical strength, mounted their attacks upon the enemy by traveling along the railroads. Some ten or fifteen versts from the rails, the terrain was unoccupied: defenders of the revolution or of the counter-revolution could have circulated there at will. For that reason, surprise attacks almost always succeeded. It is only around railway halts, towns or hamlets served by the railways that the Red Guard formations organized a front and launched their attacks.

But the rear and the immediate environs of the places under enemy threat were left undefended. The revolution's offensive action suffered counter-thrusts as a result. Red Guard units had scarcely finished issuing their appeals in a region before the counter-revolutionary forces went on to the counter-offensive and very often forced the Red Guards to beat the retreat, scrambling aboard their armored trains. So much so that the rural population never even saw them and consequently could scarcely support them.

- What are revolutionary propagandists doing in the countryside? Can they not even manage to keep the rural proletariat on stand-by to act as fresh troops to replenish Red Guard units passing through the neighborhood, or to form new Red Guard irregulars and occupy positions for the purposes of combating the counter-revolution? Lenin asked.

- Let's not get carried away. There are very few revolutionary propagandists in the countryside and there is not much that they can do. Now, every passing day brings hundreds of propagandists and secret enemies of the Revolution into the villages. In many places, we should not be waiting for revolutionary propagandists to conjure up fresh forces for the revolution and organize them to confront the counterrevolution. These are times, I told Lenin, that require decisive action of all revolutionaries in every aspect of the workers' life and struggle. Failure to take that into account, especially where we in the Ukraine are concerned, amounts to letting the counter-revolution marshaled behind the hetman expand at will and consolidate its power.

Sverdlov's eyes darted from me to Lenin and back again and he smiled with satisfaction. As for Lenin, his fingers were intertwined and he was deep in thought, his head tilted to one side. Having taken it all in, he said to me:

- Everything that you have just told me is greatly to be regretted. And, turning towards Sverdlov, he added: We are on the right track in reorganizing the Red Guard units into the Red Army, the track that leads on to the proletariat's definitive victory over the bourgeoisie.

- Yes, yes, Sverdlov responded with animation.

Whereupon Lenin said to me:

- What work have you in mind to do here in Moscow?

My answer was that I would not be staying long. As agreed by the Conference of partisan groups held in Taganrog, I was due to return to the Ukraine early in July.

- Clandestinely? Lenin asked.

- Yes, I replied.

Turning then to Sverdlov, Lenin mused:

- Anarchists are always full of the spirit of sacrifice, ready to face any sacrifice, but being blind fanatics they ignore the past and have their thoughts fixed exclusively upon the distant future.

And, begging me not to take that as applicable to me, he went on:

- You, comrade, I regard as a man with a feeling for the realities and requirements of our times. If only a third of the anarchists in Russia were like you, we Communists would be ready to work with them under certain conditions and work in concert in the interests of free organization of the producers. Right then, I felt a deep regard for Lenin develop within me, although until recently I had held him responsible for the elimination of Moscow's anarchist organizations, which had been the signal for the crushing of them in lots of other cities. And in my heart of hearts, I was ashamed of myself. Searching for what answer I should make to Lenin, I let him have it point blank:

- The Revolution and its gains are dear to anarchist-communists: and that is proof that on that count they are all alike.

- Oh, come off it! Lenin returned with a laugh. We know the anarchists as well as you do. For the most part, they have no idea of the here-and-now, or at any rate, care very little about it; now the present is so serious that not thinking about it or not adopting some positive stance with regard to it is more than shameful in a revolutionary. Most anarchists have their minds focused on the future and devote their writings to that, without making any attempt to understand the here and now: and that is another thing that sets us apart from them.

At which Lenin rose from his easy chair and pacing back and forth, added:

- Yes, yes, anarchists are big on ideas for the future, but in the here and now, their feet never touch the ground; theirs is a deplorable attitude, because their vacuous fanaticism ensures that they have no real links to that future.

Sverdlov smirked, and, turning in my direction, said:

- You cannot challenge that. Vladimir Ilitch's reasoning is spot-on. Lenin hurriedly added:

- Have anarchists ever acknowledged their lack of realism in the 'here-and-now' of life? It doesn't even occur to them.

In reply to that, I told Lenin and Sverdlov that I was a semi-literate peasant and would not get into a discussion of the, to me, overly erudite, view which Lenin had just expressed regarding anarchists.

- But I ought to tell you, Comrade Lenin, that your assertion, to wit, that anarchists have no grasp of the 'here-and-now' and have no real ties to it, etcetera, is wrong through and through. The anarchist-communists of the Ukraine, (or "Southern Russia," since you Bolshevik-Communists try to steer clear of the word Ukraine) — as I say, the anarchist-communists — have already furnished proof aplenty that they stand four-square in the 'here-and-now.' The entire struggle of the Ukrainian revolutionary countryside against the Central Rada has been conducted under the ideological direction of anarchist communists and, partly, of the Social Revolutionaries (who, to be honest, ascribe to their fight against the Rada quite different objectives than we anarchist-communists do). Your Bolsheviks are, so to speak, non-existent in our countryside; where any do exist, their influence is minuscule. Nearly all of the peasant communes or associations in the Ukraine have been launched at the instigation of anarchist-communists. And the laboring population's armed struggle with the counter-revolution generally, as well as with the counter-revolution embodied in the Austro-Hungarian and German armies of invasion, has been undertaken under the exclusive ideological and organizational aegis of anarchist-communists. True, it may not suit your party's interests to give us credit for all that, but the facts are there and you cannot dispute them. You are, I imagine, perfectly well aware of the numbers and fighting capabilities of the Ukraine's revolutionary irregulars. Not for nothing have you referred to the courage with which they have heroically defended our common revolutionary gains.

A good half of them have fought under the anarchist colors. Mokrooussov, M. Nikiforova, Cherednyak, Garin, Chernyak, Lunev and many another partisan commander — it would take too long to list them all — are all anarchist-communists. Not to mention myself and the group to which I belong, or all the other partisan groups and volunteers that we have set up to defend the revolution and of which the Red Guard command simply must be aware. All of which demonstrates rather forcefully, Comrade Lenin, the extent to which you are mistaken in alleging that we anarchist-communists do not have our feet on the ground, that our attitude in the 'here-and-now' is to be deplored, although we were fond of thinking about the 'future' a lot. What I have said to you in the course of this conversation cannot be called into question, for it is the truth. The account I have given you contradicts the verdict you pronounced upon us, and everyone, you included, can see there proof that we are four-square in the 'here-and-now,' that we operate there, keeping an eye out for whatever brings us closer to the future, about which we do think, and very seriously at that.

I glanced at Sverdlov now. He blushed, but carried on smiling at me. As for Lenin, spreading his arms, he said:

- Perhaps I may be mistaken.

- Yes, yes, as it happens, Comrade Lenin, you have been too hard on us anarchist-communists, simply, I believe, because you are misinformed as to the reality in the Ukraine and the role we play there.

- Maybe, I won't challenge that. In any case, show me who does not make mistakes, especially in the situation in which we find ourselves? was Lenin's response.

And, realizing that I had become a little agitated, he tried, in a fatherly way, to assuage me by steering the conversation very skillfully on to another topic. But my bad character, for want of another word for it, prevented me from taking any further interest in it, in spite of all the respect which I had developed for Lenin in the course of our exchanges. I felt insulted. And no matter that I had facing me a man with whom there would have been a lot more topics to explore and from whom there would have been a lot to learn, the mood had been broken. My answers now were more curt; something in me had snapped and a feeling of irritation swept over me.

Lenin could not have failed to notice this change of mood in me. He strove to smooth things over by switching to a different topic. And noticing that I was coming out of my sulk and succumbing to his eloquence, he suddenly asked me:

- So, it is your intention to return clandestinely to the Ukraine?
- Yes, I replied.
- May I be of assistance?
- Certainly, I said.

Turning then to Sverdlov, Lenin asked:

- Which of our people is presently in charge of the service for getting our lads south?
- Comrade Karpenko or Zatonski, Sverdlov answered. I'll make inquiries.

While Sverdlov made a telephone call to discover whether it was Karpenko or Zatonski that was in charge of the agency whose task it was to smuggle militants into the Ukraine for underground work there, Lenin attempted to persuade me that I ought to conclude from his treatment of me that the Communist Party's stance vis a vis anarchists was not so hostile as I seemed to believe.

- While we have been compelled — Lenin told me — to take vigorous action to remove the anarchists from the private hotel they were occupying in the Malaia Dmitrovka, where they were harboring certain bandits, locals or just passing through, the blame for that lies, not with us, but with the anarchists who had settled in there. Anyway, we won't be bothering them again. You ought to know that they have been given permission to occupy other premises not far from Malaia Dmitrovka and they are free to operate as they see fit.

- Have you any evidence — I asked Comrade Lenin — to indicate that the Malaia Dmitrovka anarchists were harboring bandits?

- Yes, the Extraordinary Commission [Cheka] collected the evidence and authenticated it. Otherwise our party would never have authorized it to proceed, Lenin replied.

Meanwhile, Sverdlov had returned to sit with us and he announced that Comrade Karpenko was indeed in charge of the smuggling agency, but that Comrade Zatonski was also conversant with things.

Whereupon Lenin burst out:

- There you go, comrade, drop in on Comrade Karpenko tomorrow afternoon, or whenever you like, and ask him about everything you'll be needing in order to make your way back to the Ukraine by clandestine means. He will work out a safe route to get you over the border.

- What border? I asked.

- Haven't you heard? A border has been drawn between Russia and the Ukraine. The troops manning it are Germans, Lenin said wearily.

- Yet you look upon the Ukraine as "southern Russia?" I replied.

- Looking upon is one thing, comrade, and keeping one's eyes open in life is quite another, returned Lenin.

And before I could answer, he added:

- Tell Comrade Karpenko that I sent you. If he has any queries, he need only telephone me. Here is the address at which you can find him.

By now we were, all three, on our feet. We shook hands and after a seemingly cordial exchange of thanks, I left Lenin's office.

Notes to Makhno's Visit to the Kremlin

1. Nikolai Bukharin (1888–1938), Bolshevik since 1906, member of the Party's Central Committee from 1917 up until his death. Leader of the "rightists" after 1928. A brilliant economist and theoretician, he was executed under Stalin.
2. From November 1917 on, the Central Rada was a sort of parliament of the new "Ukrainian democratic republic." The Treaty of Brest-Litovsk, agreed between the Bolsheviks and the German imperial government at the beginning of 1918, had opened the gates of the Ukraine to the AustroGermans. They set up a reactionary government there headed by the first "hetman" (a title formerly held by the elected leader of the Ukrainian Cossacks) Skorpadsky. But the defeat suffered by the Central empires towards the end of 1918 forced the withdrawal of German and Austrian troops from the Ukraine, while Skoropadsky took to his heels. He was replaced by a "Directory," headed by a former member of the Rada, the borgeois separatist, Petliura.
3. **Junkers** a German term meaning squires: the German officer corps being made up of aristocrats and recruits drawn from among the great land-owning families east of the Elbe.
4. At the time, only the *Left* wing of the Social Revolutionary Party had sided with the Bolsheviks.

5. On a specious pretext, the Bolshevik authorities, on the night of April 12, 1918, had had their police and military troops ransack the premises of the Moscow federation of anarchist groups, a private hotel situated in the Malaia Dmitrovka.

6. Haidamaks — military forces of the Ukrainian reactionary government: the name is borrowed from the heroes of a Ukrainian popular uprising against the troops of the Tsar and the king of Poland in the 18th century.

The Makhnovist Movement

The texts below are taken from Piotr Arshinov's 1928 book *History of the Makhnovist Movement.*

The First "Free Communes"

[In the southern Ukraine, following the expulsion of the great landowners] the land came into peasant hands. The latter were well aware that it was not all over yet, that it was not enough to seize a tract of land and leave it at that. Life, a tough teacher, had taught them that there were enemies lurking everywhere and had taught them to stick together. In a number of places, attempts were made to reorganize life along communal lines. In spite of the peasants' hostility towards the official (government) communes, in many places throughout the Gulyai-Polye region there sprang up peasant communes known as "labor communes" or "free communes." Thus the township of Pokrovskoye saw the formation of the very first free commune, called after Rosa Luxemburg. Its members were all unemployed. To begin with, this commune comprised only a few dozen members; later, their numbers expanded to over three hundred.

(. . .) With a straightforwardness and expansiveness of soul characteristic of the people, the peasants had honored the memory of a heroine of the Revolution, a stranger to them, who had perished as a martyr in the revolutionary struggle. Now, the commune's internal arrangements were based upon the anti-authoritarian principle. As it developed and grew, it began to exercise great influence over the peasants of the entire district. The "communist" authorities attempted to meddle in the commune's internal affairs, but were rebuffed.

(. . .) Another commune which brought together the poor peasants of Gulyai-Polye was launched on an old estate seven kilometers outside Gulyai-Polye. It was simply called "Commune No. 1 of the peasants of Gulyai-Polye." Communes No. 2 and No. 3 lay around twenty kilometers from there. And there were further communes elsewhere. True, taken all in all the communes were not numerous and encompassed only a minority of the population: particularly the ones who had no solidly established arable holdings. But these communes had been formed on the initiative of the poor peasants themselves. The Makhnovists' work only influenced them to the extent that the latter were pushing the idea of free communes in the region.

The communes were launched, not as the result of some dream or example, but quite simply to meet the essential needs of the peasants who had

had nothing prior to the revolution and, having achieved victory, set about organizing their economic activity along communal lines. These were not the contrived communes of the Communist Party which usually included people rounded up haphazardly who did nothing except waste the grain and ruin the ground, who enjoyed support from the State and the government and thus lived off the labors of the people whom they presumed to teach how to work.

These were genuine working communes of peasants accustomed to work since childhood and capable of appreciating the labors of others as well as their own. To begin with, the peasants worked there in order to secure their daily bread. In addition, every individual received there all the moral and material backing he could need. The principle of fraternity and equality was staunchly upheld in the communes. Everyone, man, woman or child, was expected to work there, insofar as they were able. Organizational tasks were entrusted to one or two comrades who, once those tasks had been dealt with, returned to their normal work alongside all the other members of the commune. Obviously, such healthy, responsible practices were due to the communes' having emerged in a working context and their growth having proceeded along natural lines.

However, these seeds of free communism fell far short of accounting for the whole of the peasants' creative, constructive, economic and social activities. Instead, these seeds came to light only slowly and gradually, whereas the political climate required from the peasants immediate, concerted effort on a grand scale, with widespread mobilization and activity. It was essential that a united organization be arrived at, not just within the confines of such and such a hamlet or village, but also in whole districts or even departments (governments) making up the liberated region. There was a need to work together to resolve the various questions confronting the region as a whole. Appropriate bodies had to be created, and the peasants did not fail to do so. These bodies were the regional congresses of peasants, workers and partisans. During the region's period of freedom, three such congresses were held. The peasants succeeded in establishing close links, setting guide-lines and prescribing the economic and social tasks which lay ahead.

(. . .) With regard to the organs of social self-direction, the peasants and workers supported the notion of free labor soviets. Contrary to the Bolsheviks' and other socialists' political soviets, the free soviets of the peasants and workers were to have been the organs of their social and economic "self-governance." The individual soviet was only the executor of the wishes of the district's toilers and of their organizations. The local soviets established the requisite liaison with one another, thereby forming larger-scale economic and territorial bodies.

However, the context of war made the creation and operation of these bodies extremely difficult, and for that reason complete organization of them was never successfully carried through.

Makhno's Insurgent Army Incorporated into the Red Army (Early 1919)

At the beginning of 1919, after a series of skirmishes, the Makhnovist insurgents drove Denikin's troops back in the direction of the Sea of Azov and captured around one hundred wagon-loads of wheat from them. The first thought of Makhno and the staff of the insurgent army was to despatch these captured provisions to the famished workers of Moscow and Petrograd. That suggestion was enthusiastically endorsed by the broad masses of the insurgents. The hundred wagon-loads of wheat were delivered to Petrograd and Moscow, under escort from a Makhnovist delegation that was very warmly received by the Moscow Soviet.

The Bolsheviks arrived in the region of the **Makhnovshchina** long after Denikin. The Makhnovist insurgents had by then been locked in battle with him for a good three months; they had by then driven him out of their region and established their line of defense east of Mariupol, by the time that the first Bolshevik division, headed by Dybenko[1], arrived in Sinelnikovo.

Makhno personally, and the entire insurgent revolutionary movement, were still unknown quantities as far as the Bolsheviks were concerned. In the Communist press in Moscow and in the provinces, Makhno had hitherto been mentioned as a daring insurgent of great promise. His struggle against Skoropadsky, and then against Petliura and Denikin assured him in advance of the goodwill of the Bolshevik chiefs. To them there seemed to be no doubt but that the Makhnovists' revolutionary detachments which resisted so many varieties of counter-revolution in the Ukraine, would be absorbed into the Red Army. So they arrived singing Makhno's praises, without first having acquainted themselves with him on his home turf, and whole columns of their newspapers were devoted to him.

The Bolshevik fighters' first encounter with Makhno took place under the same auspices of goodwill and praise (in March 1919). Makhno was immediately invited to join the Red Army along with all his detachments, with an eye to joining forces in order to defeat Denikin. The political and ideological idiosyncrasies of the revolutionary insurgency were regarded as quite natural and in no way potential obstacles to amalgamation on the basis of common cause. Those idiosyncrasies were to be left intact. As we shall see anon, the leaders of the **Makhnovshchina** had been mistaken in their hopes that the Bolsheviks would be ideological adversaries only. They had failed to take into consideration that they were dealing here with the most accomplished of statists and exponents of authoritarian violence. Errors, unless danger ensues, can have their uses. Theirs proved a good lesson for the Makhnovists.

The insurgent army became a component part of the Red army under the following conditions:

a) the insurgent army is to retain its former internal order.
b) it is to have seconded to it political commissars appointed by the Communist authorities.
c) it is to be subordinated to the Red high command only in relation to military operations proper.
d) it is not to be removed from the Denikin front.
e) It is to obtain munitions and provisions on the same footing as the Red Army.
f) it is to retain its title as the Insurgent Revolutionary Army and keep its black flags. The Makhnovist insurgents' army was organized in accordance with three underlying principles: volunteer service, the elective principle and self-discipline.

Volunteer service meant that the army comprised solely revolutionary combatants enlisting of their own volition.

The elective principle consisted of the fact that the commanders of every part of the army, members of the staff and council as well as all persons holding positions of importance generally in the army, had to be elected or endorsed by the insurgents of those respective parts or by the army as a whole.

Self-discipline meant that all of the army's disciplinary rules were drawn up by commissions of insurgents, then endorsed by the general assemblies of the parts of the army, and were stringently observed, on the responsibility of each insurgent and each commander.

All of these principles were retained by the Makhnovist army when it amalgamated with the Red Army. To begin with, it was awarded the designation of "Third Brigade," later altered to "First Ukrainian Revolutionary Insurgent Division." Later, it adopted the definitive title of "Insurgent Revolutionary Army of the Ukraine (Makhnovist)."

Note to Makhno's Insurgent Army Incorporated into the Red Army

1. For more about Dybenko see below. Makhno was not quite unknown to the Bolsheviks, for Lenin as we have seen, granted him an audience in June 1918.

Counter-Revolutionary? Reply to Dybenko (commander of the Bolshevik forces) April 1919.

"Comrade" Dybenko declared the congress scheduled for Gulyai-Polye on April 10, 1919 counterrevolutionary and outlawed its organizers, against whom, he claims, the severest repressive measures must be enforced. Here, verbatim, we publish his telegram:

> From Novo-Alexeyevka, No. 283. 22.45 hours, 10 [April]. Forward to comrade Batko Makhno, Alexandrovsk divisional command. Copy to Volnovakha, Mariupol, for forwarding to comrade Makhno. Copy to the Gulyai-Polye soviet:
>
> Any congress convened in the name of the military revolutionary command, disbanded by my orders, is regarded as manifestly counter-revolutionary, and the organizers of it will be liable to the severest repressive measures up to being declared outlaws. I order that steps be taken immediately to ensure that there is no repetition of such things. — Divisional Commander Dybenko.

Prior to declaring the congress counter-revolutionary, "comrade" Dybenko did not even take the trouble to inquire in what name and for what purpose this congress was convened by the "disbanded" military revolutionary staff of Gulyai-Polye, whereas in point of fact it had been summoned by the executive committee of the military revolutionary committee. So the latter, having summoned the congress, cannot tell whether it is it which "comrade" Dybenko regards as being outside of the law.

If such be the case, allow us to inform Your Excellency by whom and to what end that (in your view, manifestly counter-revolutionary) congress was convened, and then, it may, perhaps, no longer appear as frightening as you portray it.

The congress, as said, was summoned by the executive committee of the military revolutionary council of the Gulyai-Polye region, in Gulyai-Polye itself (it being the centrally situated town). It was designated as the third Gulyai-Polye regional congress. It was summoned for the purpose of determining the future policy line of the military revolutionary council. (You see, "comrade" Dybenko, three of these "counter-revolutionary" congresses have taken place already.) But the question arises: what is the provenance of the regional military revolutionary committee itself and for what purpose was it founded? If you still do not know the answer, "comrade" Dybenko, let us enlighten you.

The regional military revolutionary council was set up in accordance with the resolution from the second congress held in Gulyai-Polye on February 12th this year. (A long time ago, as you can see, long before you ever got here).

The regional military revolutionary council was formed, then, to organize combatants and oversee voluntary mobilization, for the region was encircled by the Whites, and the insurgent detachments made up of the first volunteers were no longer sufficient to hold an extended front. At that time there were no soviet troops in our region; and then again, the population expected no great help, its view being that it was up to itself to look to the defense of its region. To that end, the Gulyai-Polye regional military revolutionary council was set up; that council comprised, according to the second congress's resolution, one delegate per district, thirty-two members in all, representing the districts of the Ekaterinoslav and Tauride governments.

But we will go into the military revolutionary council later. Here the question arises: where did that second regional congress come from? who convened it? who authorized it? was the convener an outlaw, and if not, then why not? The second regional congress was summoned to Gulyai-Polye by a steering committee made up of five individuals elected by the first congress. The second congress took place on February 12 this year and, to our great astonishment, its conveners were not outlawed, for at the time there were none of those "heroes" who would dare trespass against the people's rights, won with the people's own blood. A further question therefore arises: where had the first congress come from? who had convened it? was its convener not outlawed, and if not, why not? "Comrade" Dybenko, you are, it seems, still very new to the revolutionary movement in the Ukraine and we must educate you as to its very beginnings. Which is what we are about to do; and you, once you have been educated about it, will perhaps mend your ways a little.

The first regional congress took place on January 23 this year in the first insurgent camp in Greater Mikhailovka. It consisted of delegates from the districts adjacent to the front. Soviet troops were then a long way away, a very long way away. The region was cut off from the whole world: on one side by the Denikinists, on the other by the Petliurists; consequently, there were only the insurgent detachments with Father Makhno and Shchuss at their head to match these others blow for blow. The organizers and social institutions in the towns and villages in those days did not always go by the same names. In such and such a town there might be a "soviet," somewhere else a "people's regency," in a third place a "military revolutionary staff," in a fourth a "provincial regency," etc., but the ethos was equally revolutionary throughout. In order to consolidate the front as well as to introduce a degree of uniformity of organization and action across the region, the first congress was summoned.

No one had convened it; it had come together spontaneously, in accordance with the population's wishes and with its approval. At the congress it was proposed that those of our brothers who had been forcibly enlisted in the Petliurist army be snatched back. To that end, a five man delegation was elected and instructed to call to Father Makhno's headquarters and whichever others might be necessary, and to infiltrate even the army of the Ukrainian Directory (known as Petliura's army) in order to proclaim to our conscripted brethren that they had been misled and must quit that army. In addition, the delegation was charged with summoning, upon its return, a more comprehensive second congress, with a view to organizing the entire region delivered from the counter-revolutionary bands and creating a more powerful defense front.

So, upon returning, the delegates did summon that second regional congress, outside of any "party," "authorities" or "law;" for you, "comrade" Dybenko, and other lovers and guardians of the law of the same ilk as yourself were away far away: and since the heroic leaders of the insurgent movement did not aspire to power over the people who had just, with their very own hands, torn asunder the shackles of slavery, the congress was not declared counter-revolutionary, and its conveners were not outlawed.

To return to the regional council: Even as the Gulyai-Polye regional military revolutionary council was being formed, the soviet authorities arrived in the region. In accordance with the resolution passed at the second congress, the regional congress did not leave matters in abeyance pending the arrival of the soviet authorities. It had a duty to implement the instructions from congress, unswervingly. The council was not a directing agency but merely an executive one. It carried on doing what it could and continued its efforts along revolutionary lines. Little by little, the soviet authorities began to place obstacles in the way of the council's activities; commissars and other high-ranking officials of the soviet government began to look upon the council as a counter-revolutionary organization. At which point the council members decided to summon the third regional congress for April 10 in Gulyai-Polye, in order to determine the council's future policy line or indeed to wind it up, should congress so decide. And lo and behold, the congress went ahead.

Those who attended were not counter-revolutionaries, but rather the people who had been the very first to raise the flag of insurrection in the Ukraine, the flag of social revolution. They had come in order to assist in the coordination of the overall struggle against all oppressors. Representatives from 72 cantons spread over various districts and governments, as well as several military units showed up for the congress, and they all found that the Gulyai-Polye regional military revolutionary council was needed; indeed they expanded its executive committee and enjoined the latter to carry out egalitarian mobilization of volunteers in the region. The congress was well and truly stunned by "comrade" Dybenko's telegram pronouncing the congress "counter-revolutionary," when that region had led the way in raising the banner of insurrection. Which is why the congress passed a vigorous protest against that telegram.

Such is the picture that should come as an eye-opener to you, "comrade" Dybenko. Catch yourself on! Think! Do you, on your own, have any right to declare counter-revolutionary a population of one million toilers who, with their very own horny hands, have cast off the shackles of slavery and are now rebuilding their lives as they deem fit?

No! If you are truly revolutionary, you must rally to their aid in the struggle against the oppressors and in their endeavors to build a new, free life.

Can it be that there are laws made by a handful of individuals purporting to be revolutionaries, entitling them to place the most revolutionary of peoples, in its entirety, outside of the law? (Given that the council's executive committee represents the whole mass of the people.)

Is it tolerable, is it reasonable that they should turn up to lay down laws of trespass designed to enslave a people which has just brought down all lawmakers and all laws?

Is there some law under which a revolutionary is supposedly entitled to apply the severest of punishments to the revolutionary mass of which he purports to be the defender, simply because that mass has, without seeking anyone's leave, seized the benefits which that revolutionary had promised it: liberty and equality?

Can the revolutionary mass of the people remain silent when that revolutionary strips it of the liberty so recently won?

Do the revolution's laws require that a delegate be shot because of his belief that he has a duty to carry out the mandate entrusted to him by the revolutionary mass which elected him?

What interests should a revolutionary defend? The party's interests or those of the people, the spilling of whose blood sets the revolution in motion?

The Gulyai-Polye military revolutionary council stands above party political control and influence; it acknowledges no one, except the people who have elected it. Its duty is to carry out the tasks entrusted to it by the people, and not to hamper any left-wing socialist party in the dissemination of its ideas. Consequently, should the Bolshevik idea some day find favor with the workers, the military revolutionary council, this manifestly counter-revolutionary organization as the Bolsheviks see it, will yield to another, more "revolutionary" Bolshevik organization. But in the meanwhile do not stand in our way and do not attempt to snuff us out.

If, "comrade" Dybenko, you and your like carry on with the same policy as before, if you should deem it proper and conscientious, then do your worst with your dirty work. Outlaw all of the instigators of the regional congresses and also those who were summoned when you and your party met in Kursk. Label as counter-revolutionaries all of those who led the way in raising the banner of insurrection and social revolution in the Ukraine and took action everywhere without waiting for your leave and without sticking to the letter of your program, but took a more left-wing approach. Outlaw, too, all who sent their delegates to the congresses which you have described as counter-revolutionary. And finally, outlaw too all of the fallen fighters who, without your leave, participated in the insurgent movement for the liberation of the whole toiling people. And don't forget to declare illegal and counterrevolutionary all of the congresses that proceeded without authorization from you. But know this: that in the end truth will triumph over might. In spite of all your threats, the council will not default upon the duties entrusted to it, for it is not entitled to do so, any more than it is entitled to usurp the people's rights.

>The Gulyai-Polye regional military revolutionary council:
>[followed by signatures]

Trotsky and the "Makhnovshchina" (May 31–June 4, 1919)

Regardless of all the respect due the memory of a great revolutionary such as Leon Trotsky, the squalid episode, retailed below, from his prestigious political and military career ought not to be passed over in silence. Truth alone is revolutionary.

The anti-Makhnovist propaganda of the Bolsheviks resumed with a vengeance.

It was Trotsky, who had in the meantime arrived in the Ukraine, who set the tone for this campaign; according to him, the insurgent movement was nothing but a movement of well-to-do farmers ("kulaks") bent upon consolidating their power in the area. All of the Makhnovist and anarchist prattle about the libertarian toilers' commune was merely a tactical ploy, whereas in reality the Makhnovists and anarchists were bent on establishing their own anarchist authority, which, when all was said and done, added up to that of the wealthy kulaks. (see Trotsky's article "The Makhnovshchina" in the newspaper *On the Road*, No. 51).

Simultaneously with this campaign of deliberately misinformative agitation, the surveillance, or rather blockade, maintained on the insurgent territories was taken to extremes. Revolutionary workers drawn to that proud and independent region by their sympathies from far-flung regions in Russia, from Moscow, Petrograd, Ivanovo-Voznessensk, the Volga, the Urals and Siberia had to confront the greatest difficulties before they could arrive there.

Fresh supplies of munitions, cartridges and other essential equipment, issued on a daily basis along the front, were cut off completely (...) and the situation took a disastrous turn — just when Denikin's troops were receiving considerable reinforcement in the very sector in question, through the arrival of the Kuban Cossacks and detachments raised in the Caucasus.

Did the Bolsheviks realize what they were doing and understand the implications of their policy for the already very complex situation in the Ukraine?

Certainly. They were perfectly well aware of what they were doing. They had resorted to blockade tactics with an eye to destroying and eradicating the region's military might. It is of course a lot easier to take on unarmed adversaries. It would be easier to bring to heel insurgents short of munitions and confronting the heavily armed Denikin front than those same insurgents kitted out with all the requisite equipment.

But at the same time, the Bolsheviks failed utterly to comprehend the overall situation right across the Donetz region as a whole. They had no idea of Denikin's front or the resources available to him — they did not even know what his immediate plans were. And yet, considerable numbers of soldiery had been raised, well-trained and organized in the Caucasus, and the Don and Kuban regions, preparatory to a general onslaught against the Revolution.

The stubborn resistance put up over a four month period by the Gulyai-Polye region had prevented Denikin's troops from making serious progress in their push northwards, for the Gulyai-Polye insurgents represented a standing menace to their left flank.

(. . .) With all the more commitment, the Whites laid the groundwork for their second campaign, which opened in May 1919 on a huge scale which even the Makhnovists had not anticipated. The Bolsheviks knew nothing of all this, or rather, did not want to know about it, preoccupied as they were by their plan of campaign against the **Makhnovshchina**.

In this way, the liberated region and with it, the whole of the Ukraine, was threatened on two flanks simultaneously. At which point the Gulyai-Polye military revolutionary council, cognizant of the full gravity of the situation, decided to summon an extra-ordinary congress of the peasants, workers, partisans and Red soldiers from several regions, notably from the governments of Ekaterinoslav, Kharkov, Tauride, Kherson and Donetz. This congress was to have appraised the overall position, given the mortal danger represented by Denikin's counter-revolutionary forces and the soviet authorities' incompetence to lift a finger to counter it. The congress was to have spelled out the short-term tasks and practical measures to be undertaken by the toilers in order to remedy that state of affairs.

Here is the text of the summons issued in this connection by the military revolutionary council to the toilers of the Ukraine:

SUMMONS TO THE FOURTH EXTRA-ORDINARY CONGRESS OF PEASANT, WORKER AND PARTISAN DELEGATES (TELEGRAM NO. 416)

To all district, cantonal, communal and village executive committees in the governments of Ekaterinoslav, Tauride and neighboring regions; to all units of the First Insurgent Division of the Ukraine, known as the Father Makhno Division; to all Red Army troops stationed in the same areas. To one and all.

At its sitting on May 30, the executive committee of the military revolutionary council, after scrutiny of the impact upon the front of the onslaught of White gangs, and consideration of the overall political and economic situation of soviet power, came to the conclusion that only the toiling masses themselves, and not individuals or parties, can devise a solution to this. Which is why the executive committee of the Gulyai-Polye regional military revolutionary committee has decided to summon an extra-ordinary congress in Gulyai-Polye on June 15.

Electoral procedure: 1. The peasants and workers are to choose one delegate per three thousand members of the population. 2. Insurgents and Red soldiers are to delegate one representative per troop unit (regiment, division, etc.). 3. Staffs: the staff of the Father Makhno Division will send two delegates: the brigade staffs will send one delegate per rank. 4. The district executive committees will return one delegate per fraction (party representatives). 5. District party organizations — the ones accepting the foundations of "soviet" rule — will return one delegate per organization.

Notes: a) Elections for workers' and peasants' delegates are to take place at village, cantonal, workshop of factory general assemblies. b) On their own, the assemblies of the members of the soviets or committees of these units may not proceed with these elections. c) In the event that the military revolutionary council is not sufficiently numerous, delegates will have to be issued with provisions and money on the spot.

Agenda: a) Report from the executive committee of the military revolutionary committee and delegates' reports. b) News. c) The object, role and tasks of the soviet of peasants', workers', partisans' and Red soldiers' delegates of the Gulyai-Polye region. d) Reorganization of the region's military revolutionary council. e) Military disposition in the region. f) Supply issues. g) The agrarian question. h) Financial business. i) Peasant laborers' and workers' unions. j) Public security business. k) The matter of the administration of justice in the region. I) Matters in hand.

Signed: The Executive Committee of the Military Revolutionary Council. Dated: Gulyai-Polye, May 31, 1919.

Immediately this summons was issued, the Bolsheviks launched an all-out military campaign (...) While insurgent troops marched out to face death resisting the savage onslaught of Denikin's Cossacks, the Bolsheviks, at the head of several regiments, swept into the villages in the insurgent region from the north, that is, from behind. There they seized militants, destroying the communes or kindred organizations established in the region. There can be no question but that the go-ahead for this invasion had emanated from Trotsky who had, meanwhile, arrived in the Ukraine.

With boundlessly cavalier approach, Trotsky set about "liquidating" the Makhnovist movement.

For a start, he issued the following order, by way of a reply to the summons from the Gulyai-Polye military revolutionary council:

Order No. 1824 of the Military Revolutionary Council of the Republic, June 4, 1919, Kharkov

To all military commissars and all executive committees in the Alexandrovsk, Mariupol, Berdyansk, Bakhmut, Pavlograd and Kherson districts.

The Gulyai-Polye executive committee, in concert with Makhno's brigade staff, is attempting to schedule a congress of soviets and insurgents from the Alexandrovsk, Mariupol, Berdyansk, Melitopol, Bakhmut and Pavlograd districts for the fifteenth of this month. Said congress is wholly an affront to soviet power in the Ukraine and to the organization of the Southern front, to which Makhno's brigade is attached. That congress could not produce any result other than to (...) deliver the front to the Whites, in the face of whom Makhno's brigade does nothing but fall further and further back, thanks to the incompetence, the criminal tendencies and treachery of its commanders.

1. The meeting of that congress, which will in any case not take place, is hereby forbidden.
2. The entire peasant and worker population must be warned by the spoken and the written word that participation in said congress will be regarded as an act of high treason towards the Soviet Republic and the fronts.
3. All delegates to said congress must be placed under arrest forthwith and brought before the revolutionary court martial of the 14th (formerly the 2nd) Army of the Ukraine.
4. Persons circulating calls from Makhno and the Gulyai-Polye executive committee must be placed under arrest.
5. This present order acquires the force of law once issued by telegraph and must be publicized widely everywhere, posted up in all public places and passed on to representatives from the cantonal and village executive committees, as well as to all representatives of the soviet authorities, and to the commanders and commissars of troop units.

Signed: Chairman of the Military Revolutionary Council of the Republic: Trotsky (Other signatures followed)

Without giving due attention to the matter, and swallowing the conventional view, Trotsky adjudged Makhno as responsible for everything that was going on in Gulyai-Polye and for all revolutionary dispositions in the region. He had even omitted to note that the congress had been convened, not by Makhno's brigade staff, nor indeed by the Gulyai-Polye executive committee, but by an agency wholly independent of both: by the regional military revolutionary council.

And significantly: in Order No. 1824, Trotsky hinted at treachery by the Makhnovist commanders in, he said "retreating further and further in the face of the Whites." A few days later, he and the whole of the Communist press returned to this alleged opening of the front to Denikin's troops:

(...) That front had been built up exclusively thanks to the efforts and sacrifices of the insurgent peasants themselves. It had come into existence at a particularly heroic point in their epic, at a time when the country had been rid of authorities of any sort. It was established in the south-east by way of a defensive outpost of the freedom that had been won. For more than six months, revolutionary insurgents had held the line against one of the most vigorous strands of the monarchist counterrevolution: they had offered up the lives of several thousands of their finest, mobilized all of the region's resources and were ready to defend their liberty to the death, by standing up to the counter-revolution which was now embarking upon a general offensive.

The order from Trotsky just cited was not passed on by the soviet authorities to the Makhnovists' high command which only learned of it quite by accident two or three days later. Makhno replied posthaste by telegram, declaring that he was willing to resign his command, in view of the inept and impossible position in which he had been placed. It is a manner of regret to us that we do not have the text of that telegram available.

As stated earlier, Trotsky's order acquired the force of law once telegraphed. The Bolsheviks set about implementing it in every particular by force of arms. The assemblies of Alexandrovsk factory workers at which the call issued by the Gulyai-Polye regional military revolutionary council came up for discussion were broken up by force and banned on pain of death. As for the peasants, they were quite bluntly threatened with being shot or hanged. In a variety of places around the region several individuals, such as Kostin, Polounin, Dobroluboff, etc., were seized, charged with having circulated the council's summons and executed out of hand.

In addition to Order No. 1824, Trotsky issued other orders addressed to Red Army units, enjoining the latter to destroy the **Makhnovshchina** root and branch. He also issued secret orders instructing them to at all costs capture Makhno, and members of his staff as well as the peaceable militants concerned with the cultural side of the movement, and to produce them all before a court martial, which is to say to execute them.

Makhno Offers to Take a Back Seat (June 6–9, 1919)

Makhno informed his staff and the council that the Bolsheviks had left the front in the Grishino sector unmanned and were thereby offering Denikin's troops unhindered access to the Gulyai-Polye region via the north-east flank. And in fact, the Cossack hordes burst into the region, not where they faced the insurgents' front but on the left flank where the Red Army troops were stationed. As a result, the Makhnovist army manning the front in the Mariupol-Kuteynikovo-Taganrog area found itself outflanked by Denikin's troops. The latter flooded through in huge numbers into the very heart of the region.

(. . .) The peasants throughout the region had so expected an all-out attack by Denikin that they had made preparations for it and had resolved to raise a levy of volunteer troops in reply. Ever since April, peasants in a host of villages had been despatching fresh fighters to Gulyai-Polye. But arms and munitions were in short supply. Even older units serving on the front had no munitions left and often mounted attacks on the Whites for the sole purpose of procuring some. The Bolsheviks who, under the agreement concluded, had undertaken to keep the insurgents supplied militarily, had begun their sabotage and blockade policy back in April. For which reason it was not possible to train fresh troops in spite of the influx of volunteer recruits, and the outcome of this could be predicted.

In just one day, the Gulyai-Polye peasants raised a regiment in an effort to save their village. To which end they had to arm themselves with primitive tools: axes, picks, ancient carbines, hunting pieces, etc. They set out on a march to meet the Cossacks, in an attempt to halt their progress. Around 15 kilometers outside of Gulyai-Polye, near the village of Sviatodukhovka, they clashed with significant numbers of Cossacks from the Don and Kuban. They engaged them in bitter, heroic, murderous fighting, during which they almost all perished, along with their commander, B. Veretelnikoff, a native of Gulyai-Polye who was a worker from the Putilov plant in Petrograd. Whereupon a veritable avalanche of Cossacks descended upon Gulyai-Polye, occupying it on June 6, 1919. Makhno and the army staff, having only one battery, retreated as far as the Gulyai-Polye railroad station, around seven kilometers from the village: but, towards evening, he found himself obliged to quit the station too. Having marshaled whatever forces he still could, Makhno successfully mounted a counter-attack against Gulyai-Polye the next day and managed to dislodge the enemy. But he held the village for only a very short time: a fresh onslaught of Cossacks compelled him to abandon it once again.

It should be noted that the Bolsheviks, even though they had already issued several orders targeting the Makhnovists, carried on, right from the start, to look well upon them, as if nothing was wrong. This ploy was calculated to win over the movement's leaders for sure. On June 7 they sent Makhno an armored train, urging him to hold out to the bitter end and promising that further reinforcements would follow. In fact, a few Red army detachments arrived two days later at the Gaitchur railway station in the Chaplino sector, about twenty kilometers from Gulyai-Polye; with them came the army commissars Mezhlauk, Voroshilov and others.

Contact was established between the Red Army and insurgent commands: a sort of joint staff over both camps was formed. Mezhlauk and Voroshilov rubbed shoulders with Makhno in the same armored train and they directed military operations together.

But at the same time Voroshilov had with him an order signed by Trotsky, instructing him to seize Makhno and all other ranking leaders of the **Makhnovshchina**, disarm insurgent troops and mercilessly mow down any who might attempt resistance. Voroshilov was just waiting for the right moment to carry out that mission. Makhno was alerted in time and realized what he had to do. He summed up the situation as it stood, and saw the bloody events that might erupt any day and cast around for a satisfactory resolution. He reckoned that the best thing would be for him to quit his post as commander of the insurgent front. He stated as much to the insurgent army's staff, adding that his work in the ranks as a mere enlisted man might prove more useful at a given point. And was as good as his word. To the soviet high command he tendered a written explanatory note, as follows:

4th Army staff, Voroshilov. — Kharkov, Chairman of the Military Revolutionary Council, Trotsky. Moscow, Lenin and Kamenev.

In the wake of Order No. 1284 from the military revolutionary council of the Republic, I had sent a dispatch to the staff of the 2nd Army and to Trotsky, asking to be relieved of the post I currently hold. I now reiterate my statement and here are the reasons which I hold should support it. Even though I have, with the insurgents, waged war solely upon Denikin's White bands, preaching nothing to the people save love of liberty and self-action, the entire official soviet press, as well as that of the Bolshevik-Communist Party, peddles rumors about me that are unworthy of a revolutionary (. . .) In an article entitled 'The Makhnovshchina' (in the newspaper *On the Road* No. 51) Trotsky poses the question: "Against whom are the Makhnovist insurgents revolting?." And throughout the article he is at pains to show how the **Makhnovshchina** is supposedly nothing other than a battle-front against the power of the soviets. He utters not one word about the actual front against the Whites, a front that stretches for more than one hundred versts (a little over one hundred kilometers) where, for the past six months, the insurgents have been and still are sustaining countless losses. Order No. 1824 declares me to be a plotter against the soviet republic (. . .)

I deem it the inalienable right of workers and peasants — a right earned by the Revolution — to decide for themselves to summon congresses to discuss and determine their private or general affairs. Which is why the central authorities' ban prohibition upon the calling of such congresses and the declaration which proclaims them unlawful (Order No. 1824) are a direct and insolent breach of the rights of the toiling masses.

I am perfectly well aware of the central authorities' attitude to me. I am convinced through and through that these authorities regard the insurgent movement in its entirety as incompatible with their statist activities. At the same time, the central authorities think that this movement is closely bound up with my person, and they do me the honor of all their resentment and all their hatred with regard to the insurgent movement. There could not be any better proof of that than the aforementioned article by Trotsky, in which, while knowingly peddling calumnies and lies, he makes a show of animosity directed at me personally.

This hostile attitude, now turning to aggression, on the part of the central authorities against the insurgent movement is ineluctably leading to the creation of a specific internal front, on both sides of which will be the toiling masses who have faith in the Revolution. I regard such an eventuality as a gross and unpardonable crime against the toiling people, and I believe I have a duty to do all that I can to counter it. The surest way of avoiding the authorities' committing of this crime is, in my view, for me to step down from the post which I occupy.

I imagine that, that done, the central authorities will stop suspecting me and the revolutionary insurgents of dabbling in anti-soviet conspiracies and that they will come in the end to see the Ukraine's insurrection in a serious revolutionary light, as a living, active manifestation of the masses' social Revolution, and not as a hostile clan with which relations have hitherto been dubious and fraught with mistrust, with every item of munitions begrudged and supplies of them being sometimes quite simply sabotaged: thanks to which the insurgents often had to endure great losses in men and territory won for the Revolution — which might readily have been avoided, had the central authorities adopted a different approach. I ask that arrangements be made for the collection of my records and logs.

Signed: Father Makhno
Gaitchur Station, June 9, 1919.

The Regional Peasants' and Workers Congress (October 1919)

A regional peasants' and workers' congress was held in Alexandrovsk on October 20, 1919. Upwards of two hundred delegates took part, 180 of them peasants and two or three dozen workers. The congress examined both issues of a military nature (the fight against Denikin, expansion of the insurgent army and its supply lines) and other business relating to the elements of civilian life.

The congress proceedings lasted for more than a week and were marked by a quite extraordinary vigor on the part of participants. The very ambiance of the congress made a powerful contribution to that. For one thing, the return of the victorious Makhnovist army to its native territory was an event of the utmost importance for the peasant population, virtually every peasant family having one or two members among the insurgents.

But even more telling was that the congress proceeded under the auspices of genuine and absolute freedom; no influence emanating from above was sensible there. And, to crown it all, the congress had an excellent contributor and rapporteur in the anarchist Voline, who, to the great astonishment of the peasants, was able to articulate their very deepest thoughts and desires. The idea of free soviets working in concert with the wishes of the toiling population locally; the relations between the peasants and the urban workers, based upon mutual exchanges of the products of their labors: the idea of organizing life along egalitarian and libertarian lines, all these theses, which Voline expounded in his reports, reflected the thinking of the peasant population which could not imagine the Revolution and creative revolutionary endeavor in any different shape or form.

The political parties' representatives did try, during the first day's proceedings, to introduce a note of discord, but they were promptly shouted down by the body of the congress and the gathering's efforts proceeded thereafter with perfect unanimity.

(. . .) The authentic spirit of liberty, such as is but rarely sensed, was at large in the hall. Everyone could look forward to and contemplated a truly great endeavor, deserving of all their efforts and indeed worth dying for. The peasants among whom there were many older, in fact elderly folk, said that this was the first congress at which they had felt, not just that they were completely free, but also the spirit of brotherhood and that they would never forget. And in fact the likelihood is that no one who took part in that congress will ever be able to forget it.

Manifesto of the Insurgent Army of the Ukraine (January 1, 1920)

To all of the Ukraine's peasants and workers! For transmission by telegraph, telephone or courier to all of the Ukraine's villages! For reading at peasants meetings, in factories and in firms!

Brother toilers!

The Insurgent Army of the Ukraine has been created to resist the oppression of workers and peasants by the bourgeoisie and by the Bolshevik-Communist dictatorship. It has set itself the task of fighting for the complete liberation of Ukrainian toilers from the yoke of any sort of tyranny and for the creation of a genuine socialist constitution of our own. The Insurgent Army of makhnovitsi partisans has fought with gusto on many fronts in order to achieve that goal. It is presently bringing to a successful conclusion the fight against Denikin's army, liberating region after region, wheresoever tyranny and oppression existed.

Many peasant toilers have asked themselves the question: what to do? What can and what ought we to do? How should we conduct ourselves with regard to the laws of the authorities and their organizations?

To which questions the Ukrainian Union of Toilers and Peasants will reply anon. Indeed, it must meet very shortly and summon all peasants and workers. Given that the precise date on which that assembly of the peasants and workers will proceed, at which they will have the chance to come together to debate and resolve the most important problems facing our peasants and workers, is not known, the makhnovitsi army deems it useful to publish the following manifesto:

1. All ordinances of the Denikin government are hereby annulled (. . .) Likewise annulled are those ordinances of the Communist government which conflict with peasant and worker interests. It will be for the toilers themselves to resolve the question which ordinances of the Communist government are damaging to the toilers' interests.

2. All estates belonging to monasteries, big landowners and other enemies pass into the hands of the peasants who live by the labor of their arms alone. Such transfer should be determined at meetings after discussion by the peasantry. Peasants will have to bear in mind and take account not just of their personal interests but also the common interests of the toiling people, bowed down under the exploiters' yoke.

3. Factories, firms, collieries and other means of production become the property of the working class as a whole, which assumes the responsibility for their direction and administration, encouraging and pursuing development

with the benefit of experience and seeking to gather the whole production of the country under the umbrella of a single organization.

4. All peasants and workers are invited to set up free peasants' and workers' councils. Only workers and peasants playing an active part in some useful sector of the popular economy may be elected to such councils. Representatives of political organizations are to play no part in the workers' and peasants' councils, because that might harm the interests of the toilers themselves.

5. The existence of tyrannical, militarized organizations which are at odds with the spirit of the free toilers will not be countenanced.

6. Freedom of speech, of the press and of assembly is the right of every toiler and any gesture contrary to that freedom constitutes an act of counter-revolution.

7. Police organizations are hereby abolished: in their place self-defense bodies will be set up and these may be launched by the workers and peasants.

8. The workers' and peasants' councils represent the toilers' self-defenses: each of them must struggle against any manifestation of the bourgeois and the military. Acts of banditry must be resisted and bandits and counter-revolutionaries shot where they stand.

9. Either of the two currencies, the soviet and the Ukrainian, shall be accepted as the equivalent of the other: all breaches of this ordinance will be punished.

10. The exchange of work produce or luxury goods remains free, unless overseen by peasant and worker organizations. It is proposed that such exchanges should proceed between toilers.

11. All persons hindering diffusion of this manifesto are to be deemed counter-revolutionaries.

> The Revolutionary Councils
> of the Ukrainian Army (**makhnovitsi**),
> January 1, 1920.

Program/Manifesto of April 1920[1]

1. Who are the "makhnovitsi" and for which cause do they fight?

The **makhnovitsi** are peasants and workers who rose up as long ago as 1918 against the brutality of the bourgeois, German, Hungarian and Austrian authorities and against that of the hetman of the Ukraine.

The **makhnovitsi** are toilers who have unfurled the banner of struggle against Denikin and against any form of oppression, violence and falsehood, whatever its provenance.

The **makhnovitsi** are those same toilers who, through their life-long labors, have enriched and fattened the bourgeoisie in general and, today, the soviets in particular.

2. Why are they called "makhnovitsi?"

Because, during the darkest and gravest moments of the reaction in the Ukraine, our ranks included our indefatigable friend and **condottiere**,[2] Makhno, whose voice rang out across the whole of the Ukraine, in protest at every act of violence against the toilers, summoning them all to the struggle against the oppressors, robbers, usurpers and political charlatans who deceive the toilers. To this very day that voice rings out among us, within our ranks, unchanging in its exhortation to struggle for the ultimate goal of the liberation and emancipation of toilers from each and every oppression.

3. How do you intend to bring that liberation about?

By overthrowing the monarchist coalition government, the republican, social democratic government, the Bolshevik-Communist government. In their place, through free elections, toilers' councils must be elected and these will not constitute a government, complete with written, arbitrary laws. For the soviet arrangement is not authoritarian (unlike the Social Democrats and Bolshevik Communists who purport to be the soviet authorities today). It is the purest form of anti-authoritarian, anti-State socialism, articulated through free organization of the social life of toilers, independent of authorities: a life where every worker, alone or in association, can quite independently pursue his own happiness and his own complete well-being, in accordance with the precepts of solidarity, amity and equality.

4. What is the "makhnovitsi" view of the soviet regime?

The toilers themselves must choose their own councils (soviets) which are to carry out the wishes and instructions of those same toilers: so they are to be executive councils, not authoritative councils. The land, factories, firms, mines, transport, etc., should belong to the toilers who toil, so they must be socialized.

5. Which are the paths leading to the "makhnovitsi" final objective?

A consistent and implacable revolutionary struggle against all falsehoods, arbitrariness and violence, from wherever these may emanate, a struggle to the death: free speech, just deeds and struggle under arms.

Only through the abolition of each governor, every representative of authority, through radical destruction of every political, economic and statist falsehood, through destruction of the State by social revolution can a genuine system of worker and peasant soviets be achieved and progress towards socialism assured.

Notes to Program/Manifesto of April 1920

1. Drafted by the cultural and educational branch of the Makhnovist Insurgent Army.
2. In Italy, a **condottiere** was a partisan leader.
3. Taken from the Makhnovist newspaper *The Road to Freedom*.

Anarchism and the "Makhnovshchina"[3]

The Makhnovist army is not an anarchist army, not made up of anarchists. The anarchist ideal of happiness and general equality cannot be attained through the strivings of an army, any army, even were it made up exclusively of anarchists. At best, the revolutionary army can serve to destroy the despised ancient regime; any army, which by its very nature can rely only on force and command, would be utterly impotent and indeed a hindrance to constructive endeavor, elaboration and creation. If the anarchist society is to be made possible, the workers themselves in their factories and firms and the peasants themselves in their districts and villages must set about constructing the anti-authoritarian society, awaiting decrees and laws from nowhere.

Neither anarchist armies nor isolated heroes, nor groups, nor the anarchist Confederation will introduce a new life for the workers and peasants. Only the toilers themselves, through their deliberate efforts, can build their well-being, free of State and seigneurs.

The "Makhnovitsi" Appeal to their Brethren in the Red Army

Stop! Read! Reflect! Red Army comrade! You have been despatched by your commissar-commanders to fight the **makhnovitsi** insurgents and revolutionaries.

On the orders of your commanders you will bring ruination to peaceable areas, you will carry out searches, make arrests and murder folk whom you personally do not know, but who will have been pointed out to you as enemies of the people. You will be told that the **makhnovitsi** are bandits or counter-revolutionaries. They will order, not ask, but make you march like a humble slave to your commander. You will arrest and you will kill! Who? Why? On what grounds?

Reflect, Red Army comrade! Reflect, toilers, peasants and workers forcibly subjected to the new masters who go by the ringing title of the 'worker-peasant authorities'!

We are the **makhnovitsi** revolutionary insurgents, peasants and workers like you, our Red army brethren!

We have risen up against oppression and degradation; we fight for a better and more enlightened life. Our ideal is to attain a community of toilers, with no authority, no parasites and no commissars.

The government of the Bolshevik-Communists sends you to mount punitive expeditions. It is in a hurry to make peace with Denikin and with the wealthy Poles and other White Army scum, so that it may the more easily harass the popular movement of revolutionary insurgents, of the oppressed risen up against the yoke of authority, all authority.

But the threats from the White and the Red commands do not scare us! We will answer violence with violence!

If need be, we, a tiny handful of men, will rout the divisions of the government's Red Army. Because we are free and enamored of liberty! We are insurgent revolutionaries, and the cause we champion is a just cause.

Comrade! Reflect upon whose side you are on and against whom you fight. Do not be a slave. Be a man!

                      The **makhnovitsi** revolutionary insurgents.

KRONSTADT (1921)

The Kronstadt revolt has a deserved place — a considerable place — in an anarchist anthology. Although spontaneous, it was not specifically libertarian and, to be truthful, anarchists did not play a major role in it. Ida Mett, who wrote a book on *The Kronstadt Uprising* (1938, reprinted 1948) acknowledges that the anarchist influence in it was discernible "only to the extent that anarchism too was pushing the idea of a workers' democracy." However, the Kronstadt Revolutionary Committee had invited two anarchists to join its ranks: Efim Yartchuk, who later wrote *Kronstadt*, and Voline, who devoted a substantial segment of his *The Unknown Revolution* to Kronstadt "the first wholly independent popular essay (...) at social revolution (...) mounted directly by the laboring classes themselves." But neither Yartchuk nor Voline was able to take up the Kronstadt Revolutionary Committee's invitation, in that they were both held in Bolshevik prisons at the time.

We offer, in their unpolished state, the imprecations uttered by the rebel sailors and workers. Our purpose, of course, is certainly not to join with them as they mock Lenin and Trotsky, nor to reiterate on our own account the insults and sarcastic remarks they shower upon that pair. It is all too obvious that anger pushed the revolt's language over the edge and rendered it, in part, unfair. The accumulated errors of the Bolshevik authorities between 1918 and 1921, of which Kronstadt was to be the culmination, in no way diminished the revolutionary convictions or genius of the authors of the October Revolution. But how could these sailors and workers — once the grassroots architects of the mass uprising of 1917 — who were about to perish under the gunfire of the Red officer cadets and Mongolian troops have retained the historian's objectivity and sung the praises of their executioners?

Contrary to the impression that might be obtained from a reading of the revolt's daily newspaper *Izvestia*, the crushing of the Kronstadt revolt was not the result of perverse and malignant intent on the part of Lenin and Trotsky, but rather the outcome of a conspiracy of fate attended by implacable objective circumstances (like civil war, economic disarray, famine) and daring human miscalculations (the harshness of an autocratic regime increasingly isolated from the popular forces which had hoisted it into power).

Viewed thus, the lesson of Kronstadt turns out to be a cautionary note and forewarning for all advocates of revolution from above who might be inclined not to heed it and who, in the proletariat's name, might finish up, paradoxically, turning their guns on the proletariat.

Memories of Kronstadt by Emma Goldman

Meeting with Trotsky (March 1917)[1]

(. . .) I had been aware for some time [. . .] that Trotsky was in New York [. . .] Thus far I had never met Trotsky, but I happened to be in town when a farewell rally at which he was to speak before leaving for Russia was announced.[2] I attended that rally. Trotsky was introduced after a few rather tiresome speakers. Of average height with hollow cheeks, red hair and a sparse beard, he strode forward athletically. His speech, delivered initially in Russian and then in German was powerful and electrifying. I did not see eye to eye with his politics, he being a Menshevik (Social Democrat) and as such far removed from us. But his analysis of the causes of the war was brilliant, his denunciation of the ineptitude of the provisional government in Russia scathing and his portrayal of the conditions amid which the revolution was developing enlightening. He wound up his two hour address by paying eloquent tribute to the toiling masses of his homeland. The audience was in raptures of enthusiasm and Sasha [Alexander Berkman] and I delightedly joined the ovation which greeted the speaker. We wholeheartedly subscribed to his profound faith in Russia's future.

After the rally, we sought out Trotsky to bid him farewell. He had heard tell of us and asked us when we intended to come to Russia to help with the reconstruction. "We shall assuredly meet again over there," he told us.

With Sasha I discussed the unexpected turn of events whereby we felt closer to the Menshevik Trotsky than to Peter Kropotkin, our comrade, our mentor and our friend. War made for strange bed-fellows and we wondered if we would still feel as close to Trotsky once we were in Russia (. . .)

Notes to Meeting with Trotsky (March 1917) by Emma Goldman

1. Taken from Emma Goldman *Living My Life* 1934.
2. Trotsky and his family sailed from New York bound for Russia on March 17, 1917.

Memories of Kronstadt[1]

Emma Goldman, the great Russian-born American anarchist, we have already encountered (in Volume II). Deported from the United States to Russia in 1919, she happened to be in Petrograd just when the Bolsheviks made up their minds to crush the Kronstadt revolt. She tells of this tragic episode in her book of memoirs, *Living My Life*.

(. . .) During my previous time in Russia the question of strikes had often intrigued me. People had told me that the slightest hint of anything of the sort was crushed and participants jailed. I had found that hard to credit and as ever in such cases, I had turned to Zorin[2] for clarification. He exclaimed: "Strikes! Under the dictatorship of the proletariat? No such thing." He had even chastised me for having entertained such nonsensical, impossible notions. In fact, against whom would the workers in soviet Russia go on strike? Against themselves? They were the masters of the country, politically and industrially alike. To be sure, among the workers, there were still a few whose class consciousness was not fully developed and who were not aware where their true interests lay. Such folk did indeed grumble from time to time, but they were pawns (. . .) manipulated by selfish interests and enemies of the Revolution. Skinflints and parasites very deliberately leading the ignorant astray (. . .) Obviously the soviet authorities had a duty to protect the country against saboteurs of that sort. Anyway, most of them were behind bars.

Later, I discovered from personal observation and experience that the real "saboteurs," counterrevolutionaries and bandits in the prisons of soviet Russia accounted for only a negligible minority. The vast bulk of the prison population was made up of social heretics, guilty of original sin against the Communist church. For no trespass was regarded more hatefully than that of entertaining political views different from the Party's, and of protesting against Bolshevism's mischief and crimes. I noticed that the majority were political prisoners, peasant and worker alike, guilty of having sought better treatment and living conditions. Such facts, kept strictly hidden from the public, were however common knowledge, as were all manner of things going on in secret beneath the soviet surface. How could such forbidden information leak out in spite of everything? That was a mystery to me, but leak out it did and it spread with the speed and intensity of a forest fire.

Less than twenty four hours after our return to Petrograd, we learned that the city was seething with discontent and rumors of strikes. The cause lay in the increased suffering caused by an exceptionally severe winter, and in the soviets' habitual shortsightedness. Terrible blizzards had delayed the delivery of food and fuel supplies to the city. In addition, the Petro-Soviet had made the stupid mistake of shutting down several factories and halving their workforce's rations. At the same time, it emerged that in the shops Party members had been issued with a new batch of shoes and clothing, while the rest of the workers were miserably clothed and shod. And, to cap all these errors, the authorities had banned the rally scheduled by the workers to discuss ways of improving the situation.

Among non-Communist personnel in Petrograd, the general opinion was that the situation was very grave. The atmosphere was tense and at explosion point. We of course decided to remain in the city. Not in the hope that we might avert the imminent disturbances but we wanted to be on the spot so that we might be of use to folk.

The storm broke even earlier than anticipated. It started with a strike by the workers from the Trubetskoy mills. Their demands were very modest: increased food rations, as they had been promised long ago, and distribution of whatever footwear was available. The Petro-Soviet refused to talk to the strikers until such time as they had returned to work.

Companies of armed "kursantyn"[3] made up of young Communists performing their military service, were despatched to break up the concentrations of workers around the mills. The cadets attempted to provoke the masses by shooting over their heads, but luckily the workers had disarmed them and there was no bloodshed. The strikers resorted to a much mightier weapon: the solidarity of their fellow workers. The upshot was that five plants downed tools and joined the strike. They were pouring in, as one man, from the Galernaya docks, the Admiralty yards, the Patronny mills, and the Baltysky and Laferm plants. Their street demonstration was abruptly broken up by troops. From all of the reports coming in, I concluded that the treatment meted out to the strikers was anything but fraternal.

A fervent Communist like Lisa Zorin herself was alarmed and voiced objection to the methods employed. Lisa and I had long since come to a parting of the ways, so I was startled that she felt the need to unburden her heart to me. She would never have credited that the men of the Red Army would have manhandled the workers in such a manner. She objected. Several women had fainted and others had become hysterical at the sight. One woman who had been alongside Lisa had recognized her as an active Party member and reckoned that she was responsible for this brutal display. She turned on her like a fury and slapped her right across the face, leaving her bleeding profusely.

Dear old Lisa! who had always teased me about my sentimentality. Reeling from the blow, she told her assailant that "it did not matter." Lisa told me, "In order to reassure her, I begged her to let me escort her to her home. Home? It was a vile hovel, such as I did not even dream could still exist in this country. One dark room, cold and bare, occupied by the woman, her husband and their six children. And to think that I was living in the Astoria Hotel all this time!," she sighed. She continued, telling me that she was very well aware that it was scarcely the fault of her Party if such ghastly conditions still prevailed in soviet Russia. Nor was obstinacy on the Communists' part at the back of the strike. The imperialist world's blockade and conspiracy against the workers' republic had to be held to blame for her country's poverty and suffering. But for all that, she could no longer stay in her comfortable apartment. That desperate woman's room and the image of her children, paralyzed from the cold, was to haunt her nights. Poor Lisa! She was loyal, committed and a woman of integrity. But so blinkered, politically!

The workers' demand for more bread and fuel soon became specific political demands, thanks to the arbitrary and unbending stance of the authorities. One manifesto posted on the walls by an unknown hand called for "a complete change in government policy." It stated: "First of all, the workers and peasants need freedom! They do not want to live according to the Bolshevik' decrees; they want to control their own fate." The situation was growing tenser by the day and new demands were circulating and posted on the walls and inside buildings. In the end, there emerged a demand for a Constituent Assembly, so thoroughly detested and despised by the Party in power.

Martial law was declared and workers were ordered to return to their factories, failing which they would be denied their rations. That, however, made no impact: but in addition, a number of trade unions was disbanded, their leaders and the most die-hard strikers tossed into prison.

We looked on, powerless, as gangs of men, escorted by troops and armed Chekists, passed below our windows. In the hope of persuading the soviet leaders of the folly and danger of their tactics, Sasha[4] tried to find Zinoviev, while I sought out Messrs Ravitch, Zorin and Zipperovitch, the head of the Petrograd soviet of trade unions. But they all declined to meet us, on the pretext that they were too busy defending the city against counter-revolutionary plots, dreamt up by **Mensheviks** and Social Revolutionaries. This formula was threadbare from overuse over the past three years, but was still good for pulling the wool over the eyes of Communist militants.

The strike spread, in spite of all their extreme measures. Arrests followed, but the very stupidity with which the authorities reacted acted as a spur to the ignorant. Counter-revolutionary and anti-Semitic proclamations began to appear, as mad rumors of military repression and Cheka atrocities against the strikers swept the city.

The workers were determined, but it soon became plain that hunger would be their undoing; there was no way to help the strikers, even if we had had anything to give them. All avenues leading to the industrial districts were sealed off by troops. Anyway, the population itself was in dire straits. What little food and clothing we were able to collect was but a drop in the ocean. We all understood the disparity of weapons between the dictatorship and the workers. It was too great to allow the strikers to hold out for much longer.

Into this tense and desperate situation there suddenly came a new element which held out the hope of an accommodation. The Kronstadt sailors. Keeping faith with their revolutionary traditions and with solidarity among toilers, as so loyally demonstrated during the 1905 revolution and later during the uprisings in March and October of 1917, they again came out in support of the harassed workers of Petrograd. Without blinkers. Quietly and without anyone's having realized it, they had sent out a fact-finding commission to look into the strikers' demands. The commission's report led the crews of the warships 'Petropavlovsk' and "Sebastopol' to pass a resolution in favor of their striking fellow workers. They declared their devotion to the Revolution and to the Soviets as well as their loyalty to the Communist Party. Not that that stopped them protesting at the arbitrary attitude of certain commissars and insisting strongly upon the need for the workers' organized groupings to have more powers of self-defense. In addition, they demanded freedom of association for the trade unions and peasant organizations, as well as the release of all political and trade unionist detainees from soviet prisons and concentration camps.

The example set by these crews was taken up by the First and Second Squadron of the Baltic Fleet stationed in Kronstadt. At a street rally on March 1, attended by 16,000 sailors, Red Army soldiers and workers from Kronstadt, similar resolutions were passed unanimously, except for three dissenting voices. The three against were Vassiliev, chairman of the Kronstadt soviet, who chaired the meeting, Kuzmin, commissar of the Baltic Fleet, and Kalinin, president of the federated soviet socialist republic.

Two anarchists had been at the rally and returned to regale us with the order, enthusiasm and good mood which had prevailed at it. They had not witnessed such a spontaneous display of solidarity and fervent comradeship since the early days of October. They merely deplored the fact that we had missed this demonstration. The presence of Sasha, whom the Kronstadt sailors had staunchly defended when he was in danger of being extradited to California in 1917, and myself, whom the sailors knew by reputation, would have added weight to the resolution, they said. We agreed with them that it would have been a marvelous experience to participate on soviet soil in the first great mass meeting not organized to order. Gorky had long ago assured me that the men of the Baltic Fleet were all born anarchists and that my place was with them. I had often wanted to go to Kronstadt to meet the crews and talk to them, but it was my belief that in my confused, befuddled state of mind of the time I had nothing constructive to offer. Now I would go and take my place alongside them, knowing well that the Bolsheviks would peddle the rumor that I was inciting the sailors against the regime. Sasha said that he did not care much what the Communists might say. He would join the sailors in their protests on behalf of the striking workers of Petrograd.

Our comrades labored the point that Kronstadt's expressions of sympathy with the strikers could not in any way be construed as anti-soviet activity. In fact, the sailors' frame of mind and the resolutions passed at their mass rally were markedly pro-soviet. They objected vigorously to the autocratic attitude shown towards the famished strikers, but the rally had contained not the slightest hint of opposition to the Communists. Indeed, that great meeting had taken place under the auspices of the Kronstadt Soviet. In token of their loyalty, the sailors had welcomed Kalinin with singing and music when he arrived in the town, and his address had been listened to attentively and with the utmost respect. Even after he and his colleagues had condemned the sailors and their motion, they had escorted Kalinin to the railway station with the utmost friendliness, as our informants were able to testify.

We had had wind of rumors that Kuzmin and Vassiliev had been arrested by the sailors at a meeting of three hundred delegates from the fleet, the garrison and the trade union soviet. We asked our two comrades what they knew of this. They confirmed that the pair had indeed been placed under arrest. The reason was that Kuzmin had denounced the sailors and Petrograd strikers to the gathering as traitors, (. . .) declaring that henceforth the Communist Party was going to fight them to the bitter end as counter-revolutionaries. The delegates had also learned that Kuzmin had issued orders that all provisions and munitions be removed from Kronstadt, thereby condemning the town to starve. On these grounds the Kronstadt sailors and garrison had decided to arrest the pair and to take precautions to ensure that the provisions were not removed from the town. But no way was that an indication of any intent to revolt, nor of the men of Kronstadt's having stopped believing in the revolutionary integrity of the Communists. On the contrary. They allowed Communist delegates to speak like the rest. Further proof of their confidence in the regime was that a thirty-strong committee was sent for talks with the Petro-Soviet regarding an amicable settlement of the strike.

We felt pride at this splendid solidarity on the part of the sailors and soldiers of Kronstadt with their striking brethren in Petrograd and we hoped for a speedy end to disturbances, thanks to the sailors' mediation.

Alas! our hopes crumbled when news came an hour later of developments in Kronstadt. Petrograd was stunned by an order signed by Lenin and Trotsky. The order said that Kronstadt had mutinied against the soviet government and denounced the sailors as "the tools of former tsarist generals, who, by arrangement with the Social Revolutionary traitors, had mounted a counter-revolutionary conspiracy against the proletarian republic."

"Nonsense! Utter madness!" Sasha shouted when he read a copy of that order. "Lenin and Trotsky must have been misinformed by someone. Even so, they cannot believe that the sailors are guilty of counterrevolution! What? The crews of the 'Petropavlovsk' and 'Sebastopol', who had been the staunchest supporters of the Bolsheviks in October and ever since? Didn't Trotsky himself salute them as 'the pride and glory of the Revolution'?"

"We must go to Moscow right away," said Sasha. It was absolutely essential that we see Lenin and Trotsky and explain to them that this was all a horrible misunderstanding, a mistake that could prove fatal to the Revolution itself. It was very hard for Sasha to renounce his faith in the revolutionary integrity of men who were, for millions across the globe, apostles of the proletariat. I agreed with his belief that Lenin and Trotsky had perhaps been misled by Zinoviev who telephoned every night with detailed reports from Kronstadt. Even among his own comrades, Zinoviev had never had a reputation for personal courage. He had been seized by panic at the first sign of discontent on the part of the Petrograd workers. When he learned that the local garrison had indicated its sympathy with the strikers, he lost his head completely and ordered that a machine-gun be set up in the Astoria Hotel for his personal protection. The Kronstadt business had filled him with terror and drove him to peddle nightmarish stories to Moscow. Sasha and I knew all that, but I could not believe that Lenin and Trotsky truly thought that the Kronstadters were guilty of counterrevolution, or capable of colluding with White generals, as Lenin's order accused them of doing.

An exceptional state of martial law was imposed throughout the entire province of Petrograd, and no one except officials with special passes could leave the city now. The Bolshevik press launched a campaign of calumny and venom against Kronstadt, announcing that the sailors and soldiers had made common cause with the "tsarist General Kozlovsky;" they were thereby declaring the Kronstadters outlaws. Sasha was beginning to realize that the roots of the situation went a lot deeper than simply Lenin and Trotsky acting upon bad information. The latter was to attend the special sitting of the Petro-Soviet at which the fate of Kronstadt was to be decided. We resolved to attend.

This was the first time I had heard Trotsky in Russia. I had thought that I might remind him of his farewell words in New York[5]; the hope which he had expressed that we might soon meet in Russia to help out with the great tasks now possible following the overthrow of tsarism. We were going to ask him to let us help resolve the Kronstadt problems in a spirit of fraternity, to offer our time and our energy, and even our lives, in this supreme test to which the revolution was putting the Communist Party.

Unfortunately, Trotsky's train was late in arriving and failed to make the sitting. The men who addressed that assembly were inaccessible to reason or appeal. A demented fanaticism prompted their words and a blind fear ruled their hearts.

The platform was tightly guarded by "kursanty;" bayonets fixed, Cheka troops stood between the platform and the audience. Zinoviev, who was in the chair, looked as if he was on the verge of a nervous breakdown. He stood up to speak several times, only to sit down again. When he eventually did start to speak, his head turned to right and left, as if fearing a surprise attack. His voice, weak as a child's at the best of times, rose to an extremely disagreeable and unconvincing shriek.

He denounced "General Kozlovsky" as the evil genius behind the Kronstadters, although most of those present knew that that officer had been assigned to Kronstadt as an artillery expert by Trotsky, no less. Kozlovsky was old and decrepit, and wielded no influence over the sailors or the garrison. Not that that prevented Zinoviev, chairman of the special purpose-built defense committee, from announcing that Kronstadt had revolted against the revolution and was attempting to carry out the plans of Kozlovsky and his tsarist aids.

Kalinin departed from his customary fatherly attitude and launched violently into the sailors, forgetful of the homage paid to him in Kronstadt only a few days earlier. "No measure can be too severe for counterrevolutionaries who dare raise their hand against our glorious Revolution," he declared. Secondary speakers carried on in the same tone, stirring their Communist fanaticism, ignoring the true facts, and calling for a frenzied revenge on men who, until very recently, had been acclaimed as heroes and brothers.

Above the din of the screaming, foot-stamping audience, a single voice strove to make itself heard: the strained and serious voice of a man from the front rows. He was the delegate from the striking Naval dockyard workers. He was forced, he said, to register a protest at the false accusations hurled from the platform against the courageous, loyal Kronstadters. Looking at Zinoviev and pointing him out, the fellow thundered: "It is your cruel indifference and your party's which have driven us to strike and awakened the sympathy of our sailor brothers, who have struggled alongside us in the revolution. They are guilty of no other crime and you know that! You are deliberately misrepresenting them and calling for their extermination." Shouts of "Counterrevolutionary, traitor! Menshevik! Bandit!" reduced the meeting to complete bedlam.

The elderly workman remained standing, his voice soaring above the tumult: "Barely three years ago, Lenin, Trotsky, Zinoviev and all of you were being denounced as traitors and German spies," he cried. "We workers and sailors came to your aid and rescued you from the Kerensky government. We are the ones who hoisted you into power! Have you forgotten that? Now you threaten us at sword point. You are playing with fire, remember! You are repeating the same mistakes and crimes as the Kerensky government! Watch out lest the same fate overtake you too!"

Zinoviev winced at that threat. Up on the platform, the others, embarrassed, fidgeted in their seats. The Communists in the audience seemed momentarily terrified by this sinister warning.

At which point another voice rang out. A great strapping fellow in a sailor uniform stood in the rear of the hall. Nothing had altered his brothers' revolutionary spirit, he declared. To the last man, they stood ready to defend the revolution to the last drop of their blood. And he began to read out the Kronstadt resolution passed at the mass meeting on March 1.[6] The hubbub which erupted at this act of daring drowned his voice, except for those sitting close to him. But he stuck at it and carried on reading until the end.

The sole reply to these two bold fellows, sons of the revolution, was the resolution moved by Zinoviev, demanding that Kronstadt surrender immediately and unconditionally, or face extermination. It was rushed through, amid a pandemonium of confusion and opposing voices were shouted down.

But this silence in the face of the approaching massacre was unbearable. I had to make myself heard. Not by these men possessed who would shout me down, as they had others. I would spell out my position that very night in a submission addressed to the supreme soviet defense authorities.

Once we were alone, I spoke to Sasha about this and I was glad to discover that the same thought had occurred to my old friend. He suggested that our missive should be a joint protest and should deal exclusively with the murderous resolution passed by the Petro-Soviet. Two comrades who had been with us at the meeting were of the same mind and offered to sign their names to a joint appeal to the authorities. I had no expectation that our message would have any moderating influence or would in any way impede the measures decreed against the sailors. But I was determined to register my view, by way of leaving a testament to the future that would prove that I had not stayed silent on the Communist Party's darkest act of treason to the revolution.

At 2:00 A.M., Sasha telephoned Zinoviev to tell him that he had something important to say to him regarding Kronstadt. Maybe Zinoviev thought that it could be something that might be of use to the plot against Kronstadt: otherwise he might not have taken the trouble to send Madame Ravitch to us at that hour of the night, within ten minutes of Sasha's call. She was absolutely reliable, the note from Zinoviev said, and any message should be handed to her. We gave her the following communiqué:

"To the trade union soviet and Petrograd Defense soviet.
Chairman Zinoviev.

It has become impossible to remain silent; indeed, it would be a crime! Recent events require that we anarchists speak out and spell out where we stand on the present situation.

The spirit of ferment and discontent manifest among the toilers and sailors is the product of factors demanding our serious attention. Cold and hunger have led to discontent and the absence of opportunities for discussion and criticism compels the workers and sailors to express their grievances in public.

White Guard gangs wish, and may attempt to exploit this discontent in the interests of their own class. Taking cover behind the toilers and sailors, they issue slogans demanding a Constituent Assembly, freedom of trade and articulating similar demands.

We anarchists have long since been denouncing the wrong-headedness of these slogans and to the whole world we declare that with weapons in hand, we will fight any attempt at counter-revolution, in cooperation with all friends of the socialist revolution and hand in glove with the Bolsheviks.

As regards the conflict between the soviet government and the toilers and sailors, we reckon that that should be settled, not by force of arms, but by the methods of comradeship, through a revolutionary, fraternal agreement.

The decision to spill blood which the soviet government has taken will not reassure the toilers, in the present situation. Instead, it will serve only to exacerbate things and will play into the hands of the Entente and the domestic counter-revolution.

Even more serious, the use of force by the toilers' and peasants' government against the workers and sailors will have a reactionary effect upon the international revolutionary movement and will do the greatest damage to the socialist revolution.

Comrade Bolsheviks, think before it is too late! Do not play with fire: you are about to take a decisive and very serious step.

Consequently, we offer you the following proposal: allow the election of a commission of five individuals, two of them anarchists. That commission will travel to Kronstadt to settle the quarrel by peaceable means. That, in the present situation, is the most radical approach. It will have international revolutionary significance.

Petrograd, March 5, 1921.

Alexander Berkman, Emma Goldman 'and two additional signatures'"

Proof that our appeals reached only deaf ears came that very day with Trotsky's arrival and his ultimatum to Kronstadt. By order of the workers' and peasants' government, he announced to the sailors and soldiers of Kronstadt that he was going to "go on a pheasant shoot" against all who had dared to "raise their hand against the socialist homeland." The defiant ships and crews were instructed to conform immediately with the soviet government's orders, or face being reduced by force of arms. Only those who would surrender unconditionally could expect clemency from the soviet republic.

This final warning was signed by Trotsky as chairman of the revolutionary military soviet, and by Kamenev as commander in chief of the Red Army. Once again the penalty for querying the divine right of those in government was death.

Trotsky was as good as his word. Having taken power thanks to the Kronstadters, he was now in a position to repay in full his debt to "the pride and glory of the Russian Revolution." The tsarist regime's finest military experts and strategists were in his retinue; among them was the famous Tukhachevsky[7] whom Trotsky appointed to overall command of the assault on Kronstadt. In addition, there were hordes of Chekists trained over a three year period in the arts of killing, "kursanty" and Communists specially selected for their unquestioning obedience to orders received, as well as the most dependable troops from various fronts. With such might ranged against the condemned town, it was expected that the "mutiny" would soon be broken. Especially as the sailors and soldiers of the Petrograd garrison had been disarmed and all who had expressed solidarity with their besieged comrades pulled out of the danger zone. From my window in the International Hotel, I watched them led away in small batches under escort from powerful detachments of Chekist troops. There was no spring left in their step, their arms hung limp and their heads were bowed in sadness.

The authorities had lost their fear of the Petrograd strikers. These had been weakened and broken by hunger, their energy drained. They were demoralized by the lies peddled about them and their Kronstadt brethren, their spirit crushed by the poison of doubt planted thanks to the Bolsheviks' propaganda. They had no stomach left for a fight, no hope of being able to go to the aid of their Kronstadt comrades who had, without a thought for themselves, made a stand on their behalf and were now about to pay for that with their lives.

Kronstadt was abandoned by Petrograd and cut off from the rest of Russia. It stood alone and could offer scarcely any resistance. "It will collapse at the first rifle shot!" the soviet press boasted.

Incorrectly. Kronstadt had never had any thought of "mutiny" or resisting the soviet government. Right up to the last, it was determined to spill no blood. Continually it called for a compromise and amicable settlement. But, forced to defend itself against military provocation, it fought like a lion. For a fraught ten days and nights, the besieged town's sailors and soldiers held out against continual artillery bombardment from three sides and against aerial bombardment of its non-combatant population. Heroically, it beat off the Bolsheviks' repeated efforts to storm its fortresses with specialist troops imported from Moscow. Trotsky and Tukhachevsky had every advantage over the Kronstadters. They had the backing of the entire machinery of the Communist State and the centrally-controlled press continued to spread poison about these alleged "mutineers and counterrevolutionaries." They could call upon endless reinforcements and manpower, wearing white camouflage to pass undetected across the snow blanketing the frozen Gulf of Finland, thereby concealing the night assault against the unsuspecting Kronstadters. The latter had nothing but their indomitable courage and unshakable faith in the rightness of their cause and in the free soviets they championed as the only ones capable of saving Russia from dictatorship. They lacked even an ice-breaker to hold off the Communist enemy's assault. They were worn down by hunger, cold and sleepless nights on watch. Even so, they held out well, fighting a hopeless fight against overwhelming odds.

Throughout this fearful period, not a single friendly voice was heard. During whole days and nights filled with the thunder of heavy artillery and the boom of cannons, there was no one to protest or call for a halt to the awful blood bath. Gorky... Maxim Gorky... Where was he? His voice they would heed.

"Let's go see him!" I approached some members of the "intelligentsia." Gorky, they told me, had never protested, even in serious, individual cases, not even in those involving members of his own profession, not even when he knew the condemned men to be innocent. He would not speak out now. It was hopeless.

The "intelligentsia," these men and women who had once been the spokesmen of revolution, the master-thinkers, the authors and poets, were as powerless as we and paralyzed by the futility of individual efforts. Most of their comrades and friends were in prison or in exile, and some had been executed. They felt shattered by the eradication of all human values.

I turned to the Communists of our acquaintance. Pleaded with them to do something. A few understood the monstrous crime that their party was in the process of committing against Kronstadt. They conceded that the charge of counter-revolution had been concocted. The supposed leader Kozlovsky was a nonentity, too preoccupied with his own fate to have had any hand at all in the sailors' protests. The latter were top quality, their sole concern Russia's welfare. Far from making common cause with tsarist generals, they had even declined an offer of help from Chernov, leader of the Social Revolutionaries. They sought no help from abroad. They demanded their right to choose their own deputies in the forthcoming elections to the Kronstadt soviet and justice for the Petrograd strikers.

Our Communist friends spent night after night with us. . . talking. . . and talking. . . but not a one of them dared raise his voice in public protest. We did not realize the implications of that for them, they said. They would be expelled from the party, they and their families deprived of work and rations and would be literally condemned to death by starvation. Or they would quite simply and straightforwardly vanish and no one would ever discover what had become of them. And yet they assured us that it was not fear that dictated their inaction but rather the utter futility of appeals. Nothing, absolutely nothing could stop the mill-stones of the Communist State. They had been crushed by them; they no longer had even the strength to protest.

I was haunted by the ghastly fear that Sasha and I too might be reduced to that state, all resourcefulness gone and resigned like them. Anything was better than that. . . prison, exile, even death! Or escape! Escape from this horrific fraud, this sham of a revolution.

The notion of wanting to quit Russia had never before occurred to me. The very thought disturbed and shocked me. Leave Russia to her Calvary! But my feeling was that I would brave even that rather than be a part of the grinding of this machinery, rather than become an inanimate thing manipulated at will.

The bombardment of Kronstadt continued non-stop for ten days and ten nights, ceasing abruptly on the morning of March 17. The silence which shrouded Petrograd was more daunting than the endless cannonades of the previous night. The agonizing wait gripped us all. There was no way of knowing what had happened and why the bombardment had stopped so abruptly. Later in the afternoon the tension gave way to dumb horror. Kronstadt had been brought to heel. Tens of thousands of men murdered, the town drowned in blood. The Neva, whose heavy guns had broken up the ice, became the tomb of many, kursanty and young Communists. The heroic sailors and soldiers had held their positions to their dying breath. Those unlucky enough not to have perished in combat fell into the clutches of the enemy, only to be executed or despatched to lingering torture in the frozen wastes of North Russia.

We were dumb struck. Sasha, having lost any remaining shred of belief in the Bolsheviks, roamed the streets in despair. I walked on leaden legs, every nerve overcome by tremendous weariness. I sat motionless, staring into the night (. . .)

The next day, March 18, still groggy from lack of sleep during seventeen anxious days, I woke to the tramp of many feet. The Communists were marching past to the sound of military tunes, singing the *Internationale*. Those strains, which had previously sounded so splendid to me, now sounded like a dirge sung over the fervent hopes of humanity.

March 18: the anniversary of the Paris Commune of 1871, crushed after two months by Thiers and Gallifet, the butchers of thirty thousand Communards! Re-enacted in Kronstadt on March 18, 1921.

The true implications of this "liquidation" of Kronstadt were disclosed by Lenin himself three days after the nightmare. At the Communist Party's tenth congress, held in Moscow, while the siege of Kronstadt was in progress, Lenin unexpectedly switched from his inspired paeans to communism to an equally fervent paean to the New Economic Policy. Free trade, concessions to capitalists, a free labor market in the countryside and in the factories, all things which had been vilified for more than three years as indications of counterrevolution, punishable by imprisonment or death, but now etched by Lenin upon the glorious colors of the dictatorship.

Brazenly, as ever, he confessed what honest, thoughtful people in the party and outside of it, had been aware of for seventeen days, to wit "that the Kronstadters wanted no truck with counterrevolutionaries. But they wanted no truck with us either!" The ingenuous sailors had taken seriously the revolution's watchword of "All power to the soviets!," to which Lenin and his party had solemnly promised to remain faithful. Therein lay the Kronstadters' unforgivable mistake! For which they had to die. They were to become martyrs so as to fertilize the soil for a fresh crop of slogans from Lenin, who was wiping the slate clean of his old ones. His masterpiece was the New Economic Policy, the NEP.[8]

Lenin's public admission regarding Kronstadt did nothing to halt the hunting down of sailors, soldiers and workers from the defeated town. They were arrested in their hundreds and the Cheka was busy "target-shooting."

Curiously, the anarchists were not mentioned in connection with the Kronstadt "mutiny." But at the tenth party congress, Lenin had declared that a war without quarter had to be waged against the "petite bourgeoisie," anarchist personnel included. The anarcho-syndicalist leanings of the Workers' Opposition[9] showed that this tendency had spread to the very ranks of the Communist Party itself, he had stated. Lenin's call to arms against the anarchists was taken up with alacrity. The Petrograd groups were raided and a large number of their members arrested. In addition, the Cheka shut down the presses and the offices from which *Golos Truda*, the mouthpiece of our movement's anarcho-syndicalist wing was published.

We had bought our tickets for the journey up to Moscow, before this happened. On learning of the mass arrests, we decided to stay for a little longer, in case we might be on the wanted list. We were not bothered, however;

maybe because it was thought useful to have a few anarchist celebrities at large, to show the world that only the "bandits" were in soviet prisons.

In Moscow we found all of the anarchists arrested, except for a half dozen. Yet no charge had been preferred against our comrades; no statements had been taken from them, nor were they brought to trial. In spite of which a number of them had already been sent to the penitentiary in Samara. The ones still in the Butyrky or Taganka prisons were subjected to the foulest persecution and indeed violence. Thus, one of our people, the young Kashirin, had been beaten up by a Chekist as some prison warders looked on. Maximoff[10] and other anarchists who had served on the revolutionary fronts and were well-known and well respected by many Communists, had been forced to launch a hunger strike to protest against the ghastly conditions of detention.

The first thing that was asked of us upon our return to Moscow was that we sign a manifesto addressed to the soviet authorities denouncing the concerted efforts to exterminate our comrades.

This we did, readily. Sasha was now as convinced as I was that protests from the handful of politicians still at large inside Russia were utterly pointless and futile. Then again, no effective action was to be expected of the Russian masses, even had it been possible to contact them. Years of war, civil strife and suffering had drained them of their vitality and terror had left them dumb and submissive.

Our only hopes, Sasha said, were Europe and the United States. The time had come to reveal the shameful betrayal of October to the toilers abroad. The awakened consciences of the proletariat and other liberal and radical opinions in every country must build to a mighty protest against this ruthless persecution. Only that could stay the dictatorship's hand. Nothing else.

The martyrdom of Kronstadt had already had this effect upon my friend: it had destroyed any lingering traces of the **Bolshevik myth.**[11] Not just Sasha, but other comrades who had hitherto defended the Communists' methods as inevitable in time of revolution, had been forced to gaze into the abyss between October and the dictatorship.

Notes to Memories of Kronstadt

1. Extracted from Emma Goldman *Living My Life*.
2. This Zorin, from a working class background and at this time secretary of the Bolshevik Party's Petrograd Committee, is unconnected with the Valerian Zorin who was later USSR ambassador to France: this one ended his days in the Cheka's crematoria.
3. Hand-picked officer cadets who, along with Mongolians, were employed in the destruction of the Kronstadt rebellion.
4. For more on Alexander Berkman, see Volume 11.

5. As mentioned in the preceding extract.
6. Mikhail Tukhachevsky (1893–1937), former tsarist officer and future Soviet marshal, was finally executed on Stalin's orders, on the basis of false evidence concocted by Hitler.
7. The NEP (New Economic Policy) introduced by Lenin after the failure of "war communism" was aimed at restoring private enterprise to some extent.
8. A current within the Bolshevik Party, headed by Shliapnikov and Alexandra Kollontai, and condemned at the tenth party congress.
9. Grigori Petrovitch Maximoff (1893–1950) turned into an anarchist in Russia after reading Kropotkin: he contributed to the newspaper *Golos Truda*, spokesman for the anarcho-syndicalist tendency during the Russian Revolution. He was forced to quit his native land in 1922 for Berlin, where he was active in the International Workers' Association, and then for Paris: he then emigrated to the United States, in 1925, where he published anarchist newspapers in Russian and published, in English, one of the finest books on the Russian Revolution viewed from the anarchist perspective, *Twenty Years of Terror in Russia* (1940).
11. *The Bolshevik Myth (1920–1921)* was to be the title of a pamphlet published in English by Berkman in 1922.

Resolution Passed by the General Assembly of the 1st and 2nd Squadrons of the Baltic Fleet, Held in Kronstadt

(March 1, 1921)

Having listened to reports from the representatives sent to Petrograd by the crews' general assembly to look into the situation there, the Assembly's decision is that we must,

Given that the current soviets do not reflect the wishes of the workers and peasants:

1. Proceed immediately with the re-election of the soviets by secret ballot. Electioneering among the workers and peasants must proceed with complete freedom of speech and action;
2. Establish freedom of speech and press for all workers and peasants, for anarchists and left-wing socialist parties;
3. Afford freedom of assembly to trade unions and peasant organizations;
4. Summon, over the heads of the political parties, a conference of the workers, Red soldiers and sailors of Petrograd, Kronstadt and the province of Petrograd, for no later than 10 March 1921;
5. Release all socialist political prisoners and also all workers, peasants Red soldiers and sailors imprisoned in the wake of worker and peasant disturbances;
6. Elect a commission to review the cases of those held in the prisons and concentration camps;
7. Abolish "political offices," because no political party should have privileges in the propagation of its ideas, nor should it receive State financial subsidies for that purpose. In their place we must introduce educational and cultural commissions, elected in every district and funded by government;
8. Abolish all checkpoints forthwith.
9. Standardize rations for all toilers, save for those engaged in trades involving health risks;
10. Abolish the Communist shock detachments inside every army unit: likewise the Communist Guard inside factories and plants. Should the need arise, guard corps can be appointed by companies within the army and by the workers themselves in the plants and factories;

11. Afford peasants complete freedom of action in respect of their land and also the right to own livestock, provided that they do their own work, that is, do not make use of waged labor;
12. Appoint a roving audit commission;
13. Permit the free pursuit of craft production, without use of waged labor;
14. We ask all army units and the "kursanty" military comrades to associate themselves with our resolution;

This resolution has been passed unanimously by the assembled crews of the squadron. There were two individual abstentions.

> Signed — Petritchenko, chairman of the assembly:
> and Perepelkin, secretary.

The Official Journal of the Kronstadt Uprising (Extracts from the Kronstadt *Izvestia*)[1]

And for openers, here are a few headlines:
All power to the soviets and not the parties!
The power of the soviets will free the toilers in the fields from the Communist yoke.
Lenin says: 'Communism is soviet power plus electrification,' but the people has seen that Bolshevik Communism is the absolutism of the commissars plus firing squads.
The Soviets, and not the Constituent [Assembly] are the bulwark of the toilers.
Long live red Kronstadt with the power of free soviets!
Trotsky's first shot is the Communists' distress signal.

[No. 1, March 3, 1921] To the Population of the Fortress and Town of Kronstadt

Comrades and citizens, our country is passing through a tough time. For three years now, famine, cold and economic chaos have trapped us in a vice-like grip. The Communist Party which governs the country has drifted away from the masses and proved itself powerless to rescue them from a state of general ruination. The Party has not taken any heed of the disturbances which have recently occurred in Petrograd and Moscow, which plainly demonstrated that it has lost the toiling masses' confidence. Nor has it paid any heed to the demands articulated by the workers. It looks upon all this as inklings of counter-revolution. It is profoundly mistaken.

Those disturbances and those demands are the voice of the people as a body, the voice of all who labor. All workers, sailors and Red soldiers today can clearly see that only concerted efforts, only the concerted determination of the people can afford the country bread, wood and coal, can clothe and shoe the people and rescue the Republic from the impasse in which it finds itself.

This determination on the part of all toilers, Red soldiers and sailors was demonstrated plainly at the great meeting in our town on March 1st. The meeting unanimously endorsed a resolution from the 1st and 2nd squadrons' crews.

One of the decisions made was that fresh elections to the soviets should proceed without delay.

In order to lay the fairest foundations for those fresh elections in such a way that the soviet may effectively represent the workers and the soviet be an active and vigorous body, the delegates from all of the fleet organizations, the garrison and the workers met on March 2 in the Education College. That meeting was to draw up the basis for fresh elections and thereby embark upon positive, peaceable work, the task of overhauling the soviet system.

Now, since there were grounds for fearing repression, and in the light also of threatening speeches by representatives of the authorities, the meeting decided to establish a Provisional Revolutionary Committee and invest it with full powers over the administration of the town and fortress.

The Provisional Committee has its headquarters aboard the ship of the line 'Petropavlovsk.'

Comrades and citizens! The Provisional Committee is particularly concerned that no blood shall be spilled. It has done all in its power to maintain revolutionary order in the town, in the fortress and in the forts.

Comrades and citizens! Carry on with your work. Workers, stand by your machines! Sailors and soldiers, do not leave your posts. All employees, every institution must carry on with their work.

The Provisional Revolutionary Committee calls upon all workers' organizations, all seamen's unions and others, all sea-going and land-based units, as well as every individual citizen to rally to its aid.

Its task is to assure, in fraternal collaboration with us, the requisite conditions for fair and honest elections to the new soviet.

So, comrades, order, calm, a cool head! Let us all be about honest socialist work for the good of all toilers!

   Kronstadt March 2, 1921.
   Signed: Petritchenko, chairman of the Provisional Revolutionary Committee: Tukin, secretary.

Wireless from Moscow

We publish the following wireless telegram issued by the "Rosta" agency in Moscow and intercepted by the wireless operator on the 'Petropavlovsk':

'Prepare to do battle against the White Guardist conspiracy!

The mutiny of ex-General Kozlovsky and the vessel 'Petropavlovsk' has been orchestrated by Entente spies, as has been the case in numerous earlier plots. This can seen from a reading of the French bourgeois newspaper *Le Matin* which, two weeks ahead of Kozlovsky's revolt, carried the following telegram from Helsingfors: "From Petrograd comes a report that in the wake of the Kronstadt revolt, the Bolshevik military authorities have taken steps to isolate Kronstadt and prevent the Kronstadt soldiers and sailors from nearing Petrograd. Provisions for Kronstadt are banned until further notice."

It is plain that Kronstadt's sedition has been directed from Paris and that French counter-espionage is mixed up in it. The same old story. The Social Revolutionaries, run from Paris, plotted rebellion against the soviet government, and scarcely have their preparations been completed than the real master, a tsarist general, puts in an appearance. The story of Koltchak who attempted to restore authority with the Social Revolutionaries' help is played out once again. All of the enemies of the toilers, ranging from tsarist generals through to Social Revolutionaries, are attempting to make capital out of hunger and cold. Of course, this revolt by generals and Social Revolutionaries will be crushed in short order and General Kozlovsky and his acolytes will meet the same fate as Koltchak.

But there can be no question but that the Entente's espionage network has not swooped upon Kronstadt alone. Workers and Red soldiers, rip that network asunder! Expose the whisperers and provocateurs! You must display a cool head, self-mastery and vigilance. Do not forget that the real way to overcome food shortages and other difficulties, which are passing but tiresome indeed, lies in intense effort of goodwill and not in nonsensical excesses that can only add to the misery, to the greater relish of the accursed enemies of those who toil.'

We are bringing to everyone's notice the text of a proclamation dropped from a Communist airplane over Kronstadt. Citizens will feel naught but contempt for this provocative calumny:

'To the deceived Kronstadters!

Can you see now where the wastrels have led you? Look where you are now! Even now the yawning maw of former tsarist generals looms at the back of the Social Revolutionaries and Mensheviks. All of these Petritchenkos and Tukins dance like puppets to the tune of the tsarist General Kozlovsky, Captains Borkser, Kostromitinoff, Shirmanovsky and other known White Guardists. They have deceived you! You were told that you were fighting for democracy. Barely two days have elapsed and you see that in fact you are fighting, not for democracy, but for tsarist generals!'

[No. 2, March 4, 1921] To the Population of the Town of Kronstadt

Citizens! Kronstadt begins a bitter struggle for freedom. At any moment, we may expect an attack by the Communists designed to capture Kronstadt and re-impose upon us their power, which has brought us famine, cold and economic chaos.

Everybody, every last one of us, will forcefully and steadfastly defend the freedom we have won. We will resist the attempt to capture Kronstadt. And should the Communists attempt to do so by force of arms, we will offer stiff resistance in reply.

The Provisional Revolutionary Committee urges the population not to panic should it hear gunfire. Calm and a cool head will bring us victory.

The Provisional Revolutionary Committee

Notice

The Provisional Revolutionary Committee must refute rumors to the effect that arrested Communists have been subjected to violence. The arrested Communists are completely safe.

Of the several Communists arrested, some have in any event been freed. A Communist Party representative will make up part of the commission charged with investigating the basis for the arrests. The Communist comrades Ilyin, Kabanoff and Pervushin have made overtures to the Revolutionary Committee and have been authorized to visit the detainees held aboard the vessel 'Petropavlovsk.' Which those comrades hereby confirm through their signatures here.

> Signed: Ilyin, Kabanoff, Pervushin. — This is a true copy, signed: N. Arhipoff, member of the Revolutionary Committee. — Signed on the secretary's behalf, P. Bogdanoff.

[No. 3, March 5, 1921] Victory or Death

A delegate meeting. — Yesterday, March 4th, at 6:00 P.M., there was a meeting in the Garrison Club of delegates from the military units and trade unions, summoned in order to expand the Provisional Revolutionary Committee through the election of further members, and to hear reports on developments in progress.

Twenty-two delegates, most of them directly arrived from their place of work, attended the meeting.

The seaman Petritchenko, chairman, declared that the Provisional Revolutionary Committee, being swamped with work, needed to be expanded to incorporate at least another ten new members.

Out of the twenty candidates put forward, the meeting elected, by an overwhelming majority, the comrades Vershinin, Perepelkin, Kupoloff, Ossossoff, Valk, Romanenko, Pavloff, Baikoff, Patrusheff and Kilgast.

The new members took their places on the bureau.

Then Petritchenko, chairman of the Provisional Revolutionary Committee, delivered a detailed report on the actions of the Committee since its election up to the present.

Comrade Petritchenko stressed that the entire garrison of the fortress and the ships was in battle readiness, should the need arise. He noted the great enthusiasm animating the whole working population of the town, its workers, sailors and Red soldiers.

Frantic applause greeted the newly elected members and the chairman's report. Whereupon the meeting moved on to current business.

It was revealed that the town and garrison are adequately supplied with provisions and fuel. The question of arming of the workers was examined.

It has been decided that all workers, without exception, are to be armed and charged with keeping guard within the town, for all of the sailors and soldiers were keen to take their place in the combat detachments. This decision evoked enthusiastic backing, to cries of "Victory or death!"

It was then decided that within three days, the steering commissions of all the trade unions and the trades union council should be re-elected. The latter is to be the leading worker body and keep in continual contact with the Provisional Revolutionary Committee.

Next, some sailor comrades who had, at great risk, successfully escaped from Petrograd, Strelna, Peterhof and Oranienbaum delivered their briefings.

They noted that the population and workers of all those places had been kept by the Communists in a state of absolute ignorance of what was afoot in Kronstadt. There were rumors circulating everywhere to the effect that White Guards and generals were operating in Kronstadt.

This news provoked general hilarity.

What cheered the meeting even more was the reading given to a sort of 'Manifesto' dropped over Kronstadt by a Communist airplane.

"Oh yes!" — the shout went up — "We have but one general here: the commissar of the Baltic Fleet, Kuzmin! And even *he* is under arrest!"

The meeting closed with expressions and demonstrations of enthusiasm, displaying the unanimous and steadfast determination to secure the victory or die.

[No. 4, March 6, 1921] Editorial

The horny hands of the Kronstadt sailors and workers have wrested the tiller from the Communists' hands and have taken over the helm.

The ship of soviet power will be steered, alert and sure, towards Petrograd, whence this horny-handed power is to spread right across a wretched Russia.

But take care comrades!

Increase your vigilance tenfold, for the course is strewn with reefs. One careless touch to the tiller and your ship, with its cargo so precious to you, the cargo of social reconstruction, may founder upon a rock.

Comrades, keep a close eye upon the vicinity of the tiller: enemies are even now trying to creep closer. A single lapse and they will wrest the tiller from you, and the soviet ship may go down to triumphant laughter from tsarist lackeys and henchmen of the bourgeoisie.

Comrades, right now you are rejoicing in the great, peaceful victory over the Communists' dictatorship. Now, your enemies are celebrating it too.

Your grounds for such joy, and theirs, are quite contradictory.

You are driven by a burning desire to restore the authentic power of the soviets, by a noble hope of seeing the worker engage in free labor and the peasant enjoy the right to dispose, on his land, of the produce of his labors. *They* dream of bringing back the tsarist knout and the privileges of the generals.

Your interests are different. They are not fellow travelers with you.

You needed to get rid of the Communists' power over you in order to set about creative work and peaceable construction. Whereas they want to overthrow that power to make the workers and peasants their slaves again.

You are in search of freedom. They want to shackle you as it suits them. Be vigilant! Don't let the wolves in sheep's clothing get near the tiller.

Broadcast Appeal

To all ... all ... all.

Comrade workers, Red soldiers and sailors!

Here in Kronstadt, we know the measure of your suffering, yourselves, your women and your famished children, under the yoke of the Communists' dictatorship.

We have overthrown the Communist soviet. In a few days, our Provisional Revolutionary Committee will proceed with elections to the new soviet, which, being freely elected, will mirror the wishes of the whole laboring population and garrison, and not those of a handful of "Communist" madmen.

Our cause is just. We are for soviet power, not the power of parties. We are for free election of the toiling masses' representatives. The soviets, counterfeited, captured and manipulated by the Communist Party, have always been deaf to our needs and our demands — the only answer we have ever had was the murderer's bullet.

Now, with the toilers' patience at an end, they are trying to stop your mouth with alms; by order of Zinoviev, checkpoints are to be done away with in Petrograd province and Moscow is assigning ten million gold rubles for the purchase, abroad, of provisions and basic necessities. But we know that the Petrograd proletariat will not let itself be bought off by such alms. Over the heads of the Communists, revolutionary Kronstadt stretches out its hand and offers you its fraternal aid.

Comrades! Not only do they deceive you, but they are shamelessly twisting the facts and stooping even to the foulest dissembling. Comrades, do not let yourselves be taken in!

In Kronstadt power lies exclusively in the hands of the sailors, soldiers and revolutionary workers, and not in those of "counter-revolutionaries led by a Kozlovsky," as lying Moscow radio would have you believe.

Don't delay, comrades! Join us! Make contact with us! Insist that your nonparty delegates are authorized to come to Kronstadt. Only they can tell you the truth and expose the abject slander about "Finnish bread" and Entente machinations.

Long live the revolutionary proletariat of the towns and countryside! Long live the power of the freely elected soviets!

A Letter

Rank and file Communist comrades! Look around you and you will see that we are caught in a terrible bind. We have been led into it by a handful of bureaucratic "Communists" who, under cover of being Communists, have feathered themselves very comfortable nests in our Republic.

As a Communist, I beseech you: dump these phony "Communists" who are herding you in the direction of fratricide. It is thanks to them that we rank and file Communists who are not responsible for any of it, suffer reproach from our non-party worker and peasant comrades.

The current situation frightens me.

Can it be that our brothers' blood is to be spilled for the benefit of these "bureaucratic Communists?"

Comrades, pull yourselves together! Do not let yourselves be taken in by these bureaucratic "Communists" who are provoking and inciting you into carnage. Show them the door! A true Communist should not impose his ideas, but should march alongside the whole toiling mass, among its ranks.

Rozhkali, member of the Russian (Bolshevik) Communist Party.

[No. 5, March 7, 1921] Editorial

'Field Marshal' Trotsky makes threats to the whole of free, revolutionary Kronstadt which has risen up against the absolutism of the Communist commissars.

The toilers who have thrown off the shameful yoke of Communist Party dictatorship, are threatened with a military rout by this brand new Trepoff.[2] He promises to bombard Kronstadt's peaceable population. He repeats Trepoff's order: 'Don't spare the bullets.' He must have a goodly supply for the revolutionary sailors, workers and Red soldiers.

Talks About A Delegation

The Provisional Revolutionary Committee has received the following wireless telegram from Petrograd:

Inform Petrograd by wireless whether some delegates from the soviet, chosen from among non-party and Party members can be sent from Petrograd into Kronstadt on a fact-finding visit.

The Provisional Revolutionary Committee immediately replied by wireless:

Wireless telegram to the Petrograd Soviet. — Having received the Petrograd soviet's wireless message "whether some delegates from the soviet, chosen from among non-party and Party members can be sent from Petrograd into Kronstadt on a fact-finding visit," we hereby inform you that:

We have no confidence in the independence of your non-party delegates.

We suggest that, in the presence of a delegation of ours, non-party delegates be elected from the factories, Red units and sailors. To these you may add fifteen percent of Communists. It would be a good idea if, by return, we might have 18:00 hours on March 6 as the departure date for Krondtadt's representatives to Petrograd and Petrograd delegates to Kronstadt. Should it not be possible to reply by that time, we request that you let us know the date and the reasons for delay.

Transportation will have to be arranged for the delegation from Kronstadt.
                    The Provisional Revolutionary Committee

We Wreak No Vengeance

The Communist dictatorship's oppression of the toiling masses has sparked perfectly natural indignation and resentment in the population. By reason of this state of affairs, a few individuals linked to the Communists were boycotted or dismissed. This should no longer be the case. We seek no vengeance: we defend our workers' interests. We must act with a level head and eliminate only those who, through sabotage or a slander campaign, hinder the restoration of the power and rights of the toilers.

We Red soldiers of the Red Army from the 'Krasnoarmeyetz' fort are with the Revolutionary Committee body and soul. We will defend the Committee, the workers and the peasants to the finish.

Let no one believe the lies of the Communist proclamations dropped from airplanes. We have neither generals nor masters here. Kronstadt has always been the workers' and peasants' town and will remain such.

The Communists say that we are led by spies. That is a bare-faced lie. We have always defended the freedoms won by the Revolution, and we always will. If they want to convince us, let them send us a delegation. As for generals, they are in the Communists' service. At present, when the fate of the country is at stake, we, who have taken power into our own hands and entrusted supreme command to the Revolutionary Committee, declare to the whole garrison and all toilers that we are ready to die for the freedom of the laboring people. Freed from the Communist yoke and the terror of these past three years, we would rather die than retreat a single step.

The Krasnoarmeyetz Fort detachment.

[No. 6, March 8, 1921] First "Communiqué"

At 6:45 p.m., the Communist batteries in Sestroretsk and Lissy Noss became the first to open fire on the Kronstadt forts.

The forts accepted the challenge and quickly reduced those batteries to silence.

Whereupon it was Krasnaya Gorka that opened fire. To a worthy reply from the battle-ship 'Sebastopol.' Sporadic artillery fire ensued.

On our side, two Red soldiers have been wounded and admitted to hospital. No material damage.

Kronstadt, March 7, 1921.

The First Shot

They have started to bombard Kronstadt. Well, we are ready for them! Let us have a trial of strength!

They are in a hurry to act. Understandably so: for all of the Communists' lies, the Russian toilers are beginning to grasp the grandeur of the work of liberation upon which revolutionary Kronstadt has embarked after three years of slavery.

The executioners are uneasy. Soviet Russia, victim of their ghastly aberration, is breaking out of their prison. And by the same token, they are being forced to surrender their domination over the laboring people. The Communists' government has sent up a distress signal. The eight day life of free Kronstadt is proof of their impotence.

A little while longer, and a proper response from our glorious ships and our revolutionary forts will sink the ship of the soviet pirates who have been forced to enter the lists against a revolutionary Kronstadt flying the flag reading: "Power to the soviets and not to the parties."

Let the World Know!

To all... all... all.

The first cannon shot has just been fired. "Field Marshal" Trotsky, stained with the blood of the workers, was first to open fire upon revolutionary Kronstadt which rose up against the Communists' autocracy in order to restore authentic soviet power.

Without having spilled one single drop of blood, we Red soldiers, sailors and workers of Kronstadt have shrugged off the Communist yoke. We have allowed those of their people living among us to keep their lives. Now they wish to impose their power on us again under the threat of artillery.

Wishing no bloodshed, we asked that non-party delegates from the Petrograd workers be sent here so that they might understand that Kronstadt is fighting for soviet power. But the Communists concealed our request from the Petrograd workers and opened fire: the supposedly worker and peasant government's usual answer to the demands of the laboring masses.

Let the workers of the whole world know that we, the defenders of the power of soviets, will watch over the gains of the social Revolution.

We will conquer or perish beneath the ruins of Kronstadt, fighting for the righteous cause of the working masses.

The toilers the world over will sit in judgment of us. The blood of the innocents will be upon the heads of the Communists, savage madmen drunk on power.

Long live the power of the soviets!
The Provisional Revolutionary Committee

Liberated Kronstadt Calling the Working Women of the World

Today is a world-wide holiday: the feast of the working woman. From amid the boom of cannons and the explosions of shells fired by the Communist foes of the toiling people, we workers of Kronstadt send our fraternal greetings to the working women of the world: greetings from free, revolutionary Kronstadt.

We hope that you will soon achieve your emancipation from all forms of violence and oppression. Long live the free revolutionary working women!

Long live the world-wide social Revolution!

The Provisional Revolutionary Committee

Calm Prevails in Kronstadt

Yesterday, March 7, the toilers' enemies, the Communists, opened fire on Kronstadt.

The population greeted this bombardment courageously. The workers rushed to arms with a will! It was plain that the working population of the town lived in perfect accord with its Provisional Revolutionary Committee.

In spite of the opening of hostilities, the Committee saw no point in declaring a state of siege. Indeed, what was there to fear? Certainly not its own Red soldiers, sailors, workers or intellectuals! By contrast, in Petrograd, under the state of siege in force there, one is not allowed on the streets after seven o'clock. Which is understandable: the impostors have reason to fear their own laboring population.

The Aims for Which We Fight

In making the October Revolution, the working class had hoped to secure its emancipation. But out of it came an even greater enslavement of the individual human being.

The power of the police-backed monarchy passed into the hands of usurpers, the Communists, who, instead of leaving freedom to the people, reserved for it instead fear of the Cheka's jails, the horrors of which far exceed the methods of the tsarist gendarmerie.

At the end of many a long year of struggles and suffering, the toiler in soviet Russia has received nothing but insolent orders, bayonet blows and the whistling bullets of the Cheka's "Cossacks." In fact, Communist power has replaced that glorious emblem of the toilers, the hammer and sickle, with another symbol: the bayonet and prison bars, which has allowed the new bureaucracy, the Communist commissars and functionaries, to carve out a peaceable carefree existence for themselves.

But the most abject and most criminal thing of all is the spiritual slavishness introduced by the Communists; their hand reaches out even to thought, to the toilers' moral life, forcing everyone to think in accordance with their prescription only.

With the aid of State-run trade unions, they shackled the worker to his machine and turned work into a new slavery, instead of making it pleasant.

To the protests of the peasants which extended even to spontaneous uprisings; to the demands of workers forced by their very living conditions to have recourse to strikes, they replied with mass shootings and a savagery that the tsarist generals might have envied.

The toilers' Russia, which led the way in hoisting the red banners of the emancipation of labor, has turned renegade on the blood of the martyrs, all to the greater glory of Communist rule. In that sea of blood the Communists are drowning all of the great, beautiful promises and potential of proletarian Revolution.

It was becoming more and more plain, and has now become apparent that the Communist Party is not, as it pretends to be, the toilers' champion. The interests of the working class are foreign to it. Having achieved power, it has but one concern: not to lose it. And it shrinks from no method: defamation, deceit, violence, murder and reprisals against rebels' families.

But the martyred toilers' patience has run out.

Here and there the country has been lighted by the fires of revolts in the struggle against oppression and violence. Workers' strikes have proliferated.

The Bolshevik sleuths are vigilant. All sorts of steps are taken to thwart and smother the ineluctable third revolution.

In spite of everything, it has arrived. Carried out by the toiling masses themselves. Communism's generals can see clearly that it is the people that has risen in revolt, persuaded as it is of their betrayal of the ideas of the revolution. Fearing for their own skins and knowing that they cannot hide anywhere from the toilers' wrath, the Communists try to terrorize the rebels, with the help of their "Cossacks," by means of imprisonment, execution and other atrocities. Under the yoke of Communist dictatorship, life itself has become worse than death.

The toiling people in revolt has realized that there can be no half measures in the struggle against the Communists and the restored system of serfdom. The Communists pretend to make concessions: they set up roadblocks in Petrograd province; they set aside ten million gold rubles for the purchase of produce abroad. But let no one kid themselves: lurking behind this bait is the mailed fist of the master, the dictator, of the master who, once calm has been restored, will exact a high price for his concessions.

No, no half measures! We must conquer or die!

Red Kronstadt, the terror of the counter-revolution, be it from left or right, has set the example.

It is here that the great new impetus was given to the Revolution. The flag of revolt against the tyranny of the past three years, against the oppression of a Communist autocracy that puts three centuries of the monarchist yoke to shame, has been unfurled here.

It is here in Kronstadt that the foundation stone was laid of the third revolution that will smash the last shackles on the toiler and open up before him the broad new avenue to socialist construction.

That new revolution will rouse the toiling masses of the Orient and Occident. For it will offer the example of fresh socialist construction as opposed to mechanical, governmental "Communist" construction. The toiling masses beyond our borders will then be persuaded by facts that everything that has thus far been cobbled together over here, in the workers' and peasants' name, was not socialism.

The first step in that direction was taken without a single shot's being fired, without one drop of blood's being spilled. The toilers have no need of blood. They will only spill it in self-defense. Despite all of the Communists' revolting deeds, we will have enough self-control to confine ourselves to isolating them from social life so as to prevent their hindering the work of revolution by means of their phony, malevolent agitation.

The workers and peasants are forging irresistibly ahead. They are leaving behind the Constituent with its bourgeois regime and the Communist Party's dictatorship with its Cheka and State capitalism tightening the noose around the toilers' necks and threatening to strangle them. The change which has just occurred at last offers the toiling masses the chance of ensuring that they get freely elected soviets that will operate without any violence pressure from a party. That change will also enable them to revamp the State-run trade unions into free associations of workers, peasants and intellectual workers.

The police machinery of the Communist autocracy is smashed at last.

[No. 7, March 9, 1921] Listen, Trotsky!

Over their radio stations the Communists have slung cartloads of mud at the leading lights of the third revolution who champion authentic soviet power against the commissars' usurpation and arbitrariness.

We have never concealed that from the population of Kronstadt. At all times, in our *Izvestia* we have reported these slanderous attacks.

We had nothing to fear. Citizens knew how the revolt had come about and whose handiwork it was. The workers and Red soldiers know that our garrison includes neither generals nor White Guards.

For its part, the Provisional Revolutionary Committee sent Petrograd a wireless message demanding the release of the hostages held by the Communists in their over-crowded prisons — workers, sailors and families of the same — and that political detainees be set free too.

Our second message suggested that nonparty delegates be sent to Kronstadt so that, having seen for themselves what was afoot among us, they might tell the truth to the toiling masses of Petrograd.

Well now, what have the Communists done? They have concealed that message from the workers and Red soldiers.

A few of "Field Marshal" Trotsky's troop units, having defected to us, have passed on some Petrograd newspapers. Those newspapers contain not one word about our wireless messages!

And yet, not so long ago, these tricksters, used to playing with a marked deck, were shouting that one should have no secrets from the people, not even diplomatic secrets!

Listen, Trotsky! For as long as you can give the slip to the people's verdict, you can go on shooting innocents in batches. But you cannot gun down the truth. It will eventually find a way through. You and your "Cossacks" will then be forced to give an account of yourselves.

Reorganizing the Trade Unions

Under the Communists' dictatorship, the tasks of the trade unions and their steering commissions have been cut to a minimum.

During the revolutionary trade union movement's four years in "socialist" Russia, our trade unions had no opportunity to act as class bodies.

Not that that was in any way their fault. It was, in fact, the result of the ruling party's policy of seeking to educate the masses employing the centralistic, "Communist" approach.

When all is said and done, the trade unions' work was reduced to utterly useless minutes and correspondence, the object of which was to establish the membership figures of such and such a union and then to record the specialty of each member, his standing vis a vis the Party, etc.

As for economic activity along cooperative lines, or cultural education of the unions' worker membership, not a thing was done in those areas. Which was quite understandable. For, had the unions been given the right to engage in far-reaching independent activity, the entire centralist approach to construction followed by the Communists would, of necessity, have fallen apart, which would have resulted in a demonstration of the uselessness of the commissars and the "political sections."

It was these shortcomings that alienated the masses from the trade unions, the latter having eventually turned into a gendarmerie corps hobbling all authentic trade union activity by the toiling masses. Once the Communist Party dictatorship has been overthrown, the role of the union is going to have to change radically. The trade unions and their steering commissions, once re-elected, will have to tackle the great and urgent task of educating the masses for the economic and cultural renewal of the country. They will have to breathe a new and cleansing breath into their activities. They will have to become genuine vehicles of the people's interests.

The soviet Republic cannot be strong unless its administration is handled by the laboring classes, with the aid of revitalized trade unions.

To work, then, comrade workers! Let us build the new trade unions, free of all influence: therein lies our strength.

[No. 9, March 11, 1921] To the Worker and Peasant Comrades

Kronstadt has launched a heroic struggle against the Communists' odious power, on behalf of the emancipation of the workers and peasants.

Everything that is happening now was prepared by the Communists themselves: by their bloody, ruinous work over the past three years. Letters reaching us from the countryside are filled with complaints and curses on the Communists. Our comrades returning off furlough, seething with anger and indignation, have told us of horrors perpetrated by the Bolsheviks right across the land. In addition, we ourselves have seen, heard and felt everything that has been happening around us. A tremendous, heart-rending cry of distress was reaching us from the fields and towns of our vast Russia. It ignites outrage in our hearts and steels our arms.

We do not want a return to the past. We are neither lackeys of the bourgeoisie nor hirelings of the Entente. We are for the power of all toilers, but not for the unrestrained tyrannical authority of any party.

There are no Koltchaks[3], no Denikins and no Yudenitches operating in Kronstadt: Kronstadt is in the hands of the toilers. The good sense and consciousness of simple sailors, soldiers and workers of Kronstadt have at last found the words and the path that will allow us all to escape from the impasse.

To begin with, we sought to sort everything out by peaceable means. But the Communists have refused to back down. More than Nicholas II, they cling to their power, ready to drown the whole country in blood, if only they can rule as autocrats.

And now here we have Russia's evil genius, Trotsky, hurling our brothers against us. Hundreds of their corpses already litter the ice around the fortress. For four days now the fighting has been bitter, the cannons booming, the blood of brothers flowing. For four days, the heroes of Kronstadt have successfully repulsed all enemy attacks. Trotsky hovers over our heroic town like a sparrowhawk. But Kronstadt still stands. We are all ready to die rather than surrender.

Our enemies operate with "kursanty," special Communist guards and troops drafted in from far away, misinformed and threatened by machineguns in their rear. Comrade workers! Kronstadt fights on your behalf, on behalf of the famished, on behalf of the ragged and homeless. As long as the Bolsheviks remain in power, we will not see a better life. You support all that.

In the name of what? Just so that the Communists may live in comfort and so that the commissars may grow fat? Do they still have your confidence?

Informing the Petrograd soviet that the government had set aside millions of gold rubles for the purchase of various items, Zinoviev reckoned that it worked out at 50 rubles per worker. Behold, comrade workers, the price at which the Bolshevik clique hopes that it can buy each of you.

Comrade peasants! It is you whom the Bolshevik authorities have deceived and robbed the most. Where is the land that you took back from the landlords, after centuries of dreaming about it? In the hands of Communists, or worked by the sovkhozes. And as for you, you are left to gaze upon it and lick your lips over it.

They have taken from you everything that there was to take. You are marked down for pillage and utter ruination. You are worn out by Bolshevik serfdom. You have been obliged docilely to carry out the wishes of your new masters as they starve you and stop your mouths, leaving you in the filthiest poverty.

Comrades! Kronstadters have raised the banner of revolt in the hope that tens of millions of workers and peasants would answer their call.

The dawn breaking over Kronstadt must become a sun shining over the whole of Russia.

The Kronstadt eruption must breathe new life into the whole of Russia and, first and foremost, Petrograd.

Our enemies have filled their prisons with workers. But many honest, daring workers are still at large.

Comrades, stand up for the struggle against the absolutism of the Communists!

[No. 10, March 12, 1921] Our Generals

The Communists insinuate that generals, White Guardist officers and a priest are numbered among the members of the Provisional Revolutionary Committee.

In order to have an end of these lies once and for all, let us point out to them that the Committee comprises the fifteen members that follow:

1. Petritchenko, chief clerk aboard the 'Petropavlovsk.'
2. Yakovenko, telephonist, Kronstadt district.
3. Ossossoff, mechanic on the 'Sebastopol.'
4. Arhipoff, quarter-master mechanic.
5. Perepelkin, mechanic on the 'Sebastopol.'
6. Patrushev, quarter-master mechanic on the 'Petropavlovsk.'
7. Kupoloff, first-aid doctor.
8. Vershinin, seaman on the 'Sebastopol.'
9. Tukin, electrician.
10. Romanenko, guard in the naval repair yards.
11. Oreshin, employee of the 3rd Technical School.
12. Valk, joiner.
13. Pavloff, worker in the naval mine yards.

14. Baikoff, carter.
15. Kilgast, steersman.

[No. 12, March 14, 1921] We Must Follow the Pack

We could have waited until Lenin, in the midst of the toilers' struggle for their trampled rights, stopped being a hypocrite and learned to speak the truth.

Because, as they see things, the workers and peasants made a distinction between Lenin on the one hand and Trotsky and Zinoviev on the other.

No one believed a word from Zinoviev or Trotsky, but where Lenin is concerned, confidence in him had not yet been lost.

But...

March 8th saw the opening of the Tenth Congress of the Russian Communist Party. Lenin reiterated there all of the lies about rebel Kronstadt. He declared that the rebellion's watchword was "freedom of trade." True, he did go on to say that "the movement was for soviets, but against the Bolsheviks' dictatorship"; but he could not resist invoking "White generals and petit-bourgeois anarchist elements."

So, by uttering rubbish, Lenin confuses himself. He lets slip the admission that the basis of the movement was the fight for soviet power and against the Party's dictatorship. But, rather troubled, he adds:

> This is counter-revolution of another breed. It is extremely dangerous, however insignificant the would-be amendments to our policy may appear at first glance.

There is reason to worry. The blow struck by revolutionary Kronstadt is a hard one. The Party's leaders sense that the end of their autocracy is nigh.

Lenin's great preoccupation shines through all his speeches on Kronstadt. The word "danger" recurs constantly.

For instance, he has this to say, word for word:

> We must finish off this petit-bourgeois danger which is very dangerous for us for, instead of uniting the proletariat, it disunites it: we must have maximum unity.

Yes, the Communists' chief is obliged to quiver and call for "maximum unity." For the Communists' dictatorship and the Party itself show serious fissures.

Broadly speaking, is it possible for Lenin to speak the truth?

Recently, at a Communist debate on the trade unions, he stated:

All of this bores me to death. I have had it up to here. Quite apart from my illness, I would be happy to leave it all and flee anywhere!

But his partners will not let him flee. He is their prisoner. He has to slander as they do. And, in addition, the entire policy of the Party is put out by Kronstadt's action. For Kronstadt demands, not "freedom of trade," but true soviet power.

[No. 13, March 15, 1921] The Business House of Lenin, Trotsky and Co.

It has worked well, the business house of Lenin, Trotsky and Co.

The criminal, absolutist policy of the Communist Party in power has brought Russia to the edge of the abyss and brink of ruin. After which, you might think it would be time for it to take a back seat. Alas! it seems that the toilers have not shed enough tears and blood.

Even as the historic struggle boldly launched by revolutionary Kronstadt on behalf of the rights of the toiling people, (rights ridiculed and trampled underfoot by the Communists) raged, a flock of crows has decided to hold its "Tenth Party Congress." At which it works out how to carry on, with even more malice and success, its fratricidal work.

Their effrontery knows no bounds. Blithely they talk about "trade concessions."

Lenin very simply declares as follows:

"We are starting to operate the principle of concessions. The success of this undertaking does not depend on us. But we ought to do everything within our power." And then, he admits that the Bolsheviks have brought soviet Russia to a pretty pass: "For" — he said — "we will not be able to rebuild the country without resorting to foreign technology if we want to catch up economically, to some extent, with other countries. Circumstances have forced us to look abroad to purchase not just machinery but also coal, which, however, we have in abundance." He went on to say: "In future we will still have to make further sacrifices in order to get everyday consumer goods and also what the agrarian economy needs."

So where are the famous economic feats in the name of which the worker is turned into a slave in the State factory and the peasant laborer into a serf of the sovkhozes?

That is not all. Speaking of agriculture, Lenin promises even more "well-being," if the Communists carry on with their "economic functionarism" (which was his expression).

"And if, one day" — he continues — "we do manage to rebuild great rural economics and big industry here and there, it will only be by imposing further sacrifices upon every producer, while offering nothing in return."

So much for the "well-being" which the Bolsheviks' leader dangles as a carrot before all who might docilely bear the yoke of the commissars' absolutism.

He was fairly right, the peasant who told the Eighth Congress of Soviets:

"Everything is going very well. Except, whereas we get the land, you get the bread: we get the water, but the fish is yours: the forests belong to us, but the wood belongs to you."

That aside, the toiler need have no worry.

Lenin indeed promises "to award a few incentives to small employers, to expand a little the boundaries of the free economy." Like the "good old seigneur," he prepares "a few incentives" so as to clamp the toilers' necks even tighter into the vice of the Party's dictatorship later on. As is plain from this admission: "True, we will not be able to dispense with constraint, for the country is weary and in terrible poverty."

There we have it plain: we may have the last shirt off the pauper's back.

Which is how Lenin thinks of the task of construction: trade concessions at the top, taxes at the bottom.

The Benefits of the "Commune"

"Comrades! We are going to build a splendid new life." That is what the Communists used to say and write.

"We're going to destroy the world of violence and we will build a new, socialist, quite beautiful world." Which is how they used to serenade the people.

Let us examine the reality.

All the best houses, all the best apartments are commandeered as offices and sub-offices of Communist institutions. So only the bureaucrats are agreeably, comfortably and spaciously accommodated. The number of habitable lodgings has fallen. The workers have stayed where they were. They now live there in dire straits, in worse conditions than before.

Houses, not being maintained, are going to wreck and ruin. The heating is out of order. Broken windows are not replaced. The roofs are falling apart and water is starting to seep through. Fences collapse. Pipes are half wrecked. Toilets are out of order and their contents invade the apartments, forcing citizens to answer their needs in the yard or in a neighbor's place. Staircases are still unlighted: and covered in filth. The yards are full of excrement, on account of the latrines, rubbish bins, sewage outlets and spouting being neither repaired nor emptied. The streets are filthy. The pavements, which are never repaired, are grimy and slick. Walking the streets is dangerous.

To secure accommodation, one has to have a good "connection" in the lodgings office, in the absence of which, just forget it. Only the favored few have acceptable lodgings.

Things are even worse where provisions are concerned. Irresponsible, ignorant officials have let thousands of tons of produce spoil. The potatoes distributed are always frost-bitten; the meat, in the spring and summer, always 'off.' Once upon a time, we were reluctant to set before the pigs that which citizens today get from the "builders of the splendid new life."

For quite some time, it was "honest soviet fish," herring, that saved the situation. But now even herring is turning into a rarity,

Soviet shops are worse than the factory shops of dismal memory, where the industrialists used to serve up all sorts of shoddy goods and where their slave workers could not say a thing about it.

In order to destroy family life, those who govern us have invented the collective restaurant. With what result?

The food there is even less appetizing. Before reaching the citizenry who get only the leftovers, produce is skimmed off by every conceivable means. Children's food is a little better, but still very inadequate. Above all, there is a milk shortage. For their own sovkhozes, the Communists have requisitioned all of the peasant population's dairy cattle. And a half of these beasts die before arriving at their destination. Milk from the surviving cattle goes primarily to those in government and then to functionaries. Only the leftovers reach the children

But the hardest things of all to get hold of are clothing and footwear. Old clothes are worn or swapped. Virtually nothing is distributed. (For example, one of the trade unions is currently distributing buttons: one and a half buttons per head. Is that not poking fun at everybody?) As for shoes, there just aren't any to be had.

The path to the Communist paradise is a beautiful one. But can we tread it barefoot? Meanwhile, there are lots of cracks for all necessities to slip through. The associates of the so-called "cooperatives" and those in government own everything. They have their own restaurants and special rations. They can also avail of the "coupon offices" which distribute goods as the commissars deem fit.

We have finally come to realize that this "commune" has undermined and utterly disorganized productive labor. So any urge to work, any interest in work has evaporated. Shoe-makers, tailors, plumbers, etc., have thrown it all up and gone their separate ways, to work as watchmen, messengers, etc.

So much for the paradise that the Bolsheviks have set about building.

In place of the old one, a new system of arbitrariness, insolence, "cronyism," favoritism, theft and speculation has been erected — a ghastly regime wherein one is obliged to hold out one's hands to the authorities for every crumb of bread, every button; a regime wherein one is not one's own person, not free to do as one will; a regime of slavery and degradation.

[No. 14, March 16, 1921] Self-styled "Socialism"

In making the October Revolution, the sailors, Red soldiers, workers and peasants shed their blood for the power of the soviets, to build a toilers' Republic.

The Communist Party has taken careful note of the aspirations of the masses. Having etched upon its banners attractive slogans that evoke the toilers' enthusiasm, it drew them into the struggle and promised to lead them into the splendid reign of socialism which the Bolsheviks alone are supposed to know how to build.

The workers and peasants of course were gripped by boundless delight. "At last, slavery beneath the yoke of the landlords and capitalists can be consigned to the mythology books," they reckoned. It looked as if free labor's time had come in the countryside, in the factories and in the workshops. It looked as if power was about to pass into the toilers' hands.

Skillful propaganda drew children of the laboring people into the ranks of the Party, where they were subjected to strict discipline.

After which the Communists, sensible of their strength, progressively eliminated from power, first of all, the other socialist denominations, and then ousted actual workers and peasants from many State positions, while continuing to govern in their name.

In this way the Communists substituted for the power which they had usurped tutelage by commissars with all of the whimsicality of personal authority. Contrary to all reason and contrary to the toilers' wishes, they then set about doggedly building a State socialism, with slaves, instead of erecting a society founded upon free labor.

Industry being in utter disarray, in spite of "workers' control," the Bolsheviks carried out a nationalization of the factories and workshops." The worker was transformed from a capitalist's slave into the slave of the State enterprises. Soon, even that was not enough. There were plans for the introduction of the Taylor[4] system.

The toilers, en masse, were declared enemies of the people and lumped with the "kulaks." The highly enterprising Communists then set about ruining the peasants and launching soviet ventures, which is to say, estates belonging to that new agricultural profiteer, the State. That is the sum total of what the peasants got out of Bolshevik socialism, instead of the free labor on freed soil for which they had hoped.

In return for bread and livestock, which were requisitioned virtually in their entirety, they got Cheka raids and mass shootings. A fine system of exchange for a toilers' State: lead and bayonets instead of bread!

The life of the citizen became monotonous and deadly banal, regulated according to the prescriptions of the authorities. Instead of a life enlivened by free labor and the free evolution of the individual, there was born an unprecedented, unbelievable slavery. All independent thinking, all fair criticism of the deeds of our criminal governors became crimes, punishable by imprisonment and, often, death.

The death penalty, that disgrace to the human race, became commonplace in "the socialist homeland."

So much for the splendid kingdom of socialism to which the Communist Party's dictatorship has brought us.

We have had State socialism, with its soviets of hacks blithely voting for whatever the authorities and their infallible commissars dictate to them.

The watchword "Who does not work does not eat" has been amended under this splendid "soviet" regime to read "All power to the commissars!" As for the workers, peasants and brain-workers, well! they need only get on with their work in a prison-like atmosphere.

That became unbearable. Revolutionary Kronstadt has led the way in smashing its chains and ripping out the prison bars. It fights for the authentic soviet toilers' republic where the producer himself will become the master of the products of his labors and dispose of these as he sees fit.

Notes to The Official Journal of the Kronstadt Uprising

1. This newspaper had been launched well before the uprising of March 1921. A complete French translation of the issues of the paper which came out during the revolt was published by Editions Belibaste as *La Commune de Cronstadt* (1969)
2. F. Trepoff, one of the most ferocious of Tsar Nicholas II's generals, famous for having ordered his troops during the disturbances of 1905: "Don't spare the bullets!"
3. Admiral Alexis Koltchak (1874–1920) waged war on revolutionary Russia in Siberia (1918–1919) and was shot in 1920: General Nikolai Yudenitch (1862–1919) also headed a White army in 1918 1919, specifically a Cossack army, only to perish in battle against the Bolsheviks. For Denikin, see Volume II.
4. From the name of the American Frederick Winslow Taylor (1856–1915), a system for super-exploitation of the worker, bent upon introducing "more rational" organization of labor, by timing work in order to avert "time-wasting."

Petritchenko's Testimony[1]

I have read the correspondence that has passed between the Left Social Revolutionaries' organization on the one hand and the British Communists on the other. Also at issue in that correspondence is the question of the Kronstadt uprising of 1921.

As one who presided over the Kronstadt uprising I feel that I have a moral duty to educate the British Communist Party's political bureau about that happening. I know that you have been briefed by Moscow, and I know too that such briefings are one-sided and partisan. It would do no harm for you to hear the other side of the story too.

You yourselves have conceded that the 1921 Kronstadt uprising was not inspired by outsiders; putting this another way, that means that the patience of the toiling masses, sailors, Red soldiers, workers and peasants simply had run its course.

The people's wrath against the Communist Party dictatorship, or rather, against its bureaucracy, took the form of an uprising: so began the spilling of precious blood — it was not a matter of differences of class or caste — toilers stood on both sides of the barricades. The difference consisted solely of the Kronstadters acting in knowledge and free of constraint, whereas the attackers had been misled by the Communist Party leaders and acted under coercion. I am ready to say more to you: that Kronstadters had no stomach for taking up arms and spilling blood!

Now then, what happened that Kronstadters were forced to speak in the language of cannons with the Communist Party's dictators who styled themselves the "worker and peasant government?"

The Kronstadt sailors had an active hand in the establishment of that government: they protected it against attacks from the counter-revolution: they not only guarded the approaches to Petrograd, the heart of the worldwide revolution, but also formed military detachments for service on the countless fronts against the White Guards, starting with Kornilov and finishing with generals Yudenitch and Neklyudov. But lo! those very same Kronstadters are supposed to have suddenly become enemies of the revolution; the "worker and peasant government" has depicted them as Entente agents, French spies, stalwarts of the bourgeoisie, Social Revolutionaries, Mensheviks, etc.

It is astounding that the Kronstadters should have turned abruptly into dangerous enemies at the very moment when all threat from the generals of the counterrevolutionary army had evaporated; just when the time had come to set about rebuilding the country and reaping the fruits of October's gains, to set out one's stall in its true light and spread out one's political baggage (in that promises were not enough any more and there were promises to be delivered), when it was time to draw up a balance sheet of the revolution's gains, of which no one dared even dream while the civil war was in progress. That the Kronstadters should have turned out, right at that point, to be enemies? So, what crime had Kronstadt committed against the revolution?

Once the civil war fronts had been mopped up, the Petrograd workers reckoned that they could remind the city's soviet that it was now time to turn to their economic circumstances and switch from wartime arrangements to peace-time rule.

The Petrograd soviet took the view that this demand of the workers (a demand both harmless and essential) was counter-revolutionary. It remained deaf and dumb with regard to these demands, but embarked upon search and arrest operations against the workers, declaring them to be spies and Entente agents. These bureaucrats had been corrupted during the civil war, at a time when nobody dared resist. But they had failed to see that the circumstances had changed. The workers' response was to strike. The Petrograd soviet's fury was like that of a savage beast. Abetted by its **opritchniks**[2], it penned the famished, exhausted workers inside a ring of steel and used every conceivable means to force them back to work. For all their sympathy with the workers, military units (Red soldiers and sailors) did not dare stand up for them, for those in government had warned them that Kronstadt would attack anyone who dared oppose the soviet government. But on this occasion the "worker and peasant" government did not succeed in using Kronstadt as a bogeyman. Thanks to its geographical location, adjacent to Petrograd, Kronstadt had — albeit somewhat belatedly — nonetheless discovered how things really stood in the city.

So, British comrades, you are correct in saying that the Kronstadt revolt was not inspired by anyone. And I should like to know also, what shape did the support of Russian and foreign counterrevolutionary organizations for the Kronstadters take? Let me repeat once again that the revolt did not break out at the will of any political organization; and I believe, too, that none such even existed in Kronstadt. The revolt erupted spontaneously at the wish of the masses themselves, civilian population and garrison alike. We can see that in the resolution passed and in the make-up of the Provisional Revolutionary Committee. One cannot discern there the overwhelming expression of the wishes of any anti-soviet political party.

As Kronstadters saw it, everything that happened and was done was dictated by the circumstances of the moment. The rebels placed their hopes in nobody. Not the Provisional Revolutionary Committee, not the delegates' assemblies, nor the rallies — nor, indeed, was there any question of that. The Provisional Revolutionary Committee never made any move in that direction, although that had been feasible. The **Committee strove to carry out the** people's wishes scrupulously. Was this a good thing or bad? I cannot tell, but the fact of the matter is that the mass steered the Committee and not the other way around.

We did not have among us any famous militants capable of seeing everything underground to a depth of three **arshins**[3] and knowing everything that needs to be done in order to extract everything useful from it. The Kronstadters acted without plan or program, merely feeling their way within the parameters of their resolutions and according to circumstances. Cut off from the whole world, we had no idea what was going on outside Kronstadt, in soviet Russia or abroad. It is possible that certain people might have expected much of our insurrection, as is usually the case, but in our case their pains were in vain. We could not speculate about what would have happened had events taken a different turn, for the outcome would have been quite different from the one we had had in mind. **But Kronstadters had no intention of letting the initiative slip from their grasp.**

In their press, the Communists have accused us of having accepted an offer of provisions and medicines from the Russian Red Cross based in Finland. We have to say that we saw nothing wrong in that offer. Not only the Provisional Revolutionary Committee, but also the assembly of delegates had given their approval to it. We looked upon it as a purely philanthropic offering of inoffensive assistance, without any ulterior motives. When we decided to admit the (Red Cross) delegation to Kronstadt, we escorted them under blindfold to our headquarters.

At our first meeting, we told them that we were accepting their help with gratitude, given that it came from a philanthropic organization, but that we regarded ourselves as in no way beholden to them. We acceded to their request that they second a permanent representative to Kronstadt to oversee regular distribution of the provisions which their organization proposed to send us and which would have been for distribution primarily to the women and children. It was Captain Vilken[4] who stayed behind in Kronstadt: he was lodged in an apartment which was under permanent guard so that he could not budge without authorization. What danger did Vilken pose? All he could see was the morale of Kronstadt's garrison and civilian population.

Is there anything in that adding up to help from the international bourgeoisie? Or in the fact that Victor Chernov[5] had sent greetings to rebel Kronstadt? Does that add up to backing from the Russian and international counter-revolution? Are we really to believe that the Kronstadters threw themselves into the embrace of any anti-soviet political party? In fact, when the rebels learned that the Right had plans for their uprising, they had no hesitation in warning their comrades of the fact, as the editorial in the March 6 edition of the Kronstadt *Izvestia* bears witness.

Notes to Petritchenko's Testimony

1. Published in the January 1926 edition of *Znamya Borby*: taken from Ida Mett *La Commune de Cronstadt* (Editions Spartacus, 1938, new edition 1948).
2. **Opritchniks,** the personal guard of Tsar Ivan the Terrible and simultaneously the supreme political police. In the seven years (1565-1572) of its existence, its members earned a reputation for savagery. (Ida Mett's note).
3. **Arshin,** a Russian measure of length (Ida Mett).
4. Vilken was an officer in the former Russian navy (Ida Mett).
S. Victor Chernov (1876–1952), one of the leaders of the Social Revolutionary Party, was a government minister after the revolution of February 1917 and had to quit Russia in 1920.

ANARCHISTS BEHIND BARS (SUMMER 1921)

by Gaston Leval

Gaston Leval, (born in 1895) son of a Communard and himself a French anarcho-syndicalist militant, was a participant in the foundation congress of the Red International of Labor Unions in June-August 1921 in the wake of the third congress of the Communist International, as a delegate from the Spanish CNT. During his time in Moscow, his attention turned to the fate of imprisoned Russian anarchists.

Once I discovered that there were so many of our comrades in prison, I arranged, together with the French syndicalist delegates to make overtures to Dzerzhinsky, the People's Commissar for the Interior, implicitly obedient to Lenin. Being wary of me, my fellow delegates chose Joaquin Maurin[1] to speak on behalf of the CNT delegation. Maurin reported back on their first audience. At the sight of the list of the prisoners whose release was being sought, Dzerzhinsky[2] blanched, then went red with fury, arguing that these men were counterrevolutionaries in cahoots with the White generals; he accused them of having derailed trainloads of Red Army troops and of being responsible for the deaths of thousands of soldiers, in the Ukraine especially.

We were unable to probe any further into what had happened and Maurin and his friends among our delegation won the day. Not that I gave up, any more, indeed, than a number of delegates of other nationalities did, and we pressed on with our lobbying. Not a single piece of evidence had been adduced to back Dzerzhinsky's claims, not so much as one criminal indictment. No indictment, no trial, no judges, let alone defense lawyers — there was none of that. Whatever the "people's commissar," whose job it was to defend the regime, might have said, this was a case of arbitrary imprisonment.

We persisted. As my fellow delegates took the line that it was hopeless and banished the matter from their minds, they at last left it to me to take formal charge of it. The people's commissar for Public Education, Lunacharsky[3], visibly discomfited by the role he was forced to play in the name of party discipline, was despatched to us on two occasions but, being unable to take any decisions, he merely acted as an intermediary, receiving and passing on requests and responses. After Lunacharsky, they sent us Ulrikh[4], a significant and mysterious bigwig from the prosecution office. This again was a waste of time and the weeks slipped by. They were assuredly determined to wear us down.

I regularly went to see Emma Goldman and Alexander Berkman. Through their two rooms paraded the wives whose spouses were imprisoned. Worried and distraught, they sometimes broke down in tears. And I listened to the odyssey, the lives of these men who had fallen victim to the so-called socialist State. Victor Serge himself, who from time to time sincerely kept a foot in both camps, and carried on writing articles in the western press in favor of the regime, filled me in on their background. Maximoff was an anarcho-syndicalist theoretician of stature, incapable of perpetrating an act of anti-soviet sabotage. Yartchuk was the erstwhile secretary of the soviet in Kronstadt where Zinoviev had sought refuge when Kerensky ordered him arrested. Voline, the *bête noire* of government circles, was an anarcho-syndicalist theoretician, a lecturer, a gifted writer who had been living in exile at the time of the revolution against tsarism. Such and such was now in prison, someone else banished to Siberia. And all of these authentic revolutionaries were now languishing in jails which some of them, such as Maria Spiridonova[5], had occupied years earlier.

We sought permission to visit them and although we were delegates from trade union organizations which it was hoped to win over, permission was denied. I remember that in the Spain of Alfonso XIII, where I had come from, and during one of the most fearful repressions that country ever experienced, aside from the Franco era, we were still able to visit prisoners, unless they were being held in secret. In the Modelo prison in Valencia and in the one in Barcelona, my friends had had no difficulty in seeing me. They had only to ask for me during visiting hours and the warders would escort me down to the visiting room. In the villages of Spain through which I passed later I was always able to visit my imprisoned comrades. In the Russia of Lenin and Trotsky, this was impossible. Most of the delegates did not press the matter — not knowing what else to do — but I stuck to my guns. Accusations were not enough. We were offered no proof and there were too many valid challenges contradicting the authorities' allegations. I was intent upon having proof.

Among the female comrades whom I met at Emma Goldman's place was Olga Maximoff[6], a thin, thirty year old brunette of average height, drained by her ordeals. She had met her spouse while a deportee in Siberia under tsarism, his circumstances being the same. She suggested to me that I enter the Butyrky prison the next day to speak with our comrades. I would go in with her and other prisoners' wives and would be supplied with Russian papers to get me past the guards. I might fail, but I agreed to chance it. The following day, off I went with four comrades who were traveling as a party. Their bare feet slipped upon the small cobbles and gravel of the city streets. Two of them carried, hanging from their shoulders, a huge canvas bag containing a few provisions obtained with great difficulty. The youngest of them, Yartchuk's wife, had fought on the barricades in Petrograd and Moscow, in order to bring down first tsarism and then the Kerensky government.

At the entrance to the prison, there was a female sentry on duty. She knew my female comrades and barely glanced at their visiting permits. I handed her my papers without uttering a word and she returned them to me with the comment "Da," to which I responded with a smile. Two of the women engaged her in conversation about something while I wandered off with the others.

We crossed a courtyard and entered the visiting room. The comrades called out the names of the prisoners whom they wished to see, Voline included. The gap between the visitors and the inmates was no bar to almost direct contact, and no member of staff, or policeman, listened in on the conversations, which, for me, was confirmation that this was a case of preventive detention, with no inquiry and no court proceedings involved.

In came the prisoners. "This is Gaston Leval," one of the women told Voline, a man of average height, around forty five years of age, wearing a black beard and with the splendid head of a Jewish intellectual.

My name was known to him because he had heard tell of me. Effusively, he shook my hand, speaking to me in very correct French. Then, at the risk of startling him and looking a bit ridiculous, but because I was keen to conduct an utterly impartial investigation, I asked him to brief me in detail about what he had been up to since his return to Russia.

Over an hour or an hour and a half, with painstaking precision, while I made notes, Voline explained his work as a propagandist and fighter. After a tour of the prison system, Voline had wound up in Butyrky. He related his odyssey to me in a very detailed manner, rehearsing the facts, dates, names, towns and villages. And, along with the rest of the prisoners, he demanded a public trial.

(. . .) I returned to the Lux Hotel, determined to carry on the campaign to release my comrades. But by the time the congress of the Red International of Labor Unions opened, we had not moved forward by a single concession, promise or hope. On five or six occasions already we had met with delegates from the Soviet authorities and on every occasion relations had been broken off or suspended without result. They were sticking to the tactics of attrition.

Then the comrades in the Butyrky embarked upon a hunger strike. They smuggled out a manifesto written in French in which they asked syndicalist delegates to lobby the Russian authorities on behalf of their release and freedom of thought and expression for all revolutionaries. But the disheartened delegates to whom they appealed merely deplored the strike which was an embarrassment to them. Three, four and five days passed. I could do nothing at the congress. Marginalized by my fellow-delegates and unused as I was — on account of the clandestine activity to which I had been condemned thus far — to maneuvers and counter-maneuvers, commissions and backstairs lobbying, I was reduced to inactivity and powerlessness. Although more coherent and, for the most part, oppositionist, the French delegation was likewise unable to do much more. Our comrades pressed on with their hunger strike. We were told that in Orel and in other towns whose names I cannot now recall, there were similar strikes and that two or three of the strikers had perished.

Which was not impossible, for all of Russia's jails were bulging with prisoners who had been prompted to protest by the international congresses, in the hope that their voices might reach beyond the borders of Bolshevik Russia. What else was there for them to do?

Five days, six days, seven days. One or two delegates made isolated efforts but all to no avail. At Emma Goldman's and Alexander Berkman's apartments could I still see our comrades' womenfolk, distraught and tormented and occasionally in tears in that news of executions might arrive at any time. Olga Maximoff arrived to tackle me again at the congress and, knowing no French, she tugged at my jacket while repeating in tones of supplication and with pleading eyes that I can still hear and see; "Comrade Leval, Comrade Leval!"

Seven days, eight days, nine days! We were distraught, not knowing where to turn. And I found the opposition delegates powerless and disheartened. Others, powerless to do anything, even took our comrades to task for having exploited their presence and placed them in an uncomfortable position.

Finally, on the eleventh day, after one final plea from dear, good Olga Maximoff, I managed to persuade two or three delegations at the congress to make a supreme effort. Others followed suit. Shortly afterwards around fifteen of us set off for the Kremlin. We were off to speak with the master of Russia, Lenin.

Arriving outside one of the perimeter gates at the Kremlin, we ran into the guards. One of us, Michel Kneller[7], a Russian-speaker, explained our desire to see "tovaritch" Lenin. Note was taken of our names and of the foreign delegations represented. Telephone calls, waiting. After a quarter of an hour, a positive response. Two troopers, Chekists no doubt, escorted us through the maze of streets. We passed palaces and sumptuous mansions and chapels in the ancient residence of Rurik.[8] Outside the building where Lenin was, we bumped into another guard who refused to let us proceed any further. We explained who we were. But he had had no orders. We had to write another note re-applying for an audience with comrade Lenin, who sent us, in reply, another note in rather flawed French, asking us to be specific as to the object of our visit and apologizing for the fact that he could not receive us, being swamped with work. We scribbled a further note, signed by every one of us in turn. We represented around ten foreign trade union organizations, which must have counted for something in the reckonings of the tactician who missed nothing. And back came the Chekist trooper, bearing, at last, one last note from Lenin, who agreed to see us.

We were shown up to the first floor, into a room where we waited for a long time, curious and on edge. Then a door opened behind us and Lenin appeared, quite small, with a Mongoloid face, eyes squinting and grinning in icy irony.

One by one, he shook hands with us all, asking our name and the delegation to which we belonged. And while he questioned us, and we answered, he fixed us in his amused, penetrating gaze with disconcerting indifference.

Then he invited us to go through to an adjoining room and be seated around a huge rectangular table. He took his own seat. Tom Mann[9], the English trade union delegate and the most prominent figure among us, sat near him and spelled out, in English, the purpose of our visit. We had made up our minds to seek, not just the release of our comrades jailed in the Butyrky, but of all left-wing revolutionaries. In English, Lenin answered our spokesman who heard him out attentively, his face all intelligence, smiling and ruddy: in the end, seemingly convinced, he nodded his agreement. Whereupon the master of the Kremlin translated his reply into French.

He reiterated the charges made by Dzerzhinsky, announcing that our overtures were out of place. Those in prison were not true anarchists nor idealists — just bandits abusing our good intentions. The evidence for this was that there were anarchists, real ones, collaborating with the Bolsheviks and holding official positions. And he came to Voline "who, with Makhno, has had trains derailed in the Ukraine and butchered thousands of Red Army soldiers and allied himself with the White general, Denikin, against the Bolsheviks."

On this particular matter, I was in possession of rather detailed information. Among other things, the testimony of one Red Army general who had been in the Ukraine when these things had happened and who had talked at length with our delegation in one of the rooms at the Lux Hotel. He had been categorical: "Makhno has never allied himself with the Whites against us. At times, he fought the Whites and us simultaneously, but it cannot be said that he was in cahoots with the Whites." I remember too that Voline had been in charge of propaganda and cultural affairs in districts recaptured from the Austro-Hungarian armies and counterrevolutionary generals and not of directing military operations. And if Makhno had fought the Red army, it was because Trotsky had attacked the Ukrainian revolutionary forces unwilling to kowtow to Bolshevik despotism. For, when all was said and done, the Communist Party was one of the revolutionary parties and the others had a right to defend themselves against its attempts to ride roughshod over everyone.

So I interrupted Lenin, not abruptly but clearly and firmly. I had, I told him, spoken with Voline in the Butyrky prison "to which I had gained access perfectly legally, I might add" (Lenin made a gesture indicating "very well, I do not doubt it"). And I repeated, item by item, all that I knew of my imprisoned comrade's activities. I talked for a quarter of an hour, citing dates, facts and names. Lenin heard me out attentively, eyes squinting and with a long face which made him look somewhat rat-like, staring at me curiously. Once I had finished, he was visibly rattled. But, too cute to show that he had been beaten, he picked his words, and crafted his phrases and circumlocution to buy time to recover: — Yes, obviously... if things are as you say, that is a horse of a different color... I must seek additional information about Voline... I was not aware of these very important details....

He carried on falteringly, for the point — as far as he was concerned — was not to give ground. I had bushwhacked the fellow! Finally, he improvised:

> As you appreciate, today we face a very special situation. Folk who yesterday were revolutionaries have become counterrevolutionaries and we are compelled to fight them. Look at Plekhanov, the founding father of socialism in Russia. To one of our comrades who was leaving Switzerland, bound for Russia, he said: "This vermin must be crushed!" The Bolshevik State has to struggle against these new enemies. The State is a machine for which we are answerable and we cannot allow its operation to be frustrated. Voline is highly intelligent, which makes him all the more dangerous and we must take the most strenuous steps against him. After all, along with Makhno he has played along with the White generals Denikin and Koltchak by having Red Army troop trains derailed.

The other delegates were less well informed than me and did not quibble. For they were *au fait* with certain things and had learned that one could not speak up without risking assassination at the hands of "White

Guards" on the border. Even so, they spoke up about the matter of freedom of expression for all revolutionary denominations and for the freeing of all political prisoners, across the board. While they were talking, Lenin, just as he had done with Tom Mann, and as he had done while I was speaking, stared hard at them, ever ironic, as if entertained, moving his bald head and little beard up and down, up and down. Or else, with his right cheek resting on his hand, he seemed absorbed in examination of the ceiling. So much so that, disconcerted and realizing that it was pointless to proceed, the champion of freedom and humanity simply dried up or stopped short.

The audience lasted for around three quarters of an hour, at the end of which time Lenin announced that rights for the revolutionary opposition were out of the question. The comrades on the Politburo would certainly refuse that. All that he could do was look into the cases of the hunger strikers, but it was not up to him to decide. That was a matter for the Politburo upon which he could not, in any case, impose his view, for decisions were made democratically by a majority.

Lenin lied, and we pretended to swallow his lies in order to avoid a brutal falling-out. There was playacting on both sides. And, at his request, I drew up a note in which we called upon "Comrade Lenin" to present to the Politburo our request that those on hunger strike in the Butyrky prison be released. Just them. Lenin promised to let us have the answer the next day, at ten o'clock, in the room of the French delegate Sirolle[10]. And we parted after a hand-shake, accompanied by a final probing and ironic stare.

The following day, the answer did not come until noon, which was not a good omen. Signed, not by Lenin but by Trotsky, who had the candor to acknowledge his responsibilities. A categorical refusal to free the hunger strikers. The sole firm suggestion? That they be expelled from Russia. Followed by a lecture on the necessity of learning to take account of revolutionary responsibilities and not accede to superficial sentiments when the higher interests of the revolution were at stake.

What could we do other than accept? We could not resume our overtures to high ranking persons already approached, who would doubtless not even have agreed to receive us. And that could have backfired on our comrades to whom we passed on the solution that had been offered. On the positive side, they would get out of prison. They would be expelled from their own country — quite a symbol.

For the other prisoners, the other parties, we could do nothing now.

The congress finished a few days later. Delegates to'ed and fro'ed in the streets of Moscow. We were invited to attend theater shows. At the opera, Chalyapin sang for us: ballets were mounted for us, and there were splendid gymnastic displays on the banks of the Moskova. Few delegates took notes.

But two weeks had passed and our comrades were still in prison in spite of the deal signed between the delegates and Lunacharsky, stipulating that they were to be freed and expelled from Russia. From the Russia from which some of them had had to flee in tsarist times, and where they had returned so brimful of hope when the revolution broke out. We did not trust the word of the Bolshevik leadership with whose dishonesty we were familiar and we wondered whether they were not waiting for us to leave in order to keep our comrades, who were also impatient, behind bars.

But Trotsky had it announced to the French delegation that he would one evening call to Sirolle's room on a friendly visit. The Italian and Spanish syndicalists were alerted and we decided to avail of the occasion to press for details about the implementation of the agreement signed.

A very handsome, intelligent, energetic and supercilious man, Trotsky showed up took a seat in our midst and spoke in French about various aspects of the fight being waged against the White generals and the economic straits in which the new Russia found itself. Regarding bureaucracy, which we thought a frightful danger, he said that, if he could, he would load whole ships with bureaucrats and sink them in the sea without hesitation. But the problem was not that simple. He regretted that and could not prevent it.

Other matters were broached — including the revolutionary movement in France, the policy of the CGT and the treachery of the western trade union leaders. We were in all but complete agreement, for Trotsky charmed us with his persuasive arguments and the explanations he offered. But deep-down, we were waiting for an opening to raise the topic dearest to our hearts and it seemed that he had guessed as much, for he talked unendingly of the most diverse matters. Just as he was about to leave, we raised what he assuredly had been hoping to avoid.

Whereupon he raised his eye-brows, and half-smiling, half in anger, he began by saying that it might be better not to spoil this interview by broaching our intervention on behalf of the imprisoned Russian anarchists, which was not the best thing that we had done in Russia, that we ought not to brag about it to our country's workers when we got home, that we had been deceived and that our primary duty ought to have been trust in the Soviet government. Then, changing tone and concealing his wrath from the delegates whose smiles were visibly false, he assured us that his promise would be honored.

That seemed too vague. And with the support of Arlandis,[11] I asked when it would be honored, when our comrades would get out of prison.

Then I watched as Trotsky drew himself up to his full height, inflated his chest, raising his arms while clenching his fists and, in an explosion of rage, asked me, in a near scream:

Who are you to ask me, and I don't know you, when I am going to implement the decisions I have made?

Then, seizing me by the lapels of my jacket, he added, in the same tone:

We Bolsheviks have made our revolution, and what have you done? It is not your place to give us orders, and we have nothing to learn from you!

What other phrases he uttered I cannot recall now. I was so startled, surprised and dumbfounded by this outburst that, right then and there, I could not think of an answer. I will even admit that I felt the blood drain from my face. Then, I calmly told him:

No need to answer in that tone, comrade Trotsky. We are quite within our rights to ask you a question!

The other delegates stepped in, trying to calm him down. Trotsky reiterated that he would honor his word.

Before I left, I bade good-bye to many comrades still at large, all of whom were to perish in the jails or isolators that prefigured the concentration camps. I shook hands with Voline and his friends, freed from the Butyrky prison at last and departed for Berlin, via Riga.

The revolution which had loomed after the world-wide slaughter like the dawn of liberation for the international proletariat and the whole of mankind now appeared to us as one of the deadliest threats to the future of the peoples. The methodical police terror, the Party's tightening grip upon the whole of social life, the systematic annihilation of all non-Bolshevik currents, the no less systematic extermination of all revolutionaries who thought along lines different from those of the new masters, and indeed the eradication of every hint of dissent within the Party all proved that we were on the road to a new despotism that was not merely political but also intellectual, mental and moral, reminiscent of the darkest days of the Middle Ages.

Notes to Anarchists Behind Bars (Summer 1921)

1. Joaquin Maurin (born 1897), the founder, successively, of the Communist Federation of Catalonia, then, after his break with Moscow, of the Worker and Peasant Bloc (1931) and then of the Workers' Party of Marxist Unification-POUM (1935: both teacher and trade union activist with the CNT: spent fifteen years in prison under the Primo de Rivera dictatorship and then under Franco: moved to the United States.

2. Felix Dzerzhinsky (1877–1926), of aristocratic extraction, a Lithuanian Social Democrat from 1895, arrested and convicted several times, freed from prison by the 1917 Revolution: founded the political police, the Cheka (later the GPU); died of a heart attack.
3. Anatol Lunacharsky (1873–1933) writer and literary critic. Social Democrat from 1898, turned Bolshevik in 1903, Commissar for Education from 1917 to 1929.
4. Ulrikh was to be shot during the Stalinist purges.
5. Maria Spiridonova (born 1889), active terrorist, sentenced to death for the execution of a provincial governor, a sentence commuted to life imprisonment: raped and tortured while being transferred to Siberia: after February 1917, leader of the Left Social Revolutionaries: implicated in their rebellion in July 1918: imprisoned from 1919 or 1920: never released thereafter.
6. Olga Maximoff, wife of G.P. Maximoff.
7. Michel Kneller, a French activist who, in 1919, fired revolver shots at the Elysee Palace in protest at the blockade on soviet Russia: delegate from the French CCT to the foundation congress of the Red International of Labor Unions. A Communist sympathizer with syndicalist leanings: subsequently became a left-wing "abundancist."
8. Rurik, founder of the Russian Empire, died in 879.
9. Tom Mann (1856–1941) English mechanic, secretary of the Independent Labor Party in 1894: joined the American revolutionary syndicalist Industrial Workers of the World (IWW): took part in the founding of the Communist Party of Great Britain in 1921.
10. Henri Sirolle (born 1886) joint secretary of the Rail Federation in 1920: a versatile anarcho-syndicalist: at the first congress of the CCTU in Saint-Etienne in July 1922, reporting on his experiences as a delegate in Moscow in 1921, he told how, at an audience with Lenin, the latter had shown him a few files on anarchists and that he, Sirolle, had concluded from these... that they deserved to die! Ended up in charge of Marshal Petain's Secours National.
11. One of the Spanish trade union delegates accompanying Gaston Leval.

ANARCHISM IN THE SPANISH CIVIL WAR

The reader will already have encountered the Spanish Revolution of 1936 (in Volume III of this anthology) in connection with its experiments in social reconstruction, described at the time as collectives, but which might be referred to today as self-management.

It only remains to offer a number of readings dealing with the Spanish anarchists' political and military role in the civil war. Some of these documents relate to the years between 1919 and the revolutionary victory on July 19, 1936. There are indications of the clash between Spanish anarcho-syndicalism and Bolshevism even then.

After that, we turn to the great guerrilla Buenaventura Durruti who, to borrow his own words, "made revolution and war simultaneously." The reader can thus get some notion of the Spanish libertarians' all too little known conception of self-discipline and revolutionary warfare. Durruti was another Makhno. Indeed, he had made the exiled Russian guerrilla's acquaintance in Paris and had been able to benefit from Makhno's advice, straight from his own lips.

Finally, we will turn to the anarchists' participation in government, in two governments in fact, the (autonomous) government of the Generalidad of Catalonia and the (central) government based first in Madrid and then in Valencia. Such participation, needless to say, flew in the face of the fundamental principles of "apolitical" anarchism, and, even in libertarian quarters, provoked heated arguments which have not abated to this very day.

Anarchism in Spain from 1919 to 1936

The CNT and the Third International

The texts below reveal that there was not always an unbridgeable gulf between the Bolshevik and the anarcho-syndicalist versions of social revolution. When the prestige of the recent October Revolution, victorious but suffering onslaughts on all sides from the world-wide reaction, stood at its highest point, the Spanish National Confederation of Labor (CNT), drawn like a moth to a lamp, made up its mind to participate, on a provisional basis at any rate, in the sessions of the Communist International in Moscow. But quite quickly, fundamental differences of outlook surfaced as Russian Bolshevism increasingly showed its sectarian, overbearing face, and the breakdown was not long in coming.

It is to be noted that this trend mirrored the experience of a number of French revolutionary syndicalists of the stripe of Pierre Monatte, who, after having pledged allegiance to Moscow, rather speedily came to the conclusion that they had been mistaken and distanced themselves once and for all from the Kremlin and from the French Communist Party alike.*

The December 1919 Congress of the CNT[1]

The CNT's national congress was held in Madrid from December 10 to 18, 1919. It dealt with three major issues: amalgamation of the Spanish proletariat's trade union centrals (defeated by 325,955 votes to 169,125, with 10,192 abstentions), a new organizational format based upon national federations of industry (rejected by 651,472 votes to 14,008) and a statement of libertarian communist principles (carried unanimously by acclamation).

But the most important debate was the one that focused upon the stance to be adopted with regard to the Russian revolution. Several ideas had been put forward:

What action might we take to lend support to the Russian revolution and circumvent the blockade (. . .) by the capitalist States?

Ought we to affiliate to the Third trade union International?

Should the Confederation affiliate forthwith to the International, and which one? Several propositions were accepted, including the following:

> The National Confederation of Labor declares itself a staunch
> defender of the principles upheld by Bakunin in the First

---

* See *Syndicalisme revolutionnaire et communisme. Les archives de Pierre Monatte* (1969).

International. It declares further that it affiliates provisionally to the Third International on account of its predominantly revolutionary character, pending the holding of the International Congress in Spain, which must establish the foundations which are to govern the true workers' International.

(...) Angel Pestaña[2] was charged to travel to Russia in order to attend the second congress of the Third International and communicate the decisions taken by the confederal congress.

Notes to The December 1919 Congress of the CNT

1. Extract from José Peirats, *La CNT en la revolucion espanola* 2 vols., 1958.
2. Angel Pestaña (1886–1937), watch-maker, moved from the secretariat of the Metalworkers' Union to the CNT national secretaryship in 1914: along with Salvador Segui, he had been behind the resurgence of Spanish anarcho-syndicalism between 1916 and 1923: after 1931, he was the leading light within the CNT of the reformist current known as the "Thirty" and was expelled. In 1934 he launched a Syndicalist Party which he represented in the Spanish parliament up to 1936: he died after an illness.

THE SECOND CONGRESS OF THE COMMUNIST INTERNATIONAL (JUNE 1920)[1]

The Third International's second congress opened on 28 June 1920 in its headquarters in Moscow. Straight off, Zinoviev moved that the Spanish Confederation be accepted as a member of the Third International's Executive Committee, which was agreed.

Comrade Lozovsky[2] in turn moved that a revolutionary trade union International be organized. To that end, he read out a document which declared: "In most of the belligerent countries, most of the trade unions had been supporters of neutrality (apoliticism) during the grievous war years: they had been the slaves of imperialist capitalism and had played a poisonous role in delaying the emancipation of the toilers (...); the dictatorship of the bourgeoisie must be countered by the dictatorship of the proletariat, the only one capable of breaking the resistance of the exploiters and thereby ensure that the conquest of power by the proletariat is consolidated, as the only decisive, transitional method."

Following upon which the congress decided to:

Condemn all tactics designed to remove vanguard elements from existing trade union organizations, and instead radically to remove from the leadership of the trade union movement opportunists who had collaborated with the bourgeois by embracing the war:

(. . .) Wage methodical propaganda inside trade union organizations the world over, establishing within each one a communist cell which might eventually impose its viewpoint.

(. . .) Create an international action and campaign committee to overhaul the trade union movement. That committee will operate as an international council of labor unions in conjunction with the executive committee of the Third International, observing conditions to be prescribed by congress. That council will comprise representatives from all affiliated national labor organizations.

(. . .) When my turn to speak came, I stated: 'Three items from the document will be the focus of a quick and concrete scrutiny, in that the organizations which I represent have espoused a stance which quite distances them from this document; those three items are:

1) Apoliticism; 2) the conquest of power; and, 3) the dictatorship of the proletariat.

(. . .) In effect, apoliticism is, in this document, damned by some trade union organizations, when virtually all of the trade union organizations which took a hand in the imperialist war were politicized, which runs counter to what this document asserts (. . .) So where is the logic in this document? The remaining two items relate to the conquest of power and dictatorship of the proletariat (. . .) A few words would suffice to spell out the thinking of the Confederation which I am here to represent with regard to these two matters. On this score, let me remind you that at the Confederation's first congress held in Madrid during the second fortnight of December last year, it was decided unanimously by the five hundred delegates present that the ultimate objective was the establishment of libertarian communism.

(. . .) Let me add a couple of words more on the article commending close collaboration with the politicized communist proletariat.

The Confederation is agreeable to cooperation with all revolutionary organizations fighting against the capitalist regime, while reserving the right, however, to do so as it sees fit. I do not think, indeed, that the Confederation would consent to act if its freedom of action were called into question (. . .)

There was no discussion of paragraphs one or two. In the course of discussion of paragraph three, I reaffirmed that we were apolitical and that we had to resist war by whatever means and that it was flying in the face of reason to endorse a document that condemned our action and our principles. In the end, it was agreed that the phrasing of the paragraph should be amended.

Paragraph four was the focus of protracted discussion, for several of us argued the case for complete trade union autonomy. In the end, after endless debate [the document was signed by five of the seven delegates present].

I was in a very delicate position, given that the Confederation had affiliated to the Third International. I could hardly repudiate a document which it had accepted. So I had to fall in line with the majority.

(...) However, when I came to sign that document, I wrote: Angel Pestaña "of the" National Confederation of Labor, instead of the conventional practice of signing as Angel Pestaña for the National Confederation of Labor. Thereby discharging my responsibility. When I was called as a speaker, I reminded delegates that they were already conversant with my differences with regard to the conquest of power and dictatorship of the proletariat, and that these positions were not personal to me, but reflected the Confederation's position.

I announced that, this being the case, if the majority forced me to agree to the document as it stood, I would sign it but would first issue the following caution:

> Everything having to do with conquest of political power, dictatorship of the proletariat and cooperation with the Communist political proletariat remains subject to further decisions to be made by the Confederation upon my return to Spain, and the Confederal Committee has been briefed about everything decided at this gathering.

The same thing applied to the summons due to be issued to trade union organizations the world over. It was indicated in that summons that those national and international trades' unions, local and regional unions which accepted revolutionary class struggle were invited to attend the conference.

I was not in agreement either with (...) this summons which (...) ruled out lots of organizations that would have liked to attend the conference but which were not in agreement with dictatorship or with the conquest of power. That, in my view, was a mistake (...)

Notes to The Second Congress of the Communist International (June 1920)

1. Angel Pestaña's account.

2. Salomon Lozovsky (1878–1952), worker and Bolshevik from 1903: in 1909 he emigrated and was active in the French labor movement up until 1917. Leader of the Textile Workers' Union within which he conducted oppositionist trade union activity. After 1919 he became a slavish hack. Chairman of the Red International of Labor Unions (Profintern) from 1921 to 1937.

A "Pantomime" Congress[1]

Pestaña contends that the Communists agreed to revise the phrasing of the document with regard to dictatorship of the proletariat, but while the Spanish delegate was momentarily absent, the document was issued in its original format and with Pestaña's signature. Of the progress of the congress itself, Pestaña says that the struggle that broke out over the appointment of a chairman took up all its attention. But he soon realized that the congress itself was a pantomime. The chair made the rules, amended propositions as it saw fit, turned the agenda upside down and tabled propositions off its own bat. The way in which it manipulated the congress was thoroughly abusive: Zinoviev delivered a speech lasting an hour and a half, even though no speech was to have exceeded ten minutes in duration.

Pestaña made to reply to that speech, but he was 'guillotined' after ten minutes by the chairman brandishing a watch. Pestaña himself was criticized by Trotsky in another speech that lasted over three quarters of an hour, and when Pestaña made to reply to the attacks leveled at him by Trotsky, the chairman wound up the proceedings. He also had to register a protest at the manner in which rapporteurs were appointed. In theory, every delegate was free to table a motion, but the chair itself selected the ones that were "interesting." Proportional voting [by delegation or delegate] had been provided for, but was not implemented. The Russian Communist Party ensured that it enjoyed a comfortable majority.

To top it all, certain important decisions were not even made in the congress hall, but were made behind the scenes. Which is how the following text came to be adopted:

> In forthcoming world congresses of the Third International, the national trade union organizations affiliated to it are to be represented by delegates from each country's Communist Party.

Objections to this decision were quite simply ignored. Pestaña left Russia on September 6, 1920, after a short exchange of impressions with Armando Borghi[2] (. . .) the delegate from the Italian Syndicalist Union (USI), who returned to Italy disheartened by this unfortunate experience. But before they left Moscow, both would have been aware of the circular issued regarding the organization of the Red International of Labor Unions. If, in the forthcoming congress of the Third International, the intention was to guarantee the Communist parties ascendancy over the trade union organizations, it could be supposed that the green light would have been given for the affiliated labor organizations inside the trade union International. But this unfortunate project for a Red International of Labor Unions demonstrated the very opposite. That plan was as follows:

1. A special Committee is to be organized in each country by the Communist Party there.
2. That Committee will take charge of receiving and distributing to all trade union organizations circulars and publications from the Red international organization.
3. The Committee is to appoint the editors of the trades and revolutionary newspapers, inculcating into them the viewpoint of this International as against the rival International.
4. The Committee is to commit its own resources to intervention and debate.
5. The Committee will work in close concert with the Communist Party, though a separate body.
6. The Committee will help to convene conferences at which matters of international organization are to be discussed and will select orators with a talent for propaganda.
7. In the composition of the Committee, preference must be given to Communist comrades. Elections are to be supervised by the Communist Party.
8. In a country where this approach cannot be followed, Communist Party emissaries are to be despatched to create a similar organization."

Notes to A "Pantomime" Congress

1. Taken from José Peirats, op. cit.
2. Armando Borghi (1882–1968), general secretary of the Italian Syndicalist Union, an anarcho-syndicalist labor organization, traveled to Russia in 1920 and had met Lenin there: his most important book is *Mezzo secolo de Anarchia (1898–1945)*.

THE SPANISH REVOLUTION (1936) IN RESPONSE TO FASCISM: A GENERAL STRIKE!

(July 19, 1936)

People of Catalonia! Be on the alert! Be on a war footing! The time to act is upon us. We have spent months upon months criticizing fascism, denouncing its blemishes and issuing watchwords to get the people to rise up when the time comes against the poisonous reaction in Spain which will attempt to impose its repulsive dictatorship. People of Catalonia, that time has come: the reaction (the military, the clergy, and the large banks), all of them hand in hand, aims to introduce fascism in Spain with the aid of a military dictatorship. We, the authentic representatives of the CNT in Catalonia, consistent with our revolutionary antifascist line of conduct, cannot hesitate in these grave times and we hereby formally instruct everyone to abide by the call for a general strike the moment anyone rises in revolt, in no matter which region of Spain, while abiding by the watchwords of the National Committee. Our position remains well established and we warn that our call will go out very quickly. Remember that no one should obey a call not emanating from the Committee, that being the only way to avert the irreparable. We are passing through moments fraught with gravity. We must strike vigorously, firmly and all of us together. Let no one hold aloof! Everyone must keep in touch with one another!

It is time to remain in a state of alert and ready for action. Fascism has emerged master of the city of Seville. A revolt has occurred in Cordoba. North Africa is under fascist rule. We the people of Catalonia must be on a war footing, ready to act; now that we are facing the enemy, let everyone take up his combat post.

Let there be no pointless waste of energy nor fratricidal strife! Let us fight whole-heartedly and keep our guns handy and ready for the fray! Anyone holding back is a traitor to the cause of the people's liberation. Long live the CNT! Long live libertarian communism! In response to fascism, a general strike by revolutionaries!

The CNT Regional Committee

Antifascism in Power (July 1936)[1]

The army revolt of July 19, 1936 has had profound implications for Spain's economic life. The struggle against the clerico-militarist clan was rendered possible only through the help of the working class. Left to its own devices, the republican bourgeoisie would have been overwhelmed.

That alliance could not be confined to the realm of politics. Syndicalists and anarchists had had bad experiences with the bourgeois Republic. So it was unthinkable that they should rest content with thwarting the clerico-militarist rebellion. The initiation of changes to the economic system was to be expected. Indeed, they could not carry on putting up with economic exploitation which was, in their eyes, the root of political oppression.

These were facts known to the clergy, the military cabal and the big capitalists who had ties to the first two of these clans. They were well aware of what was at stake and what the implications were.

(...) For which reason the privileged class sided with the rebel military leaders.

Whereas the generals were the actors, the big capitalists pulled the strings while remaining in the background. Some of them were not even present in the theater of operations — Juan March, Francisco Cambó and the like were not in Spain when the rebellion broke out. From abroad they awaited the outcome of events. Had the military leaders achieved victory, their masters would have come home immediately. But in Catalonia, as in the greater part of Spain, the military revolt was smashed. And the puppet-masters stayed abroad.

(...) The choice now was either to hide behind the military, clerical and fascist faction which could employ terror in defense of the ancient privileges, or seek the protection of the armed workers, leaving the paralyzed sectors of the economy and the public services to look to their own organization and administration. It goes without saying that the liberal and socialist sector hoisted back into power by the February 1936 elections after two years of black reaction was greatly upset, but the hesitancy of the bourgeois republicans who were more or less hungry for reforms, was in the last resort overruled by the audacity of more extreme elements.

This was something completely new in Spain and in the world and it ushered in a new era in history. For the first time, an entire people had stood up to fascism. In Germany and elsewhere, parliamentary stultification and bureaucratic fossilization of the workers' movement had assisted the rise of fascism: in Spain the bulk of the workers' break with parliamentary methods and bourgeois politics enabled a whole people to offer resistance to the generals. Second important observation: in Spain the distinguishing feature of development was that it plunged the country into a period of social upheavals without which these far-reaching innovations might have taken place under the aegis of some party dictatorship. Instead, change was initiated by direct participation of the broad masses in the economic process, and the burden of the requisite expropriations was assumed by the labor unions which decisively shaped the socialist construction. In political terms, the new order, primarily devised within the parameters of the war's possibilities and demands, also was not dependent upon State monopolization of power. It was rooted in democratic collaboration of very motley antifascist groupings, which had hitherto been diametrically opposed to one another.

Notes to Antifascism in Power (July 1936)

1. Taken from A. Souchy *Collectivizations, l'oeuvre constructive de la Révolution espagnole* (April 1937, reissued 1965). For Souchy, see Volume III of this anthology.

FAI MANIFESTO

On July 26, the FAI Peninsular Committee broadcast this manifesto over the radio:

People of Barcelona! Workers from every labor organization, from all left-wing parties united in the fight against fascism! In these crucial times, these historic hours for Barcelona and Spain as a whole, the Iberian Anarchist Federation (FAI), which has given generously of its blood and which has been the driving force behind the super-human heroism that secured the victory thanks to the sacrifice of many lives, also needs to make its voice heard by the masses who listen to the Radio.

Comrades! One more push and victory will be ours. We have to keep up the historical tension in which we have been living for the past seven days. Strengthened by our rage and enthusiasm, we are invincible. The first antifascist column is advancing victoriously on Zaragoza. Greeted by delirious cries of enthusiasm. Men from the liberated towns are joining the bravoes from Barcelona who are going to take Zaragoza. Defeat for fascism in Zaragoza will be a mortal blow!

The sovereign will of the masses who are capable of anything when, eager for success, they march in step, must set a great example in the eyes of the world. It must show what we are capable of, what we want and must demonstrate our determination and resistance. It will thereby influence the fate of the world. We appreciate that we are living in decisive times and with equanimity and loyalty we fight alongside our allies, of whom we require the same loyalty, the same sense of responsibility and the same heroic determination to succeed. Determination that buoyed us up during those great, unforgettable events in Barcelona.

You men and women who have taken up arms, you popular militias prompted by the most fervent enthusiasm and you obscure heroes toiling in the shadows to furnish combatants with bread and war materials, should not forget that, as Napoleon famously said as he stood before the pyramids "Twenty centuries are gazing down on us." The whole world is watching us. Let us all be a coordinated, invincible force. Let us be simultaneously models of unparalleled bravery and honesty at every level. To battle, comrades! Let us crush the fascist hydra completely! July 19 marks the beginning of a new era: the peace of the past is no more. Amid the blood bath we will build the new Spain. Long live the FAI, symbol of the revolution and emblem of the violent yearning for freedom! Long live the antifascist fighting front!

The FAI Peninsular Committee

DURRUTI (1896–1936) AND LIBERTARIAN WARFARE

BUENAVENTURA DURRUTI[1]

Buenaventura Durruti y Domingo, son of railman Santiago and Anastasia, was born on July 14, 1896 in León.

At the age of five, he started primary school, moving at the age of nine to the school in the Calle Misericordia run by Ricardo Fanjul. His teacher's evaluation of Durruti after he completed his studies was: "A pupil with a talent for literature, unruly, but good-hearted."

At fourteen, he entered a machine shop as an apprentice, leaving at the age of eighteen, having received sound training, as he proved when he got his first job in Matallana de Torio, installing baths at the pit-head. After that he joined the Northern railroad company as machine-fitter. This happened in 1914, when the First World War broke out.

Although León was under the thumb of the clergy and aristocracy, the Spanish Socialist Party (PSOE) and General Workers' Union (UGT) had a working-class core there. Durruti belonged to the latter union, joining on the very day he became a wage-slave. His rebellious nature, because of which he was forever ready to confront injustice, ensured that he was always thought well of by his workmates and it made him popular in the mining towns. He took part in trade union meetings and spoke inside the workplaces, where his militant, pugnacious mentality took shape. It was then that the revolutionary strike of August 1917 erupted; in León it ended with workers being sacked and their leaders persecuted. The León branch of the National Confederation of Labor (CNT) also participated in the strike. Durruti was drawn to the pugnaciousness of these men and joined that trade union grouping, remaining with it for the rest of his life. Sacked from the railroad workshops, blacklisted by the employers in León, he was forced into exile and settled in Gijón, a revolutionary hub in the North of Spain and the center of the anarcho-syndicalist influence in the Asturias region. There, he struck up a friendship with Manuel Buenacasa[2], who educated him to anarchist theory. After a two month stay in Gijon, he was forced out to France, in that it was, for one thing, impossible for him to find work, and for another, he had failed to report for his military service, although he had reached the age of twenty one.

In Paris he came under the influence of three people: Sébastien Faure, Louis Lecoin and Emile Cottin[3]. These men were to remain forever associated with his life.

From friends who had stayed in Spain he received news. The breath of revolution sweeping Europe prompted his return to Spain at the beginning of 1920. In San Sebastian, he found Manuel Buenacasa, who was the general secretary of the CNT Construction Union there. Within a few days of his arrival, he began work as a mechanic, which enabled him to strike up a friendship with other worker militants from Barcelona, Madrid and Zaragoza. The groundwork for an anarchist group had been laid in San Sebastian and Durruti's first affiliation was to the **Los Justicieros** (Avengers) group. But the population of San Sebastian was one of those to which "nothing ever happened," and Durruti decided to move on. Buenacasa gave him a letter of introduction for Angel Pestaña, the then general secretary of the CNT National Committee, who was in Barcelona.

He stopped over in Zaragoza where the atmosphere was heavy with labor disputes. Cardinal Soldevila, along with the governor of Zaragoza, had brought in a gang of hired killers (**pistoleros**) from Barcelona, to assassinate CNT militants and finish off the CNT in Zaragoza. There was a violent backlash and one group of CNT militants, including Francisco Ascaso[4], was incarcerated in the Predicadores prison to await sentencing to lengthy terms. This happened to coincide with the arrival of Durruti and his friends in Zaragoza. The prisoners were released while the strife escalated to new heights. In this climate, Durruti, a close friend of Ascaso and of Torres Escartin[5], made up his mind in January 1922 to go and live in Barcelona.

Like Zaragoza, Barcelona just then was a battle-field. **Pistoleros** had targeted labor leaders and were gunning them down in the streets. In the face of this onslaught which had the backing of the employers and police, trade unions could not but reply in kind.

The struggle operated like a filtering process, sifting out the best, and this led to the formation of Durruti's new group, this time called **Los Solidarios**. Men like Garcia Oliver, Gregorio Sobreviela[6], etc., joined the new group which soon became the axis of the battle against gangsterism and the bosses, thanks to the solidarity of its members. On March 10, 1923, Salvador Segui[7], a very famous militant, great public speaker and superb organizer, was murdered. Around this time militant anarchism was looking to launch a more homogeneous organization and Zaragoza's **Libre Acuerdo** anarchist group summoned an anarchist conference for the month of April in Madrid.

Durruti traveled to Madrid with the dual mission of attending the conference and speaking to the comrades imprisoned following the assassination of Eduardo Dato[8] in 1921. A price having been placed on his head, he made the prison visit to the journalist Mauro Bajatierra, held as an accessory in the Dato case, under an alias. He attended the conference and was arrested as it concluded, on suspicion of unlawful activity, but freed a few days later. The inspector by whom he was arrested (who was not aware of his true identity) was disciplined by the minister of the Interior. Following which the Barcelona chief of police pointed out that "the Madrid inspector's lack of experience had allowed the terrorist individual Durruti to escape justice."

In Barcelona a National Revolutionary Committee was set up to orchestrate an insurrection. One of the committee members was Sobreviela. This was a time when the CNT had to contend with countless difficulties: it had no money, the cream of its membership was in prison or on the run. In the wake of Segui's murder, gangsterism prevailed in the Catalan capital as well as in other towns. It was at this juncture that the **Los Solidarios** group despatched envoys to several corners of the Peninsula: Zaragoza, Bilbao, Seville and Madrid. There were tremendous nation-wide upheavals between May and June 1923. In Zaragoza, Cardinal Soldevila was executed. In the wake of that execution, Francisco Ascaso and Torres Escartin were indicted. Only Ascaso managed to escape.

Fernando Gonzalez Regueral, one-time governor of Bilbao, the stalwart of employer-subsidized gangsterism, was executed in León one fiesta night.

The groundwork was laid for insurrection, the manpower was ready, but weapons were in short supply. The National Revolutionary Committee had bought some in Brussels and loaded them aboard shipping in Marseilles, but these guns turned out to be inadequate and for that reason in June 1923 Durruti and Ascaso set out from Bilbao to purchase a sizable consignment. They procured some from an arms plant in Eibar, through the good offices of an engineer. The consignment was shipped out, bound for Mexico, but, once on the high seas, the ship's captain was to await instructions to divert to the straits of Gibraltar and put the arms ashore in Barcelona, without putting into port. Time passed very quickly. The factory was slow to meet the order, and unfortunately the weapons only reached Barcelona after General Primo de Rivera had mounted his *coup d'état* in September 1923. Given that landing its cargo was impossible, the ship was forced to make its way back to Bilbao to return the weapons to the factory.

Gregorio Sobreviela had been murdered (. . .) Ricardo Sanz[9] had been sentenced to hard labor, as had Garcia Oliver. The group had been dismantled. Gregorio Jover[10], Segundo Garcia, Durruti and Ascaso were at large, but it was very dangerous for them to stay in Spain, which is why they decided to go into exile.

Their stay in France was none too long, just long enough to devise a propaganda project in conjunction with Italian, French and Russian exile militants, the upshot of which was the launch of the Librairie internationale, the principal mission of which was to promote ideological and campaign literature as well as a trilingual (Italian, French, Spanish) review. Towards the end of 1924, Durruti and Ascaso left for Cuba (. . .) There they embarked upon a campaign of agitation in favor of the Spanish revolutionary movement. This was the first time that Durruti and Ascaso ever addressed the public. Durruti, it turned out, was a popular spokesman. They soon had to quit the country, being sought by the police as dangerous agitators and they began to live a topsy turvy existence. They were forever on the move, with more or less short stays in Mexico, Peru and Santiago de Chile, before a slightly longer sojourn in Buenos Aires, where, in spite of everything, they found themselves in danger. They left for Montevideo (Uruguay), from where they embarked on a ship bound for Cherbourg. But, once on the high seas, the ship was forced to change course several times. It was later dubbed the "ghost ship." In the end they arrived in the Canary Islands where they went ashore, only to embark upon another ship bound for England. They put ashore clandestinely in Cherbourg in April 1926. From there they traveled to Paris where they lodged in a hotel in the Rue Legendre. It was as they emerged from that hotel that they were arrested by French police one morning. The formal grounds for arrest was: "having conspired against the king of Spain, Alfonso XIII, due to visit the French capital on July 14."

In October that year, they appeared before the criminal court charged with unlawful possession of weapons, rebellion and breaches of the law on aliens. During the trial they declared that they reserved:

> the right to do all in their power to combat the dictatorial regime prevailing in Spain and that, to that end, they had intended to seize the king, Alfonso XIII, so as to contrive the downfall of the monarchy in their country.

Argentina applied for the extradition of Durruti, Ascaso and Gregorio Jover. For its part, Spain did likewise, accusing them of having killed Cardinal Soldevila. The French government was ready to accede to Argentina and Spain. At the time, the French Anarchist Union was leading a campaign seeking the release of Sacco and Vanzetti, who were facing the electric chair in the United States. A further campaign was launched, headed by Louis Lecoin, Ferandel[11] and Sébastien Faure, to press for the release of the three Spanish anarchists, who were ardently defended during the trial by Louis Lecoin. Indeed, Lecoin mobilized French political and intellectual circles as well as the working class. There was great agitation in Paris. Several newspapers backed the campaign and in July 1927 the three Spanish anarchists were freed.

Expelled from France, denied residence in Belgium, Luxemburg, Switzerland and Germany, the borders of Italy and Spain remained open for them, but that spelled certain death. The USSR offered them sanctuary, albeit with conditions attached that no anarchist could accept. Which left them with but one option: to give the police the slip and stay in France. So they returned clandestinely to the Paris area. In clandestinity, Durruti struck up a friendship with the Russian revolutionary, Nestor Makhno. Life was impossible for the Spaniards and they tried in vain to enter Germany; they had to stay in France, in Lyons to be exact, where they found work under assumed names. Discovered by the police, they were put back into prison for another six months. With a straight face, Durruti told a journalist who had asked him, on the day of his release, what they were going to do: "We will begin all over again!"

In autumn 1928, they finally succeeded in entering Germany illegally, there to make contact with Rudolf Rocker[12] and Erich Mühsam, who attempted to secure political refugee status for them. Although they made overtures to highly influential figures in the political world, they failed. It was plain that if Durruti, Ascaso and Jover were to fall into the hands of the police, they would promptly be returned to Spain. As a result, the first two named decided to go to Belgium, where they reckoned they could get false passports and embark for Mexico. But they were in dire financial straits, as they admitted to the famous German actor Alexander Granach, a great friend of the poet Mühsam. He let them have all the money he could lay his hands on at the time. Thanks to which help they crossed the border but failed to embark for Mexico, because an emissary from the CNT national committee, sent from Spain, told them that the regime had collapsed.

Whereupon the two friends resolved to stay in Belgium once they had obtained false papers. They stayed in Brussels until April 13, 1931. At this point in their career as militants they tasted a measure of tranquillity. They availed of it in order to better their intellectual and revolutionary grounding and to collaborate with the Comité Pro-Liberté (Freedom Committee) which included international militants like Hugo Treni[13], Camillo Berneri and Hem Day. Come the Republic, Durruti returned to Spain. That Republic quickly dashed the hopes raised. A revolutionary show of strength on May 1, 1931 was held in the Bellas Artes hall in Barcelona. A demonstration by a hundred thousand people followed and the demonstrators paraded through Barcelona's streets up to the Generalidad Palace, intent upon registering their demands: "Freedom for the prisoners and urgent social reforms." The army and Civil Guard broke up the demonstration. There were people killed and wounded, but Durruti persuaded the soldiers to turn their guns on the Civil Guard.

Durruti's popularity was tremendous across the peninsula and his very name guaranteed a CNT rally's success. He was not, strictly speaking, a good public speaker, but he knew how to captivate the masses and open their eyes by means of examples to social injustice.

Between April 1931 and July 19, 1936, he played a part in every one of the great social conflicts in Spain. He came to prominence in the events in Figols and was deported to the Canaries, to Puerto Cabra on the island of Furteventura, where he was obliged to spend the months between February and September 1932. He was also active in the revolutionary uprising of January 1933 and was again imprisoned from January to August that year. In December 1933, Durruti was on the National Revolutionary Committee, but from December 1933 to July 1934 was again sent to prison in Burgos and Zaragoza, only to be sentenced to penal servitude on October 5, 1934 until mid–1935. He was jailed again in September 1935, only to be freed days ahead of the elections of February 1936.

The proceedings of the CNT's third congress, in Zaragoza, a congress in which about seven hundred delegates participated, opened on May 1, 1936. Durruti was part of the Textile Union delegation, as were Garcia Oliver and Francisco Ascaso. This last congress focused on construction: the revolution was imminent. The CNT National Committee denounced the fascist conspiracy, but the government elected by the Popular Front proved unable to put paid to the generals' plotting.

Durruti whipped up such a tremendous frenzy in revolutionary militants and among the working class that the president of the Generalidad, Companys[14] sought an interview with the CNT, an interview during which it was determined that a commission would be established to liaise between the CNT and the Generalidad government. Durruti and Ascaso belonged to that commission which pressed for the arming of the people, but got nothing but fine words from the government. Given the attitude of those in leadership, it was decided that the merchant vessels at anchor in Barcelona port would be raided, with an eye to capturing a few dozen weapons to add to the few that the CNT already had, as well as those seized from armories. This was the only way of confronting the Barcelona garrison which comprised 35,000 soldiers.

Rebel troops took to the streets of Barcelona at 5:00 A.M. on July 19, and at 5.00 P.M., on the Monday afternoon, Garcia Oliver reported over Radio Barcelona that the people had beaten the fascists in the course of an unequal battle. State power had never before been seen to evaporate at such speed. In under 72 hours, the State had been reduced to a nominal existence. What little forces there were left to represent it had quickly melted into the people. The CNT and the FAI were absolute masters of the situation in Barcelona and in the provinces alike.

Companys, now president of a non-existent Generalidad, had to face facts and sought an audience with the CNT and FAI in order to hand over power. (Is "hand over" the right phrase for it?) From Garcia Oliver we have a written account of this historic audience, explaining the exact situation and showing how the new organ of power known as the Central Militias' Committee came into being.

One of the first steps that this Committee took was to organize a column to set out immediately for the Aragon region. It was known as the Durruti-Farras column, in that Major Perez-Farras was its military delegate and Durruti its political delegate. On July 23, the column set out for Lerida with fewer men than had been expected, in that it had been reckoning on 10,000 men to start with. Once revolutionary power had been established in Lerida, the column made for Caspe before reaching Bujaraloz, a strategic location nearly 30 kilometers from Zaragoza, where it dug in. It took several villages and forced back the enemy.

The Bujaraloz "shack" where Durruti established his headquarters became a magnet for journalists and VIPs; it was visited by journalists, worker militants, intellectuals and political figures like Sébastien Faure and Emma Goldman.

The international group which the Column had named as the "Sébastien Faure" group included in its ranks personalities such as Emile Cottin (who died in action) and Simone Weil.[15]

As the war developed, the Aragon front was, on account of its libertarian spirit, increasingly boycotted by the central government. Durruti spoke with the Central Militias' Committee which, once briefed on the position in which he found himself, recommended that he go to Madrid to press for arms or foreign currency. Around mid-September, Durruti went to Madrid for talks with the socialist Largo Caballero[16] who was simultaneously prime minister and minister of War, and who assured him of a loan of 1800 million pesetas for the purchase of arms and the running of the Catalan war industries. But the central government failed to honor its word and the Aragon front had to confront the enemy with makeshift means, unable to capture Zaragoza, a capture that would have been highly significant.

When Madrid came under Francoist attack in October-November 1936, fear seized government and high command figures; it was believed that the loss of the capital was imminent. The government called in Durruti, reckoning that his prestige might raise its fighters' morale. His column was summoned to defend Madrid. And so, to the delight of the capital's inhabitants, Durruti arrived on November 12 at the head of his men, and without so much as being given time to rest up, was assigned to the most dangerous sector. Between November 12 and the day he died he knew not a single day's respite.

Around 2:00 p.m. on November 19th, Durruti was hit right in the lung by a "stray bullet" while facing the Clinical Hospital, a stronghold overlooking the University City, where the fascists were dug in. He was rushed urgently to the Catalan militias' hospital in the Ritz Hotel. There he underwent several operations, before dying at 6:00 A.M. the next day, November 20.

So as to spare the morale of the Republicans fighting in Madrid, who were embroiled in bitter fighting and facing the enemy's armor, the death of the man who had come to symbolize resistance to fascism was at first kept secret and his body covertly removed to Barcelona. His funeral in the Catalan capital on November 23 was attended by upwards of a half a million people.

Similarly, it was out of a concern not to wreck the morale of anti-Francoists that the republican government and the CNT both felt obliged to issue categorical denials of rumors that were beginning to circulate regarding the questionable circumstances of Durruti's death and to affirm that he had indeed perished under enemy fire.

With hindsight, it is hard to swallow the official version and the enigma shrouding his death is undiminished. Three other versions were advanced to the effect that:

1) Durruti was killed by anarchist militants because, being obliged to fight in Madrid alongside the Communists, he was tending to lean in the direction of the Communists. This is the least likely of the hypotheses.
2) Durruti was eliminated by members of the CNT's reformist right wing, keen to build upon the political compromise with other Republican forces in order to divest the struggle of all revolutionary character, against Durruti's will, he being an advocate of all-out revolutionary struggle.
3) Finally, Durruti was executed by the GPU on Stalin's orders, for his immense popularity was an obstacle to the machinations of the Spanish Communist Party.

There is no way today that we can make an objective option in favor of any of these hypotheses. However, as in any mystery story, we are entitled to seek the truth on the basis of the question: whom might Durruti's death have profited?

Notes to Buenaventura Durruti

1. Taken from an unpublished life of Durruti written by Abel Paz, with the kind permission of the author. [This book, *Durruti: The People Armed*, has since been published in English by Black Rose and is available through AK Distribution.]
2. Manuel Buenacasa (1886–1964), former seminarian then worker, the first general secretary of the CNT, director of the newspaper *Solidaridad Obrera:* in 1936 he headed the CNT's school for militants in Barcelona: author of a *History of the Spanish Workers' Movement, 1886–1926.*
3. Louis Lecoin (1888–1971) French anarchist pacifist and anarcho-syndicalist: secretary of the French Anarchist Federation in 1912: had a hand in the trade union split in 1921, before quitting the CGTU: organized the campaign trying to save the lives of Italian anarchists Sacco and Vanzetti, who were sentenced to death and eventually electrocuted: rallied to the defense of Spanish activists Durruti and Ascaso: served over twelve years in prison for draft evasion and anti-militarist propaganda: in 1939 he drafted the manifesto "Immediate Peace": in the twilight of his life he fought for the rights of conscientious objectors: publisher of the monthly *Liberte;*
Louios-Emile Cottin (1896–1936) anarchist: while still a youth he attempted the life of premier Georges Clemenceau in 1919. Sentenced to death, his punishment was commuted to ten years' imprisonment. During the Spanish revolution, he perished in the ranks of the libertarian militias.
4. Francisco Ascaso Abadia (1900–1936), libertarian activist, friend and indefatigable companion of Durruti, killed in the storming of the Atarazanas barracks on July 20, 1936.
5. José Torres Escartin (1900–1939), libertarian activist credited with the assassination of archbishop Carlos Soldevila in Zaragoza in reprisal for the murder of the great libertarian leader Salvador Segui by the killers of the governor, Martinez Anido. Driven out of his mind by police torture, he was freed by the 1931 revolution, only to be shot by the Francoists in spite of his mental condition.
6. Juan Garcia Oliver (1897–1980) one of the activist leaders of the Iberian Anarchist Federation (FAI): from 1923 he served a prison sentence from which the revolution of 1931 and an amnesty released him: fought on the barricades on July 19, 1936: in Catalonia he organized the first militias columns and war industries: was Justice minister in the Largo Caballero government, until May 1937. Gregorio Sobreviela, metalworker and anarchist trade unionist, wanted by police-for a number of coups de main and attentats: murdered in February 1924.
7. Salvador Segui (1896–1923) Catalan and brilliant public speaker, trade union organizer and cultural promoter: protagonist of the **sindicato único** (single union) instead of the trades union. Murdered by the hired killers of Catalonia's governor Martinez Anido on March 10, 1923.

8. Eduardo Dato, ultra-reactionary Spanish premier, assassinated by CNT metalworkers on March 8, 1921 in Madrid, in reprisal for the White terror enforced in Barcelona with Dato's consent by governor Martinez Anido.
9. Ricardo Sanz (born 1900), construction worker, organized the anarchist action group "Los Solidarios" in 1922: fled to France then returned to Spain in 1926 to plot against the dictatorship of General Primo de Rivera: repeatedly jailed between 1931 and 1936: in July 1936 he belonged to the War Committee of the Central Militias' Committee: after Durruti's death, Sanz replaced him as head of the column: author of several books.
10. Gregorio Jover (1892–1964?) trade union organizer, libertarian activist who was involved in a would-be attack on King Alfonso XIII in France along with Durruti and Ascaso on July 14, 1926: during the Civil War he led a libertarian column on the Aragon front.
11. Ferandel, a friend of Louis Lecoin, was treasurer of two committees spearheading the campaigns referred to.
12. On Rudolf Rocker, see Volume II of this anthology.
Erich Mühsam (1878–1934) revolutionary poet and German anarchist, author of a "Marseillaise of the workers' councils": involved in the government of the Bavarian Councils republic which survived for only six days in Munich (April 7-13. 1919) along with Gustav Landauer (1870–1919), an anarchist writer brutally done to death: Mühsam was sentenced to 15 years' imprisonment by a court martial, then amnestied at the end of 1924. Arrested by the Nazis on February 28, 1933, he was murdered by the S.S. in a concentration camp on the night of July 9-10,1934 (See Roland Lewin's *Erich Mühsam* supplement to *Le Monde libertaire* June 1968).
13. Hugo Treni, nom de plume of Ugo Fedeli. See Volume III. For Camillo Berneri, see below.
Hem Day, alias of Marcel Dieu (1902–1969), anarchist journalist and Belgian antifascist, founder of the *Cahiers Pensee et Action*.
14. Lluis Companys, lawyer and leader of a Catalan petit bourgeois party, the **Esquerra Republicana** (Republican Left): he was the CNT's defense counsel while also relying upon small-holders and share-cropping farmers: in 1936 he became the president of the Generalidad of Catalonia: he was handed over to Franco by the Vichy government and shot in Barcelona by the Francoists.
15. Simone Weil (1909–1943), French militant and philosopher, worked in a Renault plant: she fought in Spain during the civil war: she ended up a Christian and mystic and died prematurely.
16. Francisco Largo Caballero (1869–1946), of worker extraction, reformist socialist, secretary of the General Workers' Union (UGT): radicalized during the Asturias strike in 1934: premier and minister of War from September 5, 1936 to May 15, 1937: exaggeratedly nicknamed "the Spanish Lenin."

The Spirit of Durruti[1]

The Durruti Column learned of the death of Durruti during the night, without much comment. Sacrificing one's life is commonplace among Durruti's comrades. A mumbled phrase: "He was the best of us," a shout hurled simultaneously into the night: "We will avenge him," was all the comrades had to say. "Vengeance" was the watchword of the day.

Durruti had had a profound grasp of the power of anonymous endeavor. Anonymity and communism are but one. Comrade Durruti operated at a remove from all of the vanity of the luminaries of the left. He lived alongside his comrades, and fought side by side with them as a comrade. A shining example, he filled us with enthusiasm. We had no general, but the battler's zeal, the profound modesty, and the complete self-effacement before the great cause of revolution which twinkled in his eyes swamped our hearts and made them beat in unison with his, which, for us, lives on in the mountains. We will forever hear his voice: **"Adelante, adelante!"**[2] Durruti was not a general; he was our comrade. There is a lack of decorum there, but in our proletarian column the revolution is not exploited, the lime-light unsought. We have but one thing on our minds: victory and revolution.

The comrades used to gather in his tent. He would explain the meaning of his measures and converse with them. Durruti did not command, he persuaded. Only belief in the well-foundedness of a measure guaranteed clear, resolute action. Every one of us knows the reason for his action and identifies with it. And, for that very reason, every single person will see to it that the action succeeds no matter what. Comrade Durruti set us the example.

The soldier obeys out of a feeling of fear and social inferiority, and fights for want of consciousness. Which is why soldiers always fought for the interests of their social adversaries, the capitalists. The poor devils fighting alongside the fascists are a pitiful example of this. The militian fights primarily for the proletariat and seeks to achieve victory for the laboring classes. The fascist soldiers fight on behalf of a decadent minority, their enemies: the militian for the future of his own class. So the latter appears more intelligent than the soldier. The Durruti Column is disciplined by its ideal and not by the goose-step.

Everywhere that the column goes, collectivization follows. The land is given over to the collective. From the slaves of the caciques they used to be, the farming proletariat becomes free men. Rural feudalism yields to libertarian communism. The population is supplied by the column with food and clothing. It becomes part of the village community for the duration of its stay in a locality.

The revolution imposes upon the column a stricter discipline than militarization ever could. Everyone feels answerable for the success of the social revolution, which is at the core of our struggle, and which will determine it in the future just as it has in the past. I do not believe that generals or the military salute would imbue us with an attitude more attuned to current requirements. In saying that, I am convinced that I am reflecting the thinking of Durruti and the comrades.

We do not renege upon our old anti-militarism, our healthy mistrust of the rigid militarism that has always profited capitalists only. It is precisely for the sake of this militaristic rigidity that the proletariat has been prevented from educating itself and been kept in a position of social inferiority: military rigidity was to crush the will and intellect of proletarians. When all is said and done, we are fighting against the rebel generals. Which of itself demonstrates the questionable value of military discipline.

We obey no general: we seek the realization of a social ideal that will permit, alongside lots of other innovations, precisely such optimal education of the proletarian personality. Militarization, by contrast, was and is still a favorite means of diminishing that personality. One can grasp the spirit of the Durruti Column when one understands that it will always remain the daughter and defender of the proletarian revolution. The Column embodies the spirit of Durruti and of the CNT. Durruti lives on through it: his column will faithfully preserve its inheritance. It fights in conjunction with all proletarians for the revolution's victory. In the doing of which we honor the memory of our dead comrade, Durruti.

Notes to The Spirit of Durruti

1. By Karl Einstein of the Durruti Column.
2. In English: "Forward!"

THE DEFENSE OF MADRID (NOVEMBER–DECEMBER 1936)[1]

The Government's departure for Valencia came as a cold shower for the uneasy and the careless; it replaced cant about unity and discipline with a real upsurge in responsibility and initiative in answer to the appeal from the Madrid Defense Committee. Everybody realized that he had his bit to do, that people were relying on him to do it. Everybody realized that he could rely upon others for sincere resistance, and in place of a few onslaughts of oratorical heroism, concluded by tributes of confidence in the government, we had effective work, the contagion of example, the coming into play of the broad masses. The departure of the ministers was a tonic.

The arrival of Durruti with five thousand Catalan fighters; the rough, manly proclamation he issued over the airwaves, giving a good tongue-lashing to the idlers, poseurs and phony revolutionaries; the offer he made to give every **madrileño** a rifle or a pick, and the invitation to all to dig trenches and throw up barricades — all of it helped create a sort of enthusiastic, joyous euphoria which the government's communiqués and lying speeches could never have done. Up to that point, they had organized neither the defense nor the evacuation of useless mouths for fear of upsetting morale. Durruti and the Defense Committee treated **madrileños** like men and the latter conducted themselves like men. The CNT which in Madrid comprised the extremist element of the working class, set the example by mobilizing all its members in order to form a fortifications brigade and other like formations.

The following proclamation was carried by the Madrid daily *CNT*:

> The Local Federation of the Sindicatos Unicos of Madrid, whose responsibility is bound up with the fate of the antifascist cause, yesterday, Monday, mobilized all of the workers under its control in order to make a decisive contribution to the fight against the rebels on the outskirts of the Republic's capital. All works not bearing directly upon the war have been declared suspended, and today there are forty thousand confederated workers under arms in Madrid to bolster the government.
>
> The fascist endeavor will be broken upon a rampart of proletarian flesh, unless defeated before that by our weaponry, which is mightier and more effective with every passing day. Our ranks have now been cleansed of all traitors. In the July events, it was the people that stormed the fascist redoubts with its combative spontaneity and revolutionary ardor. Now, hardened by three months of battle, it must be the people that annihilates the traitors once and for all. Energy, comrades, and the victory will be ours!

The defense of Madrid led to a confrontation between federalist, libertarian fighting methods and governmental, Stalinist methods. Experience demonstrated that the humane system practiced in anarchist ranks in no way harmed combat potential and proper organization of services. Which led a rather large number of international proletarians militarized under the Russian baton to quit their units and fall into line with Durruti. The desire to be treated like a thinking citizen and not as "cannon-fodder" made the CNT-FAI militias a magnet for all tendencies. Cognizant of their role as educators and feeling themselves to be the repositories of the revolution's soul and honor, CNT organizers largely returned to their principled stances on anti-militarism and self-discipline. Their propaganda, inspired by a preoccupation with consolidating the militias' gains within the frameworks of the people's army, took a freer, more revolutionary turn. Thus, one proclamation dated November stated:

> Knowing the psychology of our people, we know that the soldier of the revolution will not fight effectively if he is turned into a soulless automaton under the rigid discipline of a code that speaks not of right or duty but rather of obedience and punishment. The old formulas are unacceptable here, because they were not laid down by a people defending itself. They were designed for the enslavement of the people, for the defense of exploiter classes using armed force to protect their interests and their privileges.
>
> The Spanish army which vanished as of July 19 for all the rigidity of its military code, was not at all outstanding for its discipline, its courage nor its organization. The bourgeois republic should no longer look to its governors, nor rebuild a new army, but should break with all the old obsolete ideas and formulas. The proletarian revolution which we are in the process of building need not look for its model to the national, political, military or social remnants opposed to its development.
>
> Revolutionary discipline grows out of the basis of conscious duty and not out of constraint. The severest punishment that a comrade refusing to carry out his task in the proletarian revolutionary society in matters military or economic can earn is to face scorn, isolation and ultimately elimination from a society where parasites have no place.

To conclude: we believe we have a duty to set before our reader a document that encapsulates rather well the practical conclusions we are entitled to expect after the discussion upon which we have reported. It comes from the German fighters who have rallied around the Durruti Column's red and black colors and represents a minimum schedule of demands for any revolutionary, within the framework of a military organization designed to be controlled by its members in the people's interests:

The people's army and soldiers' councils

> The German comrades from the international group of the Durruti Column have taken a stand on the question of militarization in general, and in the context of the Column in particular. The comrades

take the current implementation of the principles of militarization to task for having been drawn up in the absence of any close contact with front-line personnel. They deem the measures adopted thus far to be provisional and accept them as such, until such time as a new "military code" is devised, demanding that this be drawn up as quickly as possible in order to put paid to the current state of ongoing confusion. The German comrades suggest that in the drafting of that new code, account be taken of the following demands:
1. Saluting to be abolished.
2. Equal pay for all.
3. Freedom of the press (front-line newspapers)
4. Freedom of discussion.
5. Battalion council (three delegates returned by each company).
6. No delegate to wield powers of command.
7. The battalion Council will summon a general assembly of soldiers, should two thirds of company delegates be so minded.
8. The soldiers from each unit (regiment) are to elect a delegation of three men enjoying the unit's confidence. These trustees will be able to summon a general assembly at any time.
9. One of them will be seconded to the (brigade) staff in an observer capacity.
10. This format should be extended until the army as a whole has representation in the form of soldiers' councils.
11. The general staff should also second a representative from the overall Soldiers' council.
12. Field councils of war are to comprise exclusively of soldiers. In the event of charges being brought against ranks, an officer is to be seconded to the council of war.

Notes to The Defense of Madrid

1. Taken from A. Prudhommeaux, *Catalogne 36-37*: for Prudhommeaux, see below.

Durruti Is Not Dead by Emma Goldman

Durruti, whom I saw for the last time a month ago, has perished fighting on the streets of Madrid.

I knew this great fighter from the anarchist and revolutionary movement in Spain from what I had read about him.

When I arrived in Barcelona, I heard anecdotes aplenty about Durruti and his column. Which meant that I had a great desire to go to the Aragon front, a front where he was the guiding spirit of the valiant militias fighting against fascism.

As night fell I arrived at Durruti's headquarters, utterly drained by the long journey made by car along a rocky road. A few minutes in Durruti's company proved a great comfort, tonic and encouragement to me. A muscular man, as if carved out of stone, Durruti plainly represented the most dominant figure among the anarchists I had met since my arrival in Spain. His tremendous energy impressed me, as it appeared to have the same impact on all who neared him.

I found Durruti in a veritable hive of activity. Men were coming and going, the telephone was forever summoning Durruti and at the same time there was an unbroken and formidable hubbub produced by workers busily erecting a wooden skeleton for his headquarters.

Amid this ongoing noisy activity, Durruti remained serene and patient. He greeted me as if he had known me all his life. For me, the cordial, warm audience with this man bent upon a life or death struggle against fascism was something unexpected.

I had heard a lot of talk about Durruti's strong personality and standing in the column which bore his name. I was curious to discover by what means — especially as it had not been thanks to the military — he had managed to mass ten thousand volunteers with no experience or training. Durruti seemed startled that I, as an old anarchist militant, should have put such a question to him:

"I have been an anarchist all my life" — he replied — "and I hope to remain such. That is why I took the view that it would be very disagreeable for me to turn into a general and command my men with stupid military-style discipline. They have come to me of their own free will, ready to offer their lives for our antifascist struggle. I believe as I always have, in freedom. Freedom taken in the sense of responsibility. I regard discipline as indispensable, but it must be self-discipline prompted by a shared ideal and a sturdy feeling of comradeship."

He had earned the trust and affection of his men because he had never imagined himself superior to them. He was one of their number. He ate and slept as they did. Often he would forego his ration for the sake of some sick or weak fellow more needy than himself. In every battle he shared their danger. This was but one of the secrets of Durruti's success with his column. His men adored him. Not only did they obey his every order, but they were forever ready to follow him into the riskiest actions to capture fascist positions.

I had arrived on the eve of an attack that Durruti had scheduled for the following day. At the time fixed, Durruti, like the rest of his militians, set out on the march with his Mauser slung over his shoulder. Together they forced the enemy back four kilometers. They also managed to capture a substantial amount of armaments which the enemy had abandoned when he fled. No doubt the example of simple moral equality was the explanation of Durruti's influence. There was another: his great capacity for getting militians to grasp the profound significance of the war against fascism; the significance that had dominated his existence and which he had passed on to the poorest, least capable of them.

Durruti talked to me of the difficult problems his men put to him whenever they sought leave just when they were most needed on the front. That they knew their leader is obvious; they knew his decisions, his iron will. But they were also familiar with the sympathy and kindness lurking deep within him. How could he resist when men spoke to him of sickness and suffering at home, of their fathers, wives, children?

(...) He could never be indifferent to his comrades' needs. Now he had entered into a desperate battle with fascism, in defense of the Revolution. Everyone had to take up his place. He truly did have a difficult task. He would listen patiently to the suffering, seek out its causes and suggest remedies in every instance where a wretch was beset by some moral or physical affliction. Overwork, inadequate food, lack of clean air and loss of appetite for life.

- Don't you see, comrade, that the war that you, I and we all sustain is for the salvation of the Revolution, and that the Revolution is made in order to put an end to men's misery and suffering? We have to beat our fascist enemy. We have to win this war. You are an essential part of that. Don't you see that, comrade?

Sometimes, a comrade would refuse to heed this reasoning. And insist upon leaving the front:

- Very well — Durruti would tell him — but you will leave on foot, and when you get back to your village everyone will know that you lacked courage, that you deserted rather than do the duty that you set yourself.

These words produced splendid results. The fellow would ask to stay. No military severity, no constraint, no disciplinary sanction to uphold the Durruti Column on the front. Only the great energy of the man who drove them and made them feel at one with him.

A great man, this anarchist Durruti. One born to lead, to teach. An affable, cordial comrade. All rolled into one. And now Durruti is dead. His heart beats no more. His imposing physique cut down like some giant tree. Yet Durruti is not dead. The hundreds of thousands who paid their final tribute to Durruti on November 22, 1936 bear witness to that.

No. Durruti is not dead. The fire of his ardent spirit enlightened all who knew and loved him. It will never be extinguished. Even now the masses have taken up the torch dropped from the hands of Durruti. Triumphantly, they are carrying it down the trail which Durruti lighted for many years. The trail leading to the summit of Durruti's ideal. That ideal is anarchism, the great love of Durruti's life, to which he was committed entirely. He was faithful to it to his last breath! No, Durruti is not dead.

Durruti Speaks[1]

I am satisfied with my Column. My comrades are well-equipped and when the time comes everything operates like a well-oiled machine. Not that I mean by that that they are no longer men. No. Our comrades on the front know for whom and for what they fight. They feel themselves revolutionaries and they fight, not in defense of more or less promised new laws, but for the conquest of the world, of the factories, the workshops, the means of transportation, their bread and the new culture. They know that their very life depends upon success.

We make revolution and war simultaneously — and this is my personal opinion — because the circumstances so require. Revolutionary measures are not taken in Barcelona alone, but from the firing lines too. In every village we capture, we set about developing the revolution. That is the best thing about this war of ours and when I think of it, I am all the more sensible of my responsibility. From the front lines back to Barcelona, there are nothing but fighters for our cause. All working on behalf of the war and the revolution.

One of the most important watchwords currently invoked is discipline. It is much talked about, but few strive after that goal. As for myself, discipline has no meaning beyond one's notion of responsibility. I am inimical to barrack-style discipline, the discipline that leads to brutality, horror and mechanical action. Nor do I acknowledge the wrong-headed watchword to the effect that freedom is out of place as the war currently stands and is the last refuge of the coward. Within our organization, the CNT enforces the best of disciplines. Confederation members accept and implement decisions made by the committees put up by elected comrades to shoulder these burdens of responsibility. In war-time, we should defer to our elected delegates. Otherwise no operation can be mounted. If we know that we have waverers to contend with, then let us appeal to their consciences and sense of pride. That way, we will be able to make good comrades of them.

I am satisfied with the comrades who follow me. I hope that they too are happy with me. They want for nothing. They have food to eat, reading matter and revolutionary discussions. Idleness has no place in our columns. We are forever building trench-works.

We will win this war, comrades!

Notes to Durruti Speaks

1. Text taken from Andre Prudhommeaux's *Cahiers de terre libre* and his *Catalogne 36-37* (1937): Prudhommeaux (1902–1968), a libertarian writer and journalist, ran a workers' bookstore in Paris and then a cooperative print shop in Names, connected with the German councilist movement as well as with Spanish anarcho-syndicalism: he published the newspaper *Terre libre* and a collection of pamphlets under the title *Cahiers de terre libre*, the earliest editions of *L'Espagne antifasciste* (1936) and later *L'Espagne nouvelle* (1937).

DURRUTI'S MESSAGE TO THE RUSSIAN WORKERS[1]

Many international revolutionaries who are close to our hearts and our minds live in Russia, not as free men, but in the political isolators and in penal servitude. Several of them have asked to come and fight our common foe in Spain, in the front ranks of the firing line. The international proletariat would not understand their not being released, nor would it understand that the reinforcements in weapons and man-power which Russia seems to have available for despatch to Spain should be the subject of haggling involving any abdication of the Spanish revolutionaries' freedom of action.

The Spanish revolution must take a different track from the Russian revolution. It must not develop in accordance with the formula of "One party in power, the rest in prison." But it should ensure success for the only formula ensuring that a united front would not be a deception: "All tendencies to work, all tendencies in the fray against the common foe. And the people will plump for the system that it deems best."

Note to Durruti's Message to the Russian Workers

1. Taken from A. Prudhommeaux, op. cit.

FINAL ADDRESS[1]

If the militarization being introduced by the Generalidad is supposed to intimidate us and impose an iron discipline upon us, it is sadly mistaken, and we invite the authors of the decree to travel up to the front to gauge our morale and our cohesiveness; then we will come and compare them alongside the morale and discipline in the rearguard.

Note to Final Address

1. Taken from A. Prudhommeaux, op. cit.

MILITIANS, YES! SOLDIERS, NEVER!

The workers' militias have played a crucial role in respect of the war effort against fascism. They have borne the brunt of operations. They could have imposed their own stamp upon the very nature of those operations. Logic required that the loyal army units be absorbed into the militia, not the militia incorporated into the army. This however is the miscalculation made by the Madrid and Barcelona "authorities" by proceeding with mobilization attempts which would necessarily have tipped the balance in favor of political indifference and involved militarization of the militias. In Catalonia that attempted mobilization failed.

(. . .) The streets of Barcelona have been invaded by recruits from the classes of '33, '34 and '35 who, having no confidence in the officers and considering themselves freed of the old military outlook of barrack life, refused to surrender themselves bodily. A number of these young folk enlisted in the militias, and some even wanted to set off immediately for Zaragoza. To spell out their point of view, they organized a huge gathering involving 10,000 of them, during which they passed the following resolution:

> We are not refusing to do our civic and revolutionary duty. We are keen to go and liberate our brethren in Zaragoza. We want to be militians of freedom, but not soldiers in uniform. The army has proved to be a danger to the people: the people's militias alone protect public freedoms: Militians, yes! But soldiers? Never!

The CNT has lobbied Madrid and the Catalan Generalidad on their behalf. Moreover, the new recruits' declarations were promptly turned into actions: thousands spontaneously enlisted with the militias. And mobilization without regard to class differences or revolutionary determination was dropped as far as the struggle "against the rebels" was concerned.

Let Madrid and Barcelona not delude themselves either; it is not a matter of simply repressing a "seditious" movement. We are faced here with a social phenomenon whose emergence the fascist endeavor has merely brought forward a little. Any who would stand against it will be swept aside. If, on the other hand, those in leadership grasp its power and afford it a free rein, they will avoid irreparable damage.

The CNT has told these young recruits: "Since the shirking of your duty does not enter into it, we will support your rights: you can fight as militians and not as soldiers." A solution applauded by the soldiers. We like to think that Spanish governments will not deny them this right, if need be. They must know that an army that fights under coercion ultimately winds up defeated, as witness Napoleon's armies which averted neither Waterloo nor the collapse of the Empire. Volunteer armies have a whole epic behind them, like the army of the French revolution's volunteer fighters.

The CNT knows that in summoning the militians to arms, none will shirk, for desertion in battle would amount to betrayal.

Regular Army or Libertarian Militias?

The streets were filled with posters, streamers and emblems towards the end of August, and the makeshift recruiting offices were at full stretch. What were we to do with these masses of fresh recruits at a time when fascism and antifascism made up islets, neutral zones, inextricably intertwined forces, with no established front lines? Compact masses to be sent against Franco's hastily mustered Moors and Requetés?[1] Or fighters in the revolutionary style, propagandists by insurgent deed, guerrillas and irregulars?

The military experts were divided. But, oddly enough, the civilian politicians all inclined towards a mass army, probably afraid of appearing inadequately imbued with the warrior spirit and unduly heedless of the "requirements of the hour!"

(. . .) It seems[2] increasingly necessary that we should wonder if the militarism of the seditious generals is going to impose its own modalities of struggle upon Spanish revolutionaries, or if, instead, our comrades will manage to dismantle militarism by opting instead for methods of action resulting in the liquidation of the military front and the dissemination of the social revolution throughout the length and breadth of Spain.

The factors for success available to the fascists are as follows: material galore, draconian rigidity of discipline, thoroughgoing military organization, and terror wielded against the populace with the assistance of fascism's police agencies. These factors for success are validated by the tactics of the warfare of positions, of the continuous front, with masses of troops being transported to the points where decisive clashes are expected. On the people's side, the factors for success are the very opposite: manpower galore, initiative and passionate aggressiveness in individuals and groups, the active sympathy of the toiling masses as a whole right across the entire country, the economic weapon of the strike and sabotage in fascist-occupied regions. Full utilization of these moral and physical resources, which are of themselves far superior to anything available to the enemy, can only be brought about through a generalized campaign of raids, ambushes and guerrilla warfare extending to every part of the land.

The very plainly expressed intention of certain Popular Front political elements is to combat militarism by confronting it with military technique of the same order, conducting against it a "regular" warfare with large-scale strikes by army corps and concentrations of materiel, decreeing conscription, implementing a strategic plan under a single command — in short, by aping fascism pretty well completely. Here too, we have publicized the views of comrades who have let themselves be swayed by Bolshevism to the extent of calling for the creation of one "Red Army."

That approach strikes us as dangerous from more than one point of view. We ought not to forget that the Red Army of the Bolsheviks was a peace-time creation, victory over the reaction having been primarily the handiwork of bands of "partisans" employing methods comparable to those of the Spanish guerrillas.

At present, the essential issue is not the conversion of the militia, a body of partisans suited to guerrilla warfare, into a regular army with all of the characteristics of a professional army. The point is, rather, to raise the militia units' own expertise by learning from the tactical ideas of the combat group and section school, as applied in the main armies of Europe, and kitting out the combat groups with appropriate equipment (automatic weapons, hand grenades, rifle grenades, etc.). Doing otherwise would amount to staking all upon a Napoleonic battle, all of the wherewithal of which has yet to be created as far as the Spanish antifascist camp is concerned. It would amount to putting off the decision until the Greek kalends, endlessly dragging out the current position, and, in that case, trusting to serendipity a victory that would inevitably fall to us if we knew how to make full usage of our own weaponry.

All of which leads us to believe that the decision in the contest being fought out in the four corners of Spain will be moral rather than strategic in nature.

Let us be on the alert for the interested maneuvers of the appeasers and makers of compromises, who are just biding their time before betraying the people by reaching some accommodation with the fascist segment of the bourgeoisie, for the sole purpose of annihilating and smothering forever the revolutionary élan of the proletariat.

(...) Daily, fresh popular levies are being raised in Barcelona. After a few days'- summary training, these units are issued with their equipment and bid the capital farewell in a procession through the streets. Along this march-past of volunteers, the premises of all of the affiliated organizations of the Antifascist Militias' Committee are saluted and shouts of victory are exchanged between the comrades on the point of departing and those massed at the windows and balconies above.

Each column has a character of its own, more distinctive than the emblems it displays. The Communist and Socialist detachments are distinguished by a certain military stiffness, the presence of cavalry and special weapons squadrons, more compact formations, rhythmic step and raised fists. POUM[3] troops, the police troops and Catalanists' troops are noted for the splendor and profusion of their equipment. The FAI and CNT comrades march without chanting or band music.

There they are in three widely separated ranks, out of step, excited, man after man, interspersed with milling groups, an endless snake. At their head, in a single rank, the staff, in blue workers' overalls. It comprises well-known trade union militants: in the CNT every organizer or propagandist doubles as a guerrilla, an activist and a fighter. Even in Barcelona, when evening falls, men who today hold the reins of the country's economy and sit in the armchairs vacated by bankers, pick up their handgun or militian's rifle to proceed with their own hands to liquidate fascist elements whose lairs are still numerous on Catalan soil. Thus, in the anarchist ranks, there is no dividing line between the machine gunners and the typists, between personnel in the rearguard and front-line personnel. There are no professional "chiefs," only leaders of men who have paid and daily pay a personal price. No bureaucratic specialization, but rounded militants, revolutionaries from head to toe.

Through the broad avenues trickle the three narrow streams of humanity, with a crowd in tow. Alongside the militian in his red and black forage cap, rifle slung over his shoulder, strides a friend, a child, a mother, a spouse, a sister, sometimes an entire family of relatives and friends. Greetings are exchanged, names called out, hands shaken, workmates swap fraternal embraces, and we have the column invaded by a whole populace, packing the gaps in its ranks and sweeping it along in the warmth of its fervor.

An old gray-haired woman stands in the path of the middle rank: every passing man, every one without distinction, receives a mother's farewell from this woman. Thus hundreds and hundreds of men carry away the short, vigorous hug, the clumsy, impassioned embrace, the supreme clasp of an unknown mother who acknowledges all of the lads from the FAI as her own, clinging momentarily to their arms, re-enacting a thousand times over the heart-rending moment of parting. Whereupon a cry goes up from the crowd, flapping into the breeze like the wings of a gull: "Long live the FAI! Long live Anarchy!" And anyone hearing that cry understands then that the UGT, the CNT, the PSUC, all of these party and group designations are no more than things, slogans, initials, but that the FAI ("the fai" as it is pronounced) is a woman: a fiancée, spouse, sister, daughter and idealized mother of all whose hearts beat for love of liberty.

(...) Sentimental twaddle! it will be said. But is not such twaddle what revolutions are all about?

Notes to Regular Army or Libertarian Militias?

1. *Requetés*, armed bands of Navarrese Traditionalists, organized and regimented for civil war in the name of "God, Fatherland and King."
2. Taken from *L'Espagne Antifasciste* No. 4, as reprinted in *Cahiers de terre libre* 1937.
3. POUM, the anti-Stalinist inclined Workers' Party for Marxist Unification. Catalanists, members of a Catalan autonomist party.
PSUC, the (Stalinist) Unified Socialist Party of Catalonia.

The Italian Section of the Ascaso Column Opposes Militarization (Monte Pelado, October 30, 1936)

The members of the Ascaso Column's "Italian Section" are volunteers who have come from various nations to do their bit for the cause of Spanish freedom and that of freedom worldwide. Having learned of the decree promulgated by the Generalidad Council regarding amendment of the constitution of the militias, they reiterate their commitment to the cause that has brought them on to the battle-front against fascism and must declare as follows:

1. The decree in question can refer only to those who are subject to the obligations implicit in mobilization emanating from the authorities who have promulgated it — a measure on the advisability of which we shall refrain from offering any principled opinion.

2. This confirms us in our belief that the decree in question cannot be applicable to us. However, we have to state with the requisite absolute clarity that, in the event of the authorities' deeming us as liable to implementation of it, we could not but regard ourselves as released from any moral obligation and invoke our complete freedom of action — the foundation compact of the Section as such being dissolved utterly.

An Iron Column Delegate's Address to the Regional Plenum in Valencia (endorsed by the Column and reprinted in its mouthpiece Linea de Fuego *[Teruel front] on November 17, 1936)*

The Iron Column asks that the reporting panel not deal with the structure of the CNT militias.

The Iron Column must describe its structure and its internal organization. On this score, debate ought to focus on a number of points. For one thing, the militarization issue, for there is a government decree providing for militarization of all columns, and there are comrades who believe that militarization settles everything.

We say that it will settle nothing.

In place of corporals, sergeants and officer graduates from academies who are sometimes abysmally ignorant of the problems of war, we offer our organization and accept no military structure. The Iron Column and all of the CNT and FAI columns — and, indeed, others which are not confederal columns — have not found military discipline acceptable.

Single Command or Coordination?

In a motion tabled and approved at a meeting in Valencia[1] by the CNT, the FAI, the Iron Column, etc., wherein the need was expressed for the establishment a body to liaise between the forces fighting in Teruel and on a number of fronts, a request was made that war committees and column committees be set up, with an eye to establishing a delegate operations committee, made up of two civilian delegates and a general technician in an advisory capacity per column, plus the delegate from the people's executive committee, to act as liaison between the Teruel columns and those on other fronts.

Which is to say that we, who are against what is termed the single command, propagate, by example and practice, coordination of all fighting forces. We cannot countenance some staff, some minister, with no practical acquaintance with the situation on the ground, and who have never set foot on the field of battle and know nothing of the mentality of the men they command (which ignorance may well extend also to military expertise) should direct us from behind desks and issue us with orders, mostly inane ones. And as we have virtually always had to submit to the orders from the military command, war delegates and delegations from the staff, we must protest and request that the aforesaid Valencia staff be stood down. For as long as we have abided by it, such was the extent of the disorientation that we knew nothing of the situation on other fronts, nor about the activities of other columns: we suffered bombardment without managing to discover whence it emanated. Which is why we suggest that an operations committee be established, made up of direct representatives of the columns and not, as the marxists wish, of representatives from each organizational grouping; *we* want representatives familiar with the terrain and who know their way around.

The establishment of war committees is acceptable to all confederal militias. We start with the individual and form groups of ten, which come to accommodations among themselves for small-scale operations. Ten such groups together make up one **centuria,** which appoints a delegate to represent it. Thirty **centurias** make up one column, which is directed by a war committee, on which the delegates from the **centurias** have their say.

Another point is the matter of the coordination of all fronts. This will be handled by the committees constituted by two civilian delegates with one military delegate in an advisory capacity, in addition to the delegation from the people's executive committee. Thus, although every column retains its freedom of action, we arrive at coordination of forces, which is not the same thing as unity of command.

The marxists and republicans did not want that, because they said that the columns ought not to debate and that everybody had to abide by whatever the staff orders. Thus, better a defeat under the staff than fifty victories under fifty committees.

Military Hierarchy or Federalism?

As for militarization, we will readily concede that the military, who have spent their entire lives studying the tactics of warfare, are better informed than us and that their advice is often more valuable than ours. Consequently, we accept their advice and their contribution. Inside our column, for instance, the military personnel in whom we have every confidence, work in concert with us and together we coordinate our efforts: but if we should be militarized, only one thing can happen, which is that [we switch] from a federalist structure to a barrack-style discipline, which is the very thing that we do not want.

There is talk too of amalgamating militias. We reckon that association on the basis of affinity should prevail tomorrow just as it does today. Let individuals come together in accordance with their thinking and temperament. Let those who think along such and such lines combine their efforts in order to achieve their common goals. If columns are formed along heterogeneous lines, we will achieve nothing practical.

Which means that we do not in any way surrender the columns' independence and have no wish to subject ourselves to any governmental command. We fight, first to defeat fascism, and then for our ideal, which is anarchy. Our activity ought not to tend to strengthen the State, but rather to progressively destroy it and render government redundant.

We consent to nothing that conflicts with our anarchist ideas, which are a reality, given that one cannot act in contradiction of one's beliefs.

Consequently we suggest that our organization into groups, **centurias** or column committees and war committees made up of military and civilian personnel be accepted, so as to establish coordination of all of the militias fighting on the various fronts, with a central staff.

Equipment Shortages

Final point under discussion: shortages of war materials. To date, our columns have been kept supplied feebly by the State. For example, in the column which I represent, out of its three thousand component members, we may say that only around a thousand rifles have been furnished by the State and we have had to find all the rest ourselves, 80 percent of them having been taken from the enemy. Which means to say that the State, the government, official bodies have shown no interest in the question of arming and equipping columns with the material they need. This is a matter the organization ought to have resolved and in Valencia very little heed was paid to it. The organization must see to it that we want for nothing.

It has also been said that discipline averts demoralization and desertion. That is far from certain. Courage and fear depend on many factors, for the same person may be afraid in one engagement and behave like a downright hero in another. Discipline or not, it all works out the same, since it has been established that those who are militarized are the first to turn tail and run; and when danger arises, the individual, be he anarchist, marxist or republican, is gripped by the same instinct for self-preservation and either flees or advances.

The Pay Question

Here now we have another problem, which, we contend, it is for the organization to resolve. The rapporteurs' commission says that militias must be economically dependent on the State. Our answer to that must be that to begin with, the Confederation's columns were formed spontaneously and set off for the front. Nobody spared a thought for pay, because the villages where those combatants lived looked after their families, whose needs were thus provided for: but a point came when the villages stopped looking after the families and the complaints began. We have always been against this ten peseta payrate, because the individual got used to fighting for a living and made a profession of it. Such fears were justified, for a number of our comrades have been, so to speak, corrupted. We say that the unions can meet the families' needs, so we renounce the ten pesetas and seek nothing; otherwise, we will continue to draw them as we have thus far.

The one big union in Segorbe should inform you that, as we abide by the conclusions it has adopted, it is in complete agreement with the structure of the Iron Column, the Torres-Benito column and Column No. 23. Segorbe, which is where they are concentrated and recruited from, recognizes that such a structure in the militias is necessary, for it is in a better position to judge than most of the delegations attending the plenum, because it has, in addition, by way of a delegate at our plenum a female comrade who has spent upwards of a month with the Iron Column, helping to organize our outposts.

And in that regard, we laugh at this unity of command, this militarization they are trying to introduce into our confederal columns, and we laugh at them because, as one Iron Column comrade put it so well, we already have our structure and our unity of command without resorting to militarization. And we have that because we are the first, the finest of the Levante region to have stood up against fascism and to have successfully prevented fascism from taking over that region (in Segorbe to begin with and then in Valencia); and as we were the first, we have a right to speak out and to inform this plenum how the Iron Column operates.

The Militian as a Conscious Individual

My predecessor on this rostrum talked about structure. I should like to explore the matter further. Will an absolute unity of command which decides what the role of the individual is to be in the war prove more effective in action than that individual's convictions?

Because let me tell you this: those who bridle at the Iron Column because it swoops on the rear in order to make the revolution that you do not know how to make — such people, I say, do not know what they are talking about.

The ordinary militian comes to the Column because he knows that he will find there a moral, revolutionary and intellectual unity. That is why we, who were the first on to the field of battle, cannot now allow marxism and bourgeois democracy to attempt, as the reaction did yesterday, to annihilate the cream of the crop of the revolutionary Levante countryside, that is to say, its anarchist revolutionary yield.

And it is also why we cannot agree to a single command, because the military have not seen fit to do anything other than stay in the rear. And we, who have marveled at the morale of our brother confederals, who know that among their number there are those who are worth a hundred of the militarized, we want no obstruction and do not want anyone invoking this falsehood — that we cannot win this war without unity of command.

The practices of the ancien regime's political parties, seeking to create unity of command so as to hand it to their Red Armies in order to install a dictatorship perhaps as poisonous as its predecessor, are placing the revolution in jeopardy. We cannot countenance that, and on that score I have to say that this whole plenum, misdirected, unfortunately, by the regional committee, is proceeding in a plainly reformist and political atmosphere, and that is why our feeble voice must be heard, because, later, we shall all have to pay the price for our incomprehension.

Note to The Italian Section of the Ascaso Column

1. Valencia was then the seat of the central government of the republic, which had had to quit Madrid.

ANARCHO-SYNDICALISM IN GOVERNMENT

To conclude, we turn now to a prickly, burning issue which inspired floods of words and ink at the time and which even now gives rise to bitter debate.

The anarchists' participation in two Spanish republican governments, the central government of the Republic and the autonomous regional government of Catalonia, under the umbrella of the "united front against fascism" is, in fact, one of Iberian anarchism's Achilles heels.

"Pure" anarchists and non-Stalinist marxists alike took, and with hindsight now take, anarcho-syndicalists sorely to task for having jettisoned their principles. But does such criticism not lean a little too heavily upon absolutes? Is it not a little too glib in its ignoring of the context of a civil war that the Spanish revolution had to win at all costs if it wanted to survive?

- Sorry! the die-hards reply, it was precisely absorption into the machinery of the republican government, itself increasingly infiltrated by the Stalinists, that compromised the Spanish revolution's chances of survival.

What we offer below is a fairly comprehensive dossier on the debate:

- First, the rigorously principled stance enunciated by the Spanish libertarians just prior to the Revolution; the basis of which is an scathing indictment of "Antifascist" coalition governments.

- Followed by a laborious effort to justify an abrupt and unexpected U-turn.

- Then, a violent diatribe by Camillo Berneri (the Italian anarchist who went to Spain to throw in his lot with the Spanish Revolution) written against Federica Montseny, then a minister in the central government, not long before Berneri was murdered.

- Finally, to close, the self-criticism drafted by Federica Montseny thirty years after the event and especially for this anthology.

THE USELESSNESS OF GOVERNMENT[1]
(A MANIFESTO ADOPTED BY THE CNT)

"Wealthy nations are those where poverty is the rule." That dictum from a bourgeois economist is a fine summary of the contrasts within our society, where the strength of nations comprises the weakness and poverty of the largest number. Similarly, we might say that it is weak peoples that make for strong governments.

The existence of a Popular Front government, so very far from being an essential element in the struggle against fascism, in point of fact denotes a voluntary limit set to that same struggle. We need not recall that in the face of the preparations for the fascists' putsch, the Generalidad and Madrid governments did not lift a finger, all of their authority being deployed to cover up the intrigues of which they were fated, sooner or later, to become the witting or unwitting instruments.

The war underway in Spain is a social war. The part of a moderator State, based on equilibrium and retention of class differences, could scarcely be an active part in this contest, when the very foundations of the State are being undermined with every passing day. So it is correct to say that the existence of the Popular Front government in Spain is nothing more than a reflection of a compromise between the popular masses and international capitalism.

By the very nature of things, this compromise, which is merely temporary, must give way to the claims and comprehensive program of the social revolution. Whereupon the role of negotiator and preservationist in which the republicans and liberals of Barcelona, Valencia and Madrid are presently cast will vanish.

The notion of replacing these weak governments, care-takers of the changes and of foreign finance's holdings in Spain, with a strong government based upon an ideology and a "revolutionary" political organization would in fact result only in suspension and liquidation of the autonomous action of the toiling masses in arms, suspension and liquidation of the revolution.

If marxism were to take power, it would resemble more closely a self-limitation of the people's action, prompted by opportunistic savvy. The built-to-last "worker's" State sets itself the immediate task of channeling and absorbing every single one of the forces presently at liberty within the proletariat and peasantry. The "worker's" State is the full stop concluding all revolutionary progress, the beginning of a new political enslavement.

Co-ordinating the forces of the antifascist front, organizing supplies of munitions and foodstuffs on a large scale, collectivizing all undertakings of essential interest to the people in pursuance of that end, these, self-evidently, are the tasks of the hour. Thus far, they have been carried out by non-governmental, non-centralistic, non-militaristic procedures. We need only continue. There are great improvements to be made to this approach. The CNT and UGT unions find a use for their resources there, and the best deployment of their capabilities, On the other hand, the installation of a coalition government, with its discreet strife between majority and minority, its bureaucratization of elites, the concomitant fratricidal warfare between rival tendencies, all of that is more than useless to the performance of our liberating mission in Spain. It would spell the rapid collapse of our capacity for action, our desire for union, the beginning of a fatal debacle in the face of an omnipresent enemy.

We hope that Spanish and foreign workers will appreciate the correctness of the decisions taken to this effect by the National Confederation of Labor (CNT) and by the Iberian Anarchist Federation IFAI). The withering away of the State is socialism's ultimate objective. Facts have demonstrated that in practice it is achieved by liquidation of the bourgeois State, brought to a state of asphyxiation by economic expropriation, and not by the unprompted withering away of a "socialist" bureaucracy.

The Spanish people and the Russian case bear witness to that.

Note to The Uselessness of Government

1. From *Solidaridad Obrera* in the summer of 1936

A WOULD-BE JUSTIFICATION

However, within a few weeks, in mid-September 1936, the CNT reversed its stance. In the name of "antifascist unity," it saw fit to petition the Spanish prime minister, Largo Caballero, for the establishment of a fifteen-member "National Defense Council," in which five places would be reserved for it. It was only a step from that to cabinet membership — a step that the anarcho-syndicalists took. In the end, they took up portfolios in both the Generalidad government in Catalonia and, later, in the central government. Let us see now how the CNT attempted to explain away its U-turn.

Two months have elapsed since the CNT staked its claim to a share in the running of Spain's affairs. Our view is that some new agency needed to be set up, and it was with that in mind that we suggested the formula of a National

Defense Council. We have forsworn that notion, in a sincere intent to clear away the obstacles that prompted our opposition. Yet again we yield, not for political considerations, but so as to achieve the unity necessary for victory.

This is not the time to indulge in speculation nor to quibble over trifles. Primarily, it should be remarked that the tasks of the new government are not the same as those of its predecessor, and although the portfolios held by the CNT may be without significance, its very presence in that ministry ought to amend its approach and action. Attention should be focused upon the two over-riding problems of the day: winning the war and consolidating the economic reconstruction, in such a way that the new Spain may have all she needs in order to survive. No government is viable that fails to have a care for achieving those two objectives.

The preceding government was referred to as the government of victory. The facts demonstrated that it was nothing of the sort. On the contrary: things went from bad to worse. Today, there must be no repetition of that experience. Wheresoever the ministries that gave the lead from July 19 failed, today's must succeed. And for that to happen, all who figure in the new government must set aside their partisan preferences or outlooks, in order to act as if prompted by a single thought: victory. If such open and disinterested cooperation is forthcoming, if the requirements of the war and the needs of the civilian population alone dictate everyone's every action, then victory will soon smile upon us.

Two problems arise: beating fascism and sparing revolutionary Spain privation. These are the goals, and in order to achieve them let everyone set to work in loyal, disinterested collaboration.

The CNT, the Government and the State

The CNT's entry into the central government is one of the most monumental events in the recorded political history of our country. In principle and out of conviction, the CNT has always been anti-statist and inimical to all forms of government. But circumstances, almost always stronger than men's will, though the latter determines them, have altered the nature of the Spanish government and the Spanish State.

At present, the government as the instrument regulating the agencies of the State, is no longer a force for oppression targeting the working class, just as the State is no longer that agency dividing society into classes. And with the participation of CNT personnel in both, the State and the government will refrain all the more from oppressing the people.

The State's functions will be restricted by agreement with the workers' organizations, to overseeing the workings of the country's economic and social life. And the government will have nothing to preoccupy it beyond the proper running of the war and coordinating revolutionary endeavors in accordance with an overall plan.

Our comrades will bring to government the collective or majority will of the working masses, who will first have been gathered into great general assemblies. They will not act as the spokesmen for personal views but solely for decisions freely-taken by the hundreds of thousands of workers organized inside the CNT. Historical inevitability is a burden upon us all and the CNT bows to that inevitability in order to be of service to the country, by speedily winning the war and preventing any deviation by the popular revolution.

We are absolutely certain that those of our comrades chosen to represent the CNT in government will be able to do their duty and carry off the mission entrusted to them. We ought not to look upon them as individuals but rather as the organization for which they stand. They are neither governors, nor Statists, but fighters and revolutionaries in the service of success over fascism. And that success will come all the quicker and more completely, the greater the support we lend them.

The CNT's Entry into the Government

Spanish trade unionists are called upon to share in the running of the country. This new phase of the fight against fascism, and in the development of the Spanish trade union and anarchist movement, should not be viewed in terms of doctrine only. On July 19, it was the anarchists and trade unionists who marched at the head of the revolutionary movement to confront the fascist generals. The creation of antifascist militias and the collectivization of industry in Catalonia were primarily the handiwork of the CNT-FAI.

For a time, there were two sorts of governments: on the one hand, the Generalidad, on the other the Antifascist Militias' Committee and the Economic Council. It was soon realized that this duality could not continue. Whereupon there arose the Generalidad General Council, comprising all of the antifascist organizations. In Catalonia, in Levante and in Aragon, where trade unionists and anarchists account for more than half of the antifascist forces, fascism was wiped out completely, whereas in those districts where the democratic socialists and other parties were in the ascendancy the struggle did not have such a felicitous outcome.

In Madrid trade unionists are in the minority. However their influence has grown of late. For more than two months now, the CNT has been calling for the dissolution of the government and the creation of a National Defense Council, with equal participation of the CNT and the UGT. Largo Caballero was unwilling to give up the levers of power; he wanted to be Spain's Lenin. His policy tended to weaken the antifascist fighting front. The dispensing of weapons to the various parties and organizations was conducted with partiality, and the need for unity in the conduct of the war was felt with increasing urgency.

Being merely soldiers of the Revolution and letting Communists and Socialists act as the generals was not a course that could have satisfied the trade unionists and anarchists. They too were entitled to have their say in national deliberations on the prosecution of the war. Hence the CNT's request concerning creation of a National Defense Council. Caballero was not willing to surrender one iota of his power. Meanwhile, the military situation in Madrid was growing more critical each day. Unity in the direction of the war is not feasible unless the CNT is called upon to share in that direction.

On notices posted up all over Spain by the CNT, one could read: "Two million members: 50,000 soldiers on the front; upwards of 2,000 local organizations; Catalonia, Levante and Aragon in CNT hands." This mighty organization was seeking a share in the direction of the antifascist struggle. A Regional Defense council, largely made up of CNT supporters, was formed in Aragon. At which point the Madrid government found itself compelled to accede to the CNT's request: four trade unionists joined the cabinet. The CNT is entitled to more, but this is no time for partisan strife.

THE CONTRARY VIEW
OPEN LETTER TO FEDERICA MONTSENY BY CAMILLO BERNERI[1] (APRIL 1937)

Dear Comrade

I had intended to address myself to all of you minister comrades, but once I had taken up my pen, I spontaneously addressed myself to you alone and I was unwilling to go against that instinctive impulse.

That I have not always seen eye to eye with you will come as no surprise to you, nor will it be an irritant, and you have shown yourself generously oblivious of criticisms which it would virtually always have been reasonable and human to regard as unfair and over-stated. That, in my eyes, is a quality of some significance, and it is testimony to the anarchist nature of your mind. Speaking as a friend of course, that certainty effectively makes up for the ideological idiosyncrasies which you have often displayed in your articles with their highly personal style and in your admirably eloquent speeches.

I could not blithely accept the identity which you assert exists between Bakuninist anarchism and the federalist republicanism of Pi y Margall.[2] I cannot forgive you for having written "that, in Russia, it was not Lenin who was the real builder of Russia, but rather Stalin, the spirit of accomplishment, etc." And I applauded Voline's retort in *Terre libre* to your utterly inaccurate assertions regarding the Russian anarchist movement.

But it is not about that that I wish to engage you today. I hope some day to broach those matters and many another with you directly. If I address myself publicly to you, it is in regard to infinitely more serious matters, to remind you of your enormous responsibilities, which you may well have overlooked on account of your modesty.

In your speech of January 3 [1937], you said: "Anarchists have entered the government in order to prevent deviation in the Revolution and to prosecute it beyond the war, and also to oppose the eventuality of dictatorial ambitions, from wherever these may emanate."

Well comrade! In April, three months into the collaborationist experience, we find ourselves faced with a situation which has thrown up serious events, with still worse looming ahead.

Wherever — take the Basque Country, Levante or Castile — our movement has not prevailed through grassroots strength, or, in other words, comprehensive trade union structures and overwhelming affiliation of the masses, the counter-revolution is oppressive and threatens to crush everything. The government is in Valencia and it is from there that Assault Guards set out to disarm the revolutionary nuclei formed for defensive purposes. Casas Viejas[3] comes to mind whenever one thinks of Vilanesa.[4] It is the Civil Guards and Assault Guards who get to hold on to their weapons; it is they who are to control the "uncontrollables" in the rear, which is to say, disarm the revolutionary nuclei with their few rifles and handful of revolvers. All of this is happening at a time when the internal front has yet to be liquidated. Happening during a civil war in which no surprise can be ruled out and in regions where the front-line is very close and extremely indented and not a mathematical certainty. This when there is a blatantly political dispensing of weapons whereby the Aragon front, that armed accompaniment to the agrarian collectivization in Aragon and buttress of Catalonia, that Iberian Ukraine, tends to get only the bare necessity (let us hope that that "bare necessity" will prove sufficient). You are a member of a government which has offered France and England concessions in Morocco, whereas, as long ago as July 1936, Morocco ought to have been formally declared to be politically autonomous.[5] I imagine that as an anarchist you find this business as squalid as it is stupid, but I think that the time has come to let it be known that you and the other anarchist ministers are not in agreement either with the nature or the tenor of such proposals.

On October 24, 1936, I wrote in *Guerra di classe:* "The fascist army's operational base is Morocco. Propaganda in favor of Moroccan autonomy must be stepped up throughout the whole pan-Islamic sphere of influence. We must force upon Madrid unequival declarations announcing withdrawal from Morocco and protection for Moroccan autonomy. France is anxious about the possibility of a chain reaction of uprisings in North Africa and Syria; England sees Egyptian agitation for autonomy and that of the Palestinian Arabs being strengthened. We should exploit such worries by means of a policy that threatens to unleash revolt in the Islamic world. Such a policy will require funding and as a matter of urgency we must despatch agitator and organizer emissaries to every focal point of Arab emigration in every one of the frontier areas of French Morocco. It would require only a few Moroccans to carry out propaganda work (by means of wireless, leaflets, etc.) on the fronts in Aragon, the Center, Asturias and Andalusia."

It goes without saying that we cannot simultaneously guarantee English and French interests in Morocco *and* raise insurrection. Valencia carries on with Madrid's policy. That must change. And, in order to change it, it has to spell out all its own thinking loud and clear, because there are influences at work in Valencia that favor a compromise with Franco. Jean Zyromski[6] wrote in *Le Populaire* of March 3: "The intrigues are there to be seen and they are aimed at concluding a peace which would in fact signify not just the halting of the Spanish revolution, but indeed the abolition of what social progress has been achieved. 'Neither Caballero nor Franco,' that would be the catch-phrase summing up a notion which is in the air, and I am not sure that it may not be favored by certain political, diplomatic and indeed government circles in England and in France alike."

Such influences, such maneuvers account for a variety of gray areas: the inactivity of the loyalist fleet for instance. The marshaling of forces from Morocco, the piracy by the *Canarias* and the *Baleares*[7] and the fall of Malaga are the consequences of that inactivity. And the war is not yet over! If Prieto[8] is so inept and lazy, why put up with him? If Prieto's hands are tied by a policy that has him keep the fleet paralyzed, why not denounce that policy?

You anarchist ministers make eloquent speeches and write brilliant articles, but one does not win the war and defend the Revolution with speeches and articles. The one is won and the other defended by the passage from defensive to offensive. Positional strategy cannot carry on forever. The problem can only be resolved by launching the watchwords: general mobilization, weapons to the fronts, single command, people's army, etc., The problem is resolved by doing immediately whatever is practicable.

The *Depeche de Toulouse* of January 17th [1937] wrote:

> The chief preoccupation of the Interior ministry is the reassertion of the authority of the State over that of groups and over that of uncontrollables, whatever their provenance.

It goes without saying that, while months can be spent attempting to wipe out "uncontrollables," no resolution can be found to the problem of liquidating the "fifth column."[9] A prior condition of the mopping-up of the internal front is the investigative and repressive activity which can only be conducted by tried and tested revolutionaries. A domestic policy of class collaboration and flirtation with the middle classes inevitable leads to tolerance being shown to politically dubious elements. The "fifth column" is made up, not just of elements belonging to fascist organizations, but also of all the malcontents who yearn for a moderate republic. Now, it is the latter who profit from the tolerance displayed by those who hunt down the "uncontrollables."

The mopping-up of the internal front was conditional upon wide-ranging and radical action by the defense committees set up by the CNT and the UGT.

We are witnessing the infiltration into the officer corps of the Popular Army of questionable elements who cannot offer the assurances of political and trade union affiliation. The militias' committees and political delegates exercised a salutary control which has today been undermined by the prevalence of strictly military schemes of advancement and promotional. The authority of the committees and delegates must be strengthened.

We are witnessing something new, with potentially dangerous consequences — to wit, whole battalions under the command of officers who do not enjoy the respect and affection of the militians. This is a serious matter, because the value of most Spanish militians is in direct proportion with the confidence enjoyed by their own commanders. So direct election and the rights of the rank and file to dismiss must be reintroduced.

A grave mistake was made in accepting authoritarian practices, not because they were so formally authoritarian, but because they enshrined enormous errors and political aims that had nothing to do with the demands of the war.

I have had occasion to speak with Italian, French and Belgian superior officers and I have noticed that they display a much more modern and rational understanding of discipline than certain neo-generals who purport to be realists.

I believe the time has come to form the confederal army, just as the Socialist Party has launched its own troop in the shape of the 5th Regiment of People's Militias. I believe that the time has come to resolve the command problem by moving towards an effective unity of command that may render going on to the offensive on the Aragon front feasible. I believe the time has come to create a war industry to be reckoned with. And I believe the time has come to put paid to certain glaring oddities: such as the respect for Sunday as a day of rest and certain "workers' rights" that sabotage the defenses of the Revolution.

Above all, we must keep up the morale of the fighters. Luigi Bertoni,[10] articulating feelings expressed by various Italian comrades fighting on the Huesca front, wrote, not so long ago: "The Spanish war, thus bereft of all new faith, all notion of social change, all revolutionary grandeur, all universal import, is left as a vulgar war of national independence which has to be waged in order to avert the extermination which the world plutocracy has in mind. It remains a terrifying life or death issue, but is no longer a war for the establishment of a new system and a new humanity. It will be said that all is not yet lost, but in reality all is in jeopardy and invested. Our side uses the language of renunciation, as did Italian socialism in the face of fascism's advance: "Beware of provocations! Keep calm, keep cool! Order and discipline!" All of which in practice boils down to laissez-fire. And just as Fascism wound up winning in Italy, so in Spain anti-socialism in republican garb cannot but win, failing unforeseen events. Needless to add, we are merely placing this on record and not condemning our side: we cannot say how they might act differently and with effect as long as the Italo-German pressure is growing at the front and that of the Bolsheviko-bourgeois in the rear."

I do not have Luigi Bertoni's modesty. I venture to assert that Spanish anarchists could pursue a different policy line from the prevailing one; I claim that I can, on the basis of what I know about the experiences of various great recent revolutions and what I read in the Spanish libertarian press itself, recommend a few policy lines.

I believe that you must tackle the problem of whether you defend the Revolution better by making a larger contribution to the fight against fascism by participating in government, or whether you might not be infinitely more useful carrying the torch of your magnificent oratory among the fighters and in the rear.

The time has also come to clarify the unitary import which our participation in the government may have. We must address the masses, and call upon them to judge whether Marcel Cachin[11] is right when he declares in *L'Humanite* of 23 March: "The anarchist leaders are redoubling their unitary efforts and their appeals are heeded more and more."

Or whether it is *Pravda* and *Izvestia* which are right when they vilify the Spanish anarchists by depicting them as sabotaging unity.

We must appeal to the mass to sit in judgment of the moral and political complicity of the Spanish anarchist press's silence concerning Stalin's dictatorial crimes, the persecutions visited on Russian anarchists, the monstrous trials mounted against the Leninist and Trotskyist opposition, a silence duly rewarded by *Izvestia*'s defamatory remarks about *Solidaridad Obrera*.

The masses must be called upon to judge whether certain ploys designed to sabotage supplies are not part and parcel of the plan announced on December 17, 1936 by *Pravda*: "As for Catalonia, the purging of Trotskyist and anarchist syndicalist elements has begun; this endeavor will be prosecuted with the same vigor with which it has been carried out in the USSR."

The time has come to gauge whether anarchists are in government to act as the vestals of a flame on the verge of going out, or whether they are henceforth there solely to serve as a Phrygian cap for politicians flirting with the enemy or with forces keen to restore the "republic of all classes." The problem is posed by the obviousness of a crisis deeper than the men who are its representative personalities.

The dilemma — war or revolution — no longer has any meaning. The only dilemma is this: either victory over Franco, thanks to revolutionary war, or defeat.

The problem for you and other comrades is to choose between Thiers's Versailles and the Paris of the Commune, before Thiers and Bismarck cobble together a sacred union. It is for you to answer, for you are "the light beneath the bushel."

Camillo Berneri

Notes to The Contrary View

1. Camillo Berneri (1897–1937), born in Lodi, Italy, started off in the Young Socialists which he left publicly around 1915 in order to join the anarchist movement. Exiled under the Mussolini regime, he was deported from a number of European countries and sampled the prisons of half of Europe. In Germany, he contacted the anarcho-syndicalists. On learning of the Spanish Revolution, he set off immediately and was involved in the fighting. In Barcelona he launched the newspaper *Guerra di classe* some of the articles from which were collated under the title "Guerre de classes en Espagne" in *Cahiers de terre libre* of April-May 1938. He did not stint his criticisms of the anarchists' participation in government. Arrested by police on the orders of the Stalinists on May 5, 1937, during the bloody incidents in Barcelona. He was taken from his cell and gunned down.
2. In January 1937, in a public lecture in Barcelona, Federica Montseny sang the praises of the regionalism of Francisco Pi y Margall (1821–1901), a disciple of Proudhon. This had earned her criticism from Gaston Leval, along the same lines as Berneri's.
3. In 1933, the workers of Casas Viejas had taken over their village and proclaimed libertarian communism. The Civil Guards had put this rebellion down with savagery.
4. Vilanesa, a tiny Spanish village where several CNT militants were massacred after their trade union premises were ransacked.
5. The republican government had adopted an imperialist line, refusing to de-colonize Spanish Morocco, which allowed Franco to use Moroccan troops against the Spanish republic.
6. Jean Zyromski (born 1890), leader of the left wing of the SFIO socialist party, and later a member of the French Communist Party.
7. These were two Francoist cruisers which shelled Malaga at the beginning of February 1937. The *Baleares* was sunk by the republican fleet on March 6, 1937.

The *Canarias*, which had earlier shelled Gerona and Tarragona, caused many deaths after the fall of Malaga when it shelled the coastal road by which fugitives were trying to reach republican Spain.

8. Indalecio Prieto (1883–1962), socialist minister of the Spanish republic: he died in Mexico.

9. Fifth column: name given in the Spanish press to the range of fascist organizations existing in the rear of the republican front.

10. Luigi Bertoni (1872–1947), Italian anarchist who had offered his services to the Spanish revolution.

11. Marcel Cachin (1869–1958), one-time social democrat, one of the founders of the French Communist Party and a Stalinist to his dying day.

The CNT Taken to Task by its International (Paris, June 11-13, 1937)[1]

After having heard reports from the IWA[2], from the CNT delegation and clarification and opinions from the association delegates regarding the latest happenings in Spain, and their implications, the extraordinary plenum of the IWA meeting in Paris on June 11, 12 and 13, 1937 notes:

1. That the events which occurred in Barcelona recently were essentially aimed at wresting control of firms and frontiers from the CNT and driving it from its locals and the important positions it occupied, at exterminating its militants and preventing the social revolution from getting into its full stride and at strangling it.

2. That this drive, hatched over many a long month between certain members of the Valencia and Barcelona governments, in which the CNT has a share through its representatives, but unbeknownst to these, is part and parcel of a plan devised by the political parties inspired by the Spanish Communist Party, acting on orders from the Soviet government.

3. That this plan has an international dimension and serves Anglo-American capitalist interests, Franco-Anglo-Russian diplomacy having acted as the champion of the same ever since the Revolution began, and subsequently, by means of non-intervention, blockade, land-based and sea-borne controls and mediation.

4. That mediation, which the Valencia government at present rejects on grounds of opportunity, aims at a white peace, a compromise between adversarial political forces under the auspices of France and England, with a view to getting that Valancia government formally to agree to the restoration of a "democratic and parliamentary" republic, which all are agreed in regarding as having been largely overtaken by events.

Consequently, the plenum declares: a) That the war unleashed by a military, fascist counter-revolution should increasingly take on the character of a drive for the utter liberation of the Spanish proletariat, and, for that very reason, cannot but be revolution.

b) That the salvation of the social revolution must be, more than ever, the over riding and essential preoccupation of the CNT.

c) That admiration for the invincible courage of Spain's worker and peasant masses, and more especially of the masses organized under the colors of the CNT, remains undiminished, in spite of all of the vicissitudes of an unequal contest.

d) That the solidarity of the revolutionary proletariat world-wide, united within the ranks of the IWA, hostile to marxism in all of its forms, remains unshakably the same as in the past, given that reformist social democracy, as well as dictatorial Bolshevism of the Stalinist school or the Trotskyist school with all of their ramifications and subsidiaries, such as the PSUC or the POUM, are equally noxious and dangerous for the making of the Revolution.

e) That the conduct of the revolutionary war in conjunction with the transformation of society, ought, insofar as the CNT is concerned, to rule out any direct participation or indirect compact with the Valencia and Barcelona governments, and would require that the CNT abandon all political, economic and doctrinal concessions made to these governments which have the intention of preserving intact a self-styled antifascist front made up of sectors which are negotiating with the class enemy in order to conclude the war and liquidate the revolution: [the IWA] considers that the CNT's formal withdrawal from the antifascist front is increasingly necessary, although it retains the right to accept or table circumstantial arrangements with the genuinely antifascist elements of that front, eager to see the war concluded through a liberating revolution of the Spanish proletariat directed against fascism as well as against so-called republican democracy.

While not wishing to impose upon the CNT a policy line that might be momentarily disagreeable to it, the extra-ordinary plenum remains convinced that the CNT will keep faith with the principles and doctrines enunciated by the IWA and will, as soon as circumstances permit, make the adjustment to its course which events require, such adjustment being closely bound up with the very existence of the CNT and with the salvation of the social revolution in Spain, and elsewhere.

For its part, the IWA commits itself to continuing to support the Spanish revolution more forcefully and more coherently than ever, materially and by its actions. The Plenum consequently empowers the IWA secretariat, in conjunction with all our affiliated and sympathizer associations, to make urgent examination of means of stepping up propaganda on behalf of the Spanish Revolution, increasing and adding to aid to our CNT comrades, and, in every country, making provision for the eventuality of general strikes in solidarity with the Spanish proletariat in revolution. The most immediate tasks facing the IWA are:

1. Organizing a systematic campaign against the fascist States as well as the democratic ones which are directly or indirectly interfering in the struggle in Spain, with the admitted intention of strangling the proletarian revolution.

2. Implementing the earlier decisions of IWA Congresses, so as to devise, as soon as practicable, an international economic reconstruction plan for which the Spanish experience has very specific suggestions to offer.

At the same time, the Plenum asks the IWA Secretariat to communicate to the CNT, as and when appropriate, the IWA's feelings with regard to every important event which may occur in Spain.

Notes to The CNT Taken to Task by its International

1. Drafted by Pierre Besnard, the secretary of the IWA.
2. **International Workers' Association,** the anarcho-syndicalist International, which exists to this day.

FEDERICA MONTSENY SETS THE RECORD STRAIGHT

We have certainly not offered Federica Montseny space to try to justify her past attitudes, but rather out of democratic scruples and because she deserves the right of reply.

The issue of CNT participation in government during the war and the Revolution in Spain is a burning issue. When it is mooted again, thirty years on, the intention is always to offer the most scathing of condemnations, without bothering in the least to inform oneself, to understand or to explain. Criticism is wielded like a sword, and stones are cast at the men, and above all the one woman, who were impelled by circumstance to take up government portfolios.

Back in 1937, Camillo Berneri, Emma Goldman and Sébastien Faure broached this matter. Others, like Rudolf Rocker and Max Nettlau refrained from judgment and trusted us. Maybe we ought to clarify a few points so that everyone may understand and then make a judgment.

Above all, one has to appreciate the contemporary context and view things, not through a thirty year looking-glass, but bearing in mind the situation in which the CNT and the libertarian movement were placed in 1936.

It all started the day we had to turn the Antifascist Militias Committee of Barcelona, the premier agency of the Revolution, which incorporated all political and trade union forces, into the Generalidad Council [of Catalonia]. Was that truly necessary? At any rate, the issue was raised within the

Committee itself. It was debated for nights on end, at meetings and plenums. All of the leading lights from the trade unions and anarchist groups were in attendance. A decision to go it alone and keep the Militias Committee was an option to breach the antifascist front and confront the situation all alone. Ought we to have done so? Maybe. At the time, though, the majority, cognizant of the implications for the future involved in such isolation and this sort of a coup d'état, decided otherwise. Participation in the bodies which were to reconstitute the State started then and there.

The better to understand, we should recall that we had been left to our own devices by organizations the world over, that other political forces were intriguing, that the Communist Party was already at its blackmail, exploiting Russian aid, the only aid, aside from that from Mexico, reaching a Spain defenseless in the face of a Burgos Junta that was receiving arms, men and funding from Italy and Germany.

That initial venture into participation in government was camouflaged by turning the Catalan government into a "Generalidad Council" and describing as councilors people who were in reality ministers. There was an attempt to excuse it by delegating as representatives of the CNT low-profile figures, recent recruits to the Confederation such as Fabregas. But the first step had been taken.

Later, it was drama and panic when Largo Caballero established his first "war" cabinet, incorporating two Communists and inviting the CNT to join them. The shadow of Kronstadt, of libertarian Ukraine trampled underfoot, loomed. There was the mealy-mouthed invention of a "National Defense Council." Largo Caballero would have none of it. As he saw it, facing the Burgos Junta, we could not give up the cachet internationally implicit in our having a lawful government of the Republic, democratically chosen by the Spanish people.

A further plenum was summoned. In spite of support for entry into the Largo Caballero government from the then CNT general secretary, Horacio Martinez Prieto, nothing could be done until a fresh plenum of the regional branches could be held. It was decided that we should insist upon making do with a share in a National Defense Council. But Largo Caballero would not budge.

While the CNT and the FAI were in the majority in Catalonia, Valencia and Andalusia, the composition of forces was more varied in the Centre, Asturias and the Basque Country. The Socialists had substantial organizations and the Communists, thanks as ever to Russian aid and flirtation with the right-wing forces, were soaring to new heights.

Relying upon the vote of confidence which the plenum had passed in him, and persuaded that there was no alternative, Horacio Martinez Prieto therefore entered into talks with Caballero with an eye to the CNT joining a ready-made government.

We looked for men who would be representative of the two tendencies within the CNT: Lopez and Peiro representing the moderates; Garcia Oliver and myself representing the extremists. We argued it out. And wound up by giving in. In the position we were in, any scruples seemed like "evading the issue" and was regarded as "desertion;" our belief had been that we should not take upon ourselves responsibilities in which everybody ought to have had a share.

The rest we know. We were obliged to accept posts as army corps commanders, police chiefs, prison governors, political commissars, etc. Were we carried away by ambition, by thirst for power? No. No one, right then, had a thought for his personal prospects. But we did cast around for justification. Today one cannot scan the pro-militarization contents of *Solidaridad Obrera* and *CNT* without a sense of unease and bewilderment.

In spite of everything that the men of the CNT-FAI did, scurrying around and popping up everywhere, things went from bad to worse every day. So I said: "We cannot be on the streets and in the government at one and the same time." We were in the government, but the streets were slipping away from us. We had lost the workers' trust and the movement's unity had been whittled away. On the day when we quit the Caballero government, after the May 1937 events in Barcelona — a coup carefully contrived by Russian agents casting around for an excuse to stamp out the anarchist movement in Spain — I was immensely relieved, as I imagine my colleagues were too.

The war, meanwhile, was virtually lost — the Revolution too. We were split by controversy over what policy to adopt during those final months. There were comrades who shared the republicans' opinion and believed that some way had to be found of averting the final catastrophe. Others, on the other hand, called for a fight to the finish, even where hope had evaporated. Juan Negrin[1] was the leading light of the die-hard line, arguing that a world war would erupt before the year was out. Was he sincere? Be that as it may, Mariano R. Vazquez, then the CNT's general secretary, was of the same mind. So too were most comrades. Had we held out until September 1939, war would have been upon us. Would things have changed for us? Judging by the way Hitler handled the initial fighting, and in light of the lightning-quick invasion of France which reached the Pyrenees within a few days, that is questionable. Once the war was lost and the vast majority of the membership in exile, the moral rehabilitation of the CNT began. A huge number of comrades in occupied France and, a few months later, in North Africa, forcefully denounced political deviationism — there were many who reckoned that we should carry on collaborating with every antifascist force, including any governments-in-exile that might be established — at the Muret plenum in 1944 a motion to that effect was passed.

Meanwhile, once the Liberation made it feasible to have open debate and organize CNT groups right across France, the lobby that was eager to bring to a conclusion a period which they considered regrettable — during which the principles and tactics by which the CNT had been informed ever since its creation had been badly mangled — grew by leaps and bounds each day.

At the Congress of Local Federations held in Paris on May 1, 1945, after eight days of heated arguments, the adversaries of political collaboration won the first round. We had made our self-criticism. I myself, attending as delegate from the Bessieres Local Federation, spoke at length about my personal experience and the futility of our participation in government, declaring that my beliefs had come through that ordeal all the stronger for it. The fact that I had been a minister and was espousing a plainly "anti-reformist" stance, to borrow the idiom of the day, made me one of the standard-bearers of what the "reformists" termed "the classicals."

The years of exile were to be replete with protracted battles and countless ups and downs. When, at the end of 1945, the national committee of the (underground) CNT inside Spain decided, flying in the face of the majority view among the exiles, to second two ministers to the Giral government — Leiva, from inside Spain, and Horacio Martinez Prieto, who was living in Orleans — the reformist wing split from the Libertarian Movement-CNT-in-exile. The supporters of collaboration, a minority in France, may well have been in the majority inside our country.

But helped by the passage of time and by disappointments that opened the eyes of those who still believed in the feasibility of acting within the framework of a government-in-exile, our cause gained support day by day. Our movement defined its thinking clearly. At the Toulouse Congress in 1947, a motion was passed unanimously, since the opposition "reformists" had already broken away. That motion closed the door once and for all upon political participation in any government.

Here are some excerpts from it:

Statement of Principle

The Congress (...) meeting in Toulouse of October 20, 1947 and ensuing days; takes the view that all first-hand experience and all of the events which have occurred in the world in recent years merely endorse the line taken since 1870 by the proletariat organized in accordance with the watchwords of the First International;

considers that all concessions made to the State have resulted only in consolidation of the latter and that any acceptance — even provisional acceptance — of the principle of authority, represents an effective loss of ground and implies renunciation of comprehensively liberating ultimate goals;

(...) considers that the experiences of the war and the Revolution in Spain have confirmed the enduring value of efforts undertaken at the people's instigation and the endorsement by the force of events of the tactics of direct, anti-State, revolutionary action.

(...) in the light of the foregoing, the Congress declares: that it ratifies the principles and revolutionary anti-State direct action tactics which are consubstantial with anarchism and anarcho-syndicalism;

(...) that all power constituted on the principle of the political and economic State, whatever its name and whichever the parties and organizations supporting it may be, is but one of the many faces of authority;

(...) that our movement has as its ultimate aim the introduction of libertarian communism, with no transitional stage, and with tactics consonant with our principles (...)

I honestly believe that the Spanish CNT's case is a unique one in the history of all of the world's labor and political movements. After a slide towards politics, after a taste of government, as a result of which some went astray and were forever lost, an overwhelming majority returned to its roots, cured forever of any political yearnings, persuaded that only direct action by the workers can bring about the social transformation that frees man and does away with the class society. Honestly and sincerely, all who had a taste of military, administrative and political leadership positions emerged from them nauseated and more opposed to the State than ever.

Some may well wonder:

- Would the same have been true if you had won the war? If the Republic had prevailed over Francoism, what would then have become of our participation in the government?

- Had we won the war, the Revolution would have proceeded on its way. Nothing and nobody would have prevented the expansion and completion of what the majority of the people had begun on July 19. Which is probably precisely the reason why the war had to be lost and the Revolution done to death.

Note to Federica Montseny Sets the Record Straight

1. Juan Negrin (1889–1956), professor of medicine, right-wing socialist and fellow-traveler with the Stalinists. Starting as minister of Finance, he replaced Largo Caballero on May 17, 1937 in charge of the republican government. After April 1938 he was minister of War. He died in exile in London.

Kate Sharpley Library

Comrades and Friends —

No doubt some of you will be aware of the work of the **Kate Sharpley Library and Documentation Centre**, which has been in existence for the last eight years. In 1991 the Library was moved from a storage location in London to Northamptonshire, where we are now in the process of creating a database of the entire collection. At the same time, a working group has been formed to over see the organisation and running of the Library. The catalogue of the Library material will be published by AK Press (Edinburgh).

The Library is made up of private donations from comrades, deceased and living. It comprises several thousand pamphlets, books, newspapers, journals, posters, flyers, unpublished manuscripts, monographs, essay, etc. , in over 20 languages, covering the history of our movement over the last century. It contains detailed reports from the IWA (AIT/IAA), the Anarchist Federation of Britain (1945-50), the Syndicalist Workers Federation (1950-1979) and records from the anarchist publishing houses, *Cienfuegos Press*, ASP and others. Newspapers include near complete sets of *Black Flag*, *Freedom*, *Spain and the World*, *Direct Actions* (from 1945 onwards), along with countless others dating back 100 years. The Library also has a sizeable collection of libertarian socialist and council communist materials which we are keen to extend.

The Kate Sharpley Library is probably the largest collection of anarchist material in England. In order to extend and enhance the collection, we ask all anarchist groups and publications worldwide to add our name to their mailing list. We also appeal to all comrades and friends to *donate* suitable material to the Library. *All* donations are welcome and can be collected. The Kate Sharpley Library (KSL) was named in honour of Kate Sharpley, a First World War anarchist and anti-war activist — one of the countless "unknown" members of our movement so ignored by "official historians" of anarchism. The Library regularly publishes lost areas of anarchist history.

Please contact us if you would like to use our facilities. To receive details of our publications, send a stamped addressed envelope to:

KSL
BM Hurricane
London WC1N 3XX
England

THE KATE SHARPLEY LIBRARY

SOME RECENT TITLES FROM AK PRESS

THE FRIENDS OF DURRUTI GROUP 1937-1939
by Agustin Guillamón; translated by Paul Sharkey. ISBN 1-873176-54-6; 128pp, two color cover, 6x9; $9.95/£7.95. This is the story of a group of anarchists engaged in the most thoroughgoing social and economic revolution of all time. Essentially street fighters with a long pedigree of militant action, they used their own experiences to arrive at the finest contemporary analysis of the Spanish revolution. In doing so they laid down essential markers for all future revolutionaries. This study — drawing on interviews with participants and synthesizing archival information — is the definitive text on these unsung activists. "Revolutions without theory fail to make progress. We of the "Friends of Durruti" have outlined our thinking, which may be amended as appropriate in great social upheavals but which hinges upon two essential points which cannot be avoided. A program, and rifles." — *El Amigo del Pueblo* No. 5, July 20, 1937

THE SPANISH ANARCHISTS: THE HEROIC YEARS 1868–1936
by Murray Bookchin. ISBN 1-873176 04-X; 336 pp, two color cover, perfect bound 6 x 9; $19.95/£13.95. A long-awaited new edition of this seminal history of Spanish Anarchism. Hailed as a masterpiece, it includes a new prefatory essay by the author. This popular, well-researched book opens with the Italian Anarchist Fanelli's stirring visit to Spain in 1868 and traces the movement's checkered but steady growth for the next 70 years. Intimate portraits are vividly juxtaposed with striking descriptions of events: peasant revolts, labor unrest, the saintly Fermin Salvochea, official repression, the terrorists and the evolution of exciting organizational forms. Bookchin weaves his way geographically through the whole of Spain, revealing the shadings and subtleties of each small section. From the peasants of Andalusia to the factory workers of Barcelona, the Spanish people — and their exuberant belief in and struggles for freedom and self-determination — come alive. *"I've learned a great deal from this book. It is a rich and fascinating account.... Most important, it has a wonderful spirit of revolutionary optimism that connects the Spanish Anarchists with our own time."* — Howard Zinn.

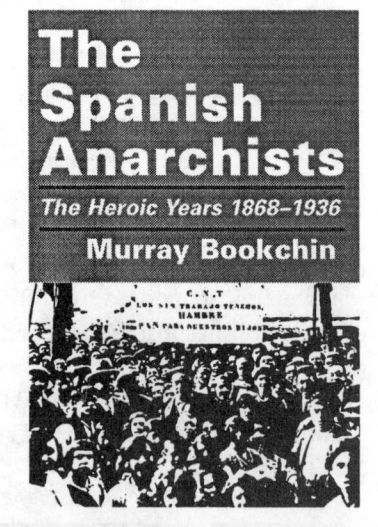

THE STRUGGLE AGAINST THE STATE AND OTHER ESSAYS

by Nestor Makhno (translated by Alexandre Skirda). ISBN 1-873176 87-2; 128 pp, two color cover, perfect bound 5-1/2 x 8-1/2; $9.95/£7.95. Born of pasant stock in Bwlyog-Polye, Ukraine, Makhno became an anarchist after the Russian Revoltuion of 1905. Sentenced to death for armed struggle, his sentence was commuted to life imprisonment. Liberated in 1917, he organized an army of anarchist resistance against both the Bolsheviks and the White counter-revolutionaries. Forced to flee by the Bolsheviks, he eventually ended up in exile in Paris. He remained poltically active, contributing to Delo Truda and other papers, and helped create the Organizational Platform of the Libertarian Communists. Makhno was determined that the next time anarchism, revamped and more disciplined thanks to its Organizational Platform, might reap the rewards proportionate with the commitment and sacrifice of its activists. The essays in this volume date from his period in exile.

SOCIAL ANARCHISM OR LIFESTYLE ANARCHISM: AN UNBRIDGEABLE CHASM

by Murray Bookchin; ISBN 1 873176 83 X; 96pp two color cover, perfect bound 5-1/2 x 8-1/2; $7.95/£5.95. This book asks — and tries to answer — several basic questions that affect all Leftists today. Will anarchism remain a revolutionary social movement or become a chic boutique lifestyle subculture? Will its primary goals be the complete transformation of a hierarchical, class, and irrational society into a libertarian communist one? Or will it become an ideology focused on personnel well-being, spiritual redemption, and self-realization within the existing society? This small book, tightly reasoned and documented, should be of interest to all radicals in the "postmodern age," socialists as well as anarchists, for whom the Left seems in hopeless disarray. Includes the essay *The Left That Was*.

AK Press publishes and distributes a wide variety of radical literature. For our latest catalog featuring these and several thousand other titles, please send a large self-addressed, stamped envelope to:

AK Press
PO Box 40682
San Francisco, CA
94140-0682

AK Press
P.O. Box 12766
Edinburgh, Scotland
EH8 9YE

SOME RECENT TITLES FROM AK PRESS

TALES FROM THE CLIT: A FEMALE EXPERIENCE OF PORNOGRAPHY
edited by Cherie Matrix.
ISBN 1-873176 09-0; 160 pp, two color cover, perfect bound 5-1/2 x 8-1/2; $10.95/£7.95. Get wet with the wildest group of feminists yet!! True stories by some of the world's most pro-sex feminists, these women have provided intimate, anti-censorship essays to re-establish the idea that equality of the sexes doesn't have to mean no sex. From intimate sexual experiences and physical perception through to the academic arena, this groundbreaking volume documents women's positive thoughts, uses and desires for, with and about pornography. Essays include such diverse topics as how various authors discovered porn, what porn means to a blind and deaf woman, running a sex magazine, starting a sex shop, and what the contributors would actually like to see. Contributors include: Deborah Ryder, Annie Sprinkle, Tuppy Owens, Carol Queen, Avedon Carol, Jan Grossman, Sue Raye, and Caroline Bottomley.

SCUM MANIFESTO
by Valerie Solanas.
ISBN 1-873176 44-9; 64 pp, two color cover, perfect bound 5-1/2 x 8-1/2; $5.00/£3.50. This is the definitive edition of the SCUM Manifesto with an afterword detailing the life and death of Valerie Solanas. "Life in this society being, at best, an utter bore and no aspect of society being at all relevant to women, there remains to civic-minded, responsible, thrill-seeking females only to overthrow the government, eliminate the money system, institute complete automation and destroy the male sex.... On the shooting of Andy Warhol: I consider that a moral act. And I consider it immoral that I missed. I should have done target practice." —Valerie Solanas

SEIZING THE AIRWAVES: A FREE RADIO HANDBOOK
edited by Ron Sakolsky & Stephen Dunifer
ISBN 1-873176-99-6; 224 pp, four color cover, perfect bound 6 x 9; $12.95/£8.95. Let us conjure up a vision of a Wild Radio Stampede disrupting the territorialized lines of Authority artificially drawn in the air surrounding Mother Earth.... Within this book, the myriad voices of the Free Radio Movement come alive with the same urgency that has challenged both corporate and governmental control of radio-activity.... If seizing the airwaves is a crime, then welcome to the millennial police state. Contributors include: Lee Ballinger, Jon Bekken, Carol Denney, Ricardo Omar Elizalde, Lorenzo Komboa Ervin, Charles Fairchild, Paul W. Griffin, Mbanna Kantako, Jerry M. Landay, Robert W. McChesney, Kiilu Nyasha, Sheila Nopper, Meme Sabon, Sal Salerno, DJ Tashtego, and Napoleon Williams.

FORTHCOMING BOOKS FROM AK PRESS

SHIBBOLETH: MY REVOLTING LIFE

by Penny Rimbaud; ISBN 1 873176 40 6; perfect bound, 4 1/8 x 6 7/8; two color cover; 352 pages; $9.95. The inside story of CRASS, the anarchist punk band who politicised a generation and put revolutionary activism back on the map for the first time since the 60s. An engaging autobiography of Jeremy John Ratter, aka Penny Rimbaud. From his strict lower-middle class childhood, to art-school, the hippies and Free Festivals, including the now legendary Stonehenge Festival, of which Rimbaud was a co-founder. The majority of the book is unsurprisingly taken up with the story of CRASS, a band unique in the history of rock n roll, and of which Rimbaud was the founder, lyricist, and drummer. Crass took the idealism of punk seriously. In the space of seven short years, from 1977 to their break-up in 1984, Crass almost single-handedly breathed life back into the then moribund peace and anarchist movements. They birthed a huge underground network of do-it-yourself activism, fanzines, record labels, activist action groups, concert halls. While remaining on their own independent record label, and steadfastly refusing any interviews etc with the major press, they managed to sell literally millions of records. Their political 'pranks' included the now infamous 'KGB tapes,' trumpeted amongst others, on the front page of the 'New York Times,' and the duping of 'Total Loving' magazine to include a CRASS song (ranting against the patriarchy of marriage) as the "perfect song to play on your wedding day." Shibboleth also includes for the first time, the full story of Wally Hope — 'The Last Of The Hippies,' close friend of Rimbaud, co-founder of the Stonehenge Festival, and murdered by the state while incarcerated in a mental institution.

THE DIAMOND SIGNATURE — A NOVEL IN FOUR BOOKS & THE DEATH OF THE IMAGINATION — A DRAMA FOR FOUR READERS

Penny Rimbaud aka J J Ratter; ISBN 1 873176 55 4; perfect bound, 4 1/8 x 6 7/8; two color cover; 256 pages; $9.95. The first collection of prose (and a play) from the father of political punk. "The first draft of 'The Diamond Signature' was completed in 1974 and since then has been revised countless times. I have always regarded it as an organic work that could be added to or taken away from at will — several sections of it were adapted for us by CRASS, the anarchist punk band with whom I was drummer and lyricist, other sections have been liberally scattered through subsequent novels." [from the preface] 'The Diamond Signature' is what Penny Rimbaud considers his most important work. It formed the basis for the band CRASS, who literally revolutionized both punk rock, and politics in a blistering seven year career, which found them reviled by the mainstream, and revered by hundreds of thousands in the underground they helped to create. It is presented here together with his other significant piece of prose, 'The Death Of The Imagination,' a new piece of work created specifically for live performance.

A CAVALIER HISTORY OF SURREALISM

by Francois Dupuis (Raoul Vaneigem) translated by Donald Nicholson-Smith. ISBN 1-873176-94-5; 128pp two color cover, perfect bound; $9.95/£7.95. A down-and-dirty survey of the Surrealist movement written under a psuedonym in 1970 by leading Situationist theorist Raoul Vaneigem. Intended for a high-school readership, Vaneigem's sketch bars no holds: disrespectful in the extreme, blistering on Surrealism's artistic and political aporias, and packed with telling quotations, it also gives respect where respect is due.

The Friends of AK Press

In the last 12 months, AK Press published around 15 new titles. In the next 12 months we should be able to publish roughly the same, including a collection of essays and interviews by Murray Bookchin, the first book from Jello Biafra, three books from members of Crass, a stunning new cyber-punk novel, and the animal rights revenge novel to end all novels, as well as a new audio CD from Noam Chomsky.

However, not only are we financially constrained as to what (and how much) we can publish, we already have a huge backlog of excellent material we would like to publish sooner, rather than later. If we had the money, we could publish sixty titles in the coming twelve months.

Projects currently being worked on include: **Morris Beckman**'s short history of British Fascism; previously unpublished early anarchist writings by **Victor Serge**; **Raoul Vaneigem**'s *A Cavalier History of Surrealism*; two volumes of the collected writings of Guy Aldred; first-hand accounts from Kronstadt survivors; an English translation of Alexandre Skirda's classic work on anarchist history and organization, and his acclaimed biography of Makhno, *The Black Cossack*; *History's Lost Orgasms*, a history of insurrection from antiquity to the present day; the autobiography of perennial revolutionaries, the Thaelmans; new work from Freddie Baer; the first translation in English (running to eight volumes) of the complete works of **Bakunin**; a new edition of the Ex's glorious Spanish Revolution book/CD package; a collection of prison stories from ex-Angry Brigader **John Barker**; new editions of 'outsider' classics *You Can't Win* by **Jack Black** and **Ben Reitman**'s *Boxcar Bertha*; a comprehensive look at the armed struggle groups of the 1960s and 1970s, both in Europe and North America; and much, much more. We are working to set up a new pamphlet series, both to reprint long neglected classics and to present new material in an affordable, accessible format.

The Friends of AK Press is a way in which you can directly help us to realize many more such projects, much faster. Friends pay a minimum monthly amount, into our AK Press account. There are also yearly and life-time memberships available. Moneys received go directly into our publishing.

In return, Friends receive (for the duration of their membership), automatically, as and when they appear, one FREE copy of **every** new AK Press title. Secondly, they are also entitled to a 10 percent discount on **everything** featured in the AK Press Distribution catalog, on **any** and **every** order.

To receive a catalog and find out more about Friends of AK Press please write to:

AK Press
PO Box 40682
San Francisco, CA
94140-0682

AK Press
P.O. Box 12766
Edinburgh, Scotland
EH8 9YE